L-95 (=100)

# LIFE

# ON

# THE

# COLOR

# LINE

D

# LIFE ON THE COLOR LINE

## The True Story

## of a White Boy

## Who Discovered

## He Was Black

# GREGORY HOWARD WILLIAMS

A DUTTON BOOK

DUTTON
Published by the Penguin Group
Penguin Books USA Inc., 375 Hudson Street,
New York, New York 10014, U.S.A.
Penguin Books Ltd, 27 Wrights Lane,
London W8 5TZ, England
Penguin Books Australia Ltd, Ringwood,
Victoria, Australia
Penguin Books Canada Ltd, 10 Alcorn Avenue,
Toronto, Ontario, Canada M4V 3B2
Penguin Books (N.Z.) Ltd, 182–190 Wairau Road,
Auckland 10, New Zealand

Penguin Books Ltd, Registered Offices:
Harmondsworth, Middlesex, England

First published by Dutton, an imprint of Dutton Signet,
a division of Penguin Books USA Inc.
Distributed in Canada by McClelland & Stewart Inc.

First Printing, February, 1995
10 9 8 7 6 5 4 3 2 1

CIP data is available.
ISBN 0-525-93850-8

Printed in the United States of America
Set in Palatino
Designed by Leonard Telesca

My old man's a white old man
And my old mother's black.

If ever I cursed my white old man
I take my curses back.

If ever I cursed my black old mother
And wished she were in hell,

I'm sorry for that
And now I wish her well.

My old man died in a big fine house
My ma died in a shack.

I wonder where I'm gonna die,
Being neither white nor black!
   —Langston Hughes, "Cross"

To the memories of my father, James A. "Buster" Williams, and my "truly mother," Dora Weekly Smith.

They gave me the strength to live this story.

And to

Sara Whitney Williams,
who gave me the courage to tell it.

# Contents

P

# Acknowledgments

This book was ten years in the making and fifty years in the living. Unfortunately, many people from my past are no longer alive, and I had to rely on my memory and those of a few others who shared the struggle with me. I have tried to be accurate and honest and portray events as best I could recall them. Fortunately, or unfortunately, those learned in the area tell us that often our most vivid and accurate memories are those of our adolescence. I have changed some names to protect the privacy of persons mentioned in the book.

I am deeply indebted to my family, friends, and colleagues who read so many drafts of the manuscript over the years. Their questions and suggestions helped me immeasurably. However, there are too many of them in Iowa City, Iowa, Columbus, Ohio, and elsewhere to mention them all. Nonetheless, at risk of overlooking others who were extremely helpful, I must express special thanks to a few. Sara Whitney Williams envisioned this book long before it was a reality. Her encouragement, memories, and creative energy were invaluable along the way and greatly enriched the end result. My agents, Jonathon and Wendy Lazear, believed in this project. Jonathon supported and counseled me longer than anyone could reasonably expect. My editor at Dutton, Deborah Brody, was never without a word of encouragement and help. My longtime pal and Iowa City companion James Alan McPherson was always willing to help me reflect on a past that mirrored his in many ways. Cameron Stracher, Steve Rhodes, and Christina Baldwin made some excellent suggestions and gave me good advice on writing. Nancy Whetstine, Harriet Dana, Annette Ebright, and many other typists over the years maintained their good cheer as I handed them one draft after another. To Natalia, Zach, Carlos, and Anthony, thanks for all the sacrifices you made to help Dad finish "The Book."

# LIFE

# ON

# THE

# COLOR

# LINE

# Chapter 1

# The Open House Cafe

The white frame building dwarfed all the other beer joints on U.S. 1 between Alexandria and Fort Belvoir, Virginia. Dad said we had "the best location in the country, right smack-dab in the middle of the Eastern Seaboard, and less than five miles from the number one tourist attraction in America." But it was the summer of 1950 and Americans were more interested in events occurring thousands of miles away than in Mount Vernon, George Washington's ancestral home.

A collective fear gnawed at the country. The North Koreans had just launched a full-scale invasion of South Korea and my family was in the middle of it all. Every afternoon green army jeeps roared into our gravel parking lot and disgorged Fort Belvoir soldiers. In fatigues and webbed gun belts, they swaggered to the broad mahogany bar of the Open House Cafe. Tales of death and destruction wreaked by the Communists as they swarmed down the Korean peninsula sent shivers down my spine as I sat at the cash register. It was hard to concentrate on my job as the tavern buzzed with stories of America in retreat, just one step away from being pushed into the sea at our final outpost. I thought the world was coming to an end.

Talk of America's imminent demise left me feeling insignificant, but Dad said my job was just as important as the soldiers' at the "front line." Nonetheless, I found it hard to believe that trying to catch waitresses pocketing our cash was as important as whether General MacArthur could rush troops from Japan in time to turn back the North Koreans. Then again, I was only six years old and had a lot to learn.

My father, a World War II army draftee when I was born, named me Gregory Howard Williams. Gregory after his captain, Gregory Barnes, and Howard after his major, Howard Schultz. For some unknown reason I ended up being called "Billy" by everyone around the tavern. When my mother was pregnant with my younger brother, "Mike," Dad was still in the army—actually, in the Fort Belvoir stockade. He was trying to convince the military police that he didn't intend to steal the five hundred army sheets found in his car during a routine inspection. Apparently unsuccessful, he moved his appeal to higher ground and christened my brother Lehman Mark Alain Williams. Lehman for General Lehman W. Miller, his commanding officer at Fort Belvoir, and Mark for General Mark Clark, who reached the height of his fame during the Korean War. Alain was for Dr. Alain Leroy Locke, the first African-American Rhodes scholar, though I didn't learn about him until much later. General Miller, either impressed with the persistence of Sergeant James A. (Tony) Williams, or the naming of my brother after him, discharged my father a few days before it was time to impanel a court-martial board.

Though Dad left the army, he didn't desert the Fort Belvoir soldiers. Within a year our bright neon sign

OPEN HOUSE CAFE
A.B.C. Lic. 6188

took its place alongside the beacons for all the other rough and tumble roadhouses scattered up and down Route 1 catering almost exclusively to America's fighting men. And that was where we sat the summer of 1950.

I have no conscious memories of life before the tavern. What I remember most are the long hours logged at the cash register. Oftentimes I terrified myself by fantasizing that the next person barging through the front door in combat regalia would be a North

Korean soldier. I planned to crack him across the head with our trusted Louisville Slugger, kept under the bar to settle late night arguments. Most of the time, though, I was just plain bored as I endlessly spun back and forth on the bar stool.

It was part of our "army" training that soldiers never deserted their posts. Though Dad couldn't court-martial me, I did fear him. In our one-room living quarters off the kitchen, he often yelled at Mom and twisted her arms until she cried, especially when he had too much to drink. So when assigned to the cash register I stayed there—from early morning until late afternoon—though sometimes the sizzle of french fries beckoned me and I sneaked into the kitchen.

Percy, our cook, ruled the kitchen. A light-brown-skinned man in his mid-fifties, he often challenged Dad's authority and constantly threatened to quit. He complained about my father's incessant drinking and how it interfered with his work. Percy really hated the way Dad teased him about being gay, or as we said in those days, "funny."

When workers gathered in the kitchen, Dad would often sneak up behind Percy and buss him on the cheek, causing the group to erupt in laughter. In the late evenings after a long day of drinking, Dad imitated Sally Rand's famous fan dance for the midnight patrons. He'd wave for Percy, who stood frowning behind the bar, to join him. Percy's brown face would turn almost purple with anger, but Dad's burlesque pantomime and coy twirling of two cloth napkins always left the crowd roaring.

After Percy's and Dad's angry exchanges, my mother usually stepped in as the peacemaker. It's hard to recall much about her. She was a part of our lives for such a brief time, and I was so young. I remember her as being tall and I had to look straight up to talk to her. Her hair was auburn just a half shade short of red. To me she was a real-life image of Esther Williams, who I saw in the Open Air Drive-In Theatre movies across from the tavern. However, I can't recall my mother being warm and friendly like the bathing beauty of the silver screen. I am only able to re-capture the memory of a forbidding, no-nonsense style that matched her sharp angular features. Perhaps it was the growing family—a sister and another brother arrived in rapid succession—and the constant strain of keeping the tavern running smoothly that gave my mother so little time for joy.

Her personality contrasted sharply with Dad's, whose charisma

and camaraderie with employees and patrons enhanced the popu-
larity of the Open House Cafe. While Dad always seemed to enjoy
himself, I never saw my mother smile. His easygoing manner com-
plemented his exceptional good looks, and even as a child I perceived that his alluring smile, wavy hair, and golden complexion
had a powerful impact on women. Waitresses who ignored my
mother never denied Dad's plea to work extra hours or do all types
of favors for us, and as I later discovered, for him.

The tavern had two distinct serving areas, the "front end" and
the "back end." The "front end" had a bar, booths and tables that
seated over seventy customers, and a shiny tile floor—which I
helped Dad lay one Sunday, cutting, fitting, torching, and gluing
squares well into the night. The "back end" was down a landing
from the kitchen. Half the size of the main bar, it had gray cinder
block walls, bare except for a Coca-Cola clock, a tattered Camel
cigarette poster, and a dust-encrusted picture of Perry Como. An
ancient bar with a cracked top was just beyond the kitchen steps,
and scratched Formica tables were scattered about the room. The
real difference between the two areas was that whites were served
in the "front end" and blacks in the "back end." Mom worked only
the "front end," but Dad was everywhere at once, managing both
with ease.

From time to time I heard the Virginia Alcoholic Beverage Commission agent, the "ABC man," say it was "against the law to serve
whites and coloreds under the same roof." Yet the official tolerated
our technical violation, perhaps because of Dad's incredible per-
suasiveness—and the fact that our spot on Route 1 was kind of a
racial dividing line. Across from us, on the east side of the highway,
it was all white, starting with Mary Vavola's trailer court and con-
tinuing down past the Twin Barrels Tavern all the way to Engleside.
West of the highway we were surrounded on three sides by the all-
black community of Gum Springs, home of former slaves and their
descendants since the time of George Washington.

I guess there has never been a time in my life that I haven't been
right on the color line. Although in those Virginia days I didn't
really understand what it meant, let alone begin to appreciate the
irony and symbolism of our life and location. Even though most of
my playmates were black, I saw segregation of the races as part of
the natural order of life. One afternoon a black soldier, in dress
uniform and shiny corporal's stripes, staggered through the door

and slid into one of our "front end" booths. Alert, I tensed, fearful we would lose our liquor license if the ABC man discovered the soldier drinking with whites. A waitress, well schooled on Virginia laws and etiquette, quickly approached him and began to recite the familiar litany. Leaning across the bar, I strained to hear the exchange, and was blasted with a thundering response. "Whaddaya mean, I can't be served? I gave a leg for this fucking country!"

Angrily, the soldier jerked his khaki trousers to his calf and knocked on a brown artificial limb to emphasize his point. As I gaped at the shiny plastic, my world suddenly became very complicated. I struggled to reconcile the contradiction of what the country required of the soldier and what the state permitted him to do.

Dad, unfazed, moved quickly from behind the bar and strode to the table. He clicked his heels, snapped to attention, and saluted the soldier.

"Sir, I'm Tony Williams. This is my establishment. It's an honor to have a fighting man like you here. Would you allow me to serve you a steak dinner, gratis?"

The soldier, disarmed, fixed a glassy-eyed stare at my father. I was also puzzled. I'd never seen Dad give away a steak dinner.

"Surely you would enjoy a change from army cooking, Corporal," Dad continued. The soldier mustered a nod. Dad touched his shoulder and said, "Let's get a couple of beers and go to our private dining area."

He then escorted the combat veteran to our family's cramped living quarters adjacent to the front end. Several rounds of beer dissolved the tension, but the memory of the soldier stayed with me.

To serve the crowds that flocked to the Open House Cafe, we needed a lot of help. We always had five or six waitresses, few of whom stayed with us very long. There were only two mainstays at the tavern in addition to Percy. Raymond and Harvey, both black, lived in nearby Gum Springs. Raymond, a slightly built man, drove our panel delivery truck to Alexandria, Washington, Weschler's Auction, and a hundred other places for beer, supplies, toilet paper, and whatever was needed. More important, he was a true buddy and willingly let Mike and me tag along with him on errands. Harvey, over six feet tall with dark brown skin, must have weighed at least 240 pounds. He mopped and cleaned the tavern late at night, rarely appearing during the day.

One of those nights is indelibly etched in my memory. It was after closing. Dad was out for the night, accepting a special business-man's award at the all-white American Legion Forty-and-Eighth Post. Percy and Raymond had left for home. Mom, after she put me, Mike, my sister and baby brother to bed, sat at the cash register counting the day's profits. I had just drifted off to sleep when I awoke to the sound of her racing into our room, slamming and latching the door. She grabbed the phone and yelled,

"Operator! Operator! Send police to the Open House Cafe on Route 1! A worker's gone crazy . . ."

Suddenly the door buckled, almost breaking away from the hinges.

"Get Mike, Billy!" Mom shouted. "Harvey's gonna kill us!"

I leaped from my top bunk and jerked Mike's shoulder. It was impossible to awaken him. I pulled him from the bed. Only when his butt hit the floor did his eyes open. He swung at me, but I shouted, "Come on, Mike! Harvey's after us!"

*Bam! Bam! Bam!* The banging and buckling continued. Mom grabbed the baby. I took my sister's hand and we all raced out the side door into the driveway alongside the building. We ran toward Gum Springs Road, which veered off Route 1 in front of the tavern. Glancing over my shoulder I saw Harvey standing inside our room, hatchet in hand. His eyes locked with mine, and he bolted to the door. We sped off again. In less than a block we were all gasping for air. "Let's hide here," Mom whispered, and pointed to a dark-ened yard. The five of us huddled on wet grass behind a row of hedges. Seconds later we heard the heavy clop of boots on the pave-ment. Peering through the bushes, I saw Harvey racing toward us. My mother placed a finger on her lips, then her hand across the baby's mouth. I closed my eyes. The footsteps came closer and closer. Finally, he stopped, right in front of us. Burying my face in the wet morning grass, I held my breath and waited to feel cold steel across my neck. He was going to chop off our heads—one, two, three, four, and five. I remained frozen, afraid to breathe. After what seemed like an eternity, there was the scrape of boots on con-crete, and I raised my head tortoiselike to see Harvey disappearing into the darkness. I exhaled, sapped of all strength and energy. We lay in the cold grass for another ten minutes, fearful he might return. Finally, my mother allowed us to crawl from behind the bushes. We scurried back to the tavern. I shook uncontrollably until I saw the flashing red light of a Fairfax County police car reflecting in the midnight sky over the tavern. The police located Harvey later that night. After six months at the state hospital, he was released as cured. Harvey returned to the tavern that same day. Dad immediately gave him a congratulatory slap on the back, pronounced him "ready to work," and handed him a bottle of beer.

Despite Mom's occasional efforts to spruce up the menu with spaghetti, ravioli, and lasagna, and put red-checkered tablecloths and candles on the front end tables, the more genteel aspect of the restaurant business never quite took off. Rather, the Open House Cafe flourished as a wild and wide-open beer joint. The successful Inchon landing in September 1950, and the Korean War—or as Dad and President Truman called it, the "United Nations Police Action"—brought thousands of soldiers, black and white, to Fort Belvoir. And most of them found their way to us. Dad, always public-spirited, did his best to give every group a grand send-off before they left for the Far East.

Though never privy to the party planning, Mike and I were generally able to guess when one was about to take place, although debarkation dates were shrouded in secrecy. Many soldiers befriended us by allowing us to play with their army gear. Some left helmets, canteens, and gun belts with us for weeks at a time. When the soldiers asked for the return of the equipment, we knew a wild and crazy "Tony Williams" party must be in the offing. Mike and I skillfully capitalized on the noise and confusion to observe those momentous occasions.

Squinting through the smoky haze from the door of our living quarters one night, Mike and I discovered over a hundred soldiers crowded in the front end. All were in their Class A dress uniforms, jackets were unbuttoned and beer-stained ties askew. A dozen white soldiers slouched in front-row chairs. The rest, black and white, stood behind them, drunk, leaning on each other. During the send-off parties, Dad totally ignored Virginia's segregation laws and deftly managed to bring everyone together. That night he had just warmed up the crowd with his fan dance, when all eyes turned to Lois, a shapely redheaded waitress. She emerged from the kitchen clad only in high heels, shiny black panties, and a red satin bra with black fringe. Music blared from the jukebox as she strutted from one side of the room to the other. Whistles and catcalls filled the air.

"Take it off! Take it off!" She paused in front of one GI, laced her fingers behind his head, and smothered him between her breasts. Then she roughly pushed him away. I began to breathe again. Gliding slowly across the floor, she paused to grind her hips toward the crowd. At the wall she pivoted smoothly and thrust her pelvis to the soldiers once more. Reaching behind her back, she unsnapped her bra. It slid down her milky arms and dropped to the floor. She tossed her long red tresses backward. Arms wide, she revealed two grapefruit-sized breasts. The crowd roared again. Mike whispered, "Her titties are bigger'n Mom's." We stared openmouthed. Lois slid her hands over her smooth torso and tucked her thumbs into the top of her panties. Slowly she rolled them down her hips. The crowd howled. With an exaggerated pout, she stopped and tugged them up again. Sweat trickled down my cheeks. My mouth felt dry. Lois faced the crowd and with one quick motion whisked them off. Her bare backside glistened in the harsh barroom light.

By now Mike and I had unconsciously crept almost to the dance floor. Dad spotted us from his front-row seat. Striding toward us, he said, "You boys get back to bed. This is adult entertainment!"

He herded us to the door, but was unable to close it before Lois turned in our direction. We caught one glimpse of a triangle of pale red hair as she parted her shielding hands.

Hoopla surrounded American victories in Korea that fall, but my seventh birthday, in November 1950, was followed by the shocking news that 200,000 Chinese Communists had joined the North Koreans. Hopes of troops "home by Christmas" vanished overnight. Even the constant swilling of beer and occasional striptease party could not lessen the fear of heading into a long, cold war.

Turmoil and violence escalated in my own small world as well. Arguments between Mom and Dad were increasingly physical, and tension mounted in the tavern. Late one evening while loading beer into the front end chiller, I heard cursing and shouts from the back end and raced to the kitchen door. Dad was yelling at two black soldiers seated at the bar.

"Okay, that's it! I'm shutting you fellows off! Take the argument back to the base. Don't bring it in here. If you can't conduct yourself civilly, I don't need your business!"

A muscular chocolate-skinned private lunged across the bar.

"Fuck you, man. This is between us. Keep your ass outta it. I don't care if you *do* own this goddam juke joint."

"That's it! Hit the door!" Dad quickly skirted the counter and jerked the soldier off the bar stool. Bodies came together in a sudden, swirling mass. Dad fell backward and crashed to the floor. Glass shattered. A fist holding a broken bottle flew toward his head. He raised his right hand to block it, but it was too late. The jagged edge peeled flesh down the side of his neck. A wave of relief overcame me when I saw no blood, but within an instant dark red gushers pumped from what seemed to be a thousand places. The soldier poised to strike again. Mom screamed, "Oh my God, he's gonna kill Tony!"

A dark blur sped through the kitchen. Baseball bat in hand, Harvey shoved Mom out of the way. The attacking soldier, distracted by the noise, paused a split second. Harvey connected squarely against the back of his head. The soldier tumbled unconscious to the concrete floor.

Harvey held the Louisville Slugger menacingly, seeking out the soldier's allies. No one stepped forward. Percy grabbed Dad by the shoulders, Raymond took his feet. His body slumped between them as they scurried up the kitchen steps. Mom pushed me aside and raced to the phone. Percy and Raymond gently laid Dad on the chopping block and urgently pressed cotton towels on his neck to staunch the flow of blood.

Concerned white faces crowded the kitchen door from the front end, and worried brown faces peered from the back. The din of voices was deafening. Blood immediately saturated the towels, seeped onto the table, and splattered onto the floor. Percy pressed harder to stop the bleeding, but only seconds passed before he dropped another bloody towel beside him. The pile at his feet grew, and I began to wonder if the ambulance would arrive in time. Percy shouted over his shoulder to Mom.

"Mary, I hope you told them this was a white man stabbed, and they don't think it's a nigger cut up down here in Gum Springs!"

Just as I began to fear that the police had mistaken my daddy for a colored man, I heard the wail of a siren in the parking lot. Two white men burst through the front door holding a green canvas stretcher between them. Dad was loaded into the ambulance, and Mom crawled in beside him. I watched the flashing red lights disappear down Route 1 toward Alexandria. While Mike, Sissy, and the baby slept, I sat with Percy, Raymond, and Harvey at the front end bar waiting for news.

About three a.m. the phone rang. Percy spoke softly. He nodded his head, then placed his hand over the receiver. "Your daddy done lost more than two pints of blood and got ninety stitches, but he's gonna be all right." That night I thanked God and Harvey for my father's life.

# Chapter 2

## The Midas Touch

Barely days after his brush with death, Dad was back at the tavern. I can't recall him ever resting. If he wasn't drinking, he was working day and night on one moneymaking scheme after another. If a watermelon truck was going to have a breakdown while winding its way from Georgia to New York, it seemed to do so right in front of our tavern. Dad would buy the whole truckload for a pittance, and for three days Mike and I stood alongside Route 1 hawking watermelons to passing motorists. Then there was the Christmas season when Dad somehow managed to put his hands on one hundred surplus army gas masks. How to parlay them into cash stumped him only momentarily. The upcoming holiday prompted him to sell them as gifts for young boys who wanted to play "soldier." His stock was exhausted in three days.

The year 1951 saw the expansion of the Tony Williams financial empire into the septic tank business. Northern Virginia housing mushroomed after World War II, and sleepy, rural Fairfax County struggled to keep up with the postwar boom. Rapid home construction quickly outpaced the growth of sewer systems, so even some of the fanciest Fairfax County homes had septic tanks. Early one morning in the spring of 1951, I awoke to find myself heir to a fortune built on this technological gap. Dad had won a brand-new Ford septic tank truck in an all-night crap game with Gypsy buddies passing through northern Virginia.

My brother Mike and I, at ages six and seven, could barely crawl on top of the truck, but we soon became the youngest employees of the A.B.C. (Always Better Cleaning) Septic Tank Service. Dad had wanted to call it Tony Williams and Sons, but practicality prevailed over sentimentality. Selecting A.B.C. placed us first in the yellow pages.

Dad really didn't need helpers. He drug us along with him because he said he wanted his boys to learn the "honey-wagon" business and life. Mike was an eager pupil. Up and dressed early every morning, he was always in the truck before being summoned. Even under the cloud of sewer gasses his face beamed as he handed Dad the crud-encrusted black hoses, crowbars, and wrenches. I was the reluctant "draftee."

In fact I always felt a bit self-conscious as the truck chugged up the streets of the Fairfax County subdivisions. The huge freshly painted houses were resplendent in the summer sun. The children, well scrubbed and neatly dressed, looked at us with disdain. It was hard to believe they needed us for anything. However, any doubts about the urgency of our visit vanished the minute Dad jimmied the manhole cover open. Once the septic tank motor was purring, Dad raced around the truck, tightening bolts and connections, and repositioning the hose inside the tank. Though normally talkative, he always ignored the homeowners who tried to chat with him, and ordered us to sit quietly on the truck. We were in and out of a job in under an hour, and generally pumped three tanks before lunchtime.

Dad was paid per visit, so there was a strong incentive to return as often as possible. One afternoon he divulged that he only emptied half of the tank on each trip—and thus came back twice as often. When I expressed concern that his "scam" might be discovered, he chuckled. "Find me the man who is going to check if I got all his shit!"

Though I loathed my seat atop the vibrating truck as we pumped the nauseous sludge from the black holes, I didn't complain, because I knew what came next. As soon as we finished Dad would say, "We're off to the races." First, we'd stop at a fast-food joint and grab a sack of half-dollar-size hamburgers. We sat in the cab chomping the burgers as Dad crossed the Fourteenth Street bridge and sped to the savings and loan to cash his checks. Well fed and flush with money, we'd then make our way to a favorite downtown department store. He had barely switched off the engine when shoppers spilling out of the revolving doors began to hold their noses. Customers and salesclerks shrank back from us as the aroma of raw sewage preceded us down the aisles.

We didn't care. We could buy whatever captured our fancy. Vivid in my memory is a red-and-silver satin jacket I found on one visit. It was expensive, but Dad counted out cash like it was play money. Then it was on to the men's section, where he snatched a Botany 500 sport coat off the rack; to Appliances, where he ordered the newest gadgets; then always to the girls' section, for a floor-length "Gypsy" dress for my sister. Dad peeled off bill after bill and the wad in his hand didn't seem to get any smaller. Finally, when we were so laden with packages we could barely balance them in our arms, we returned to the truck. As we weaved through the frowning sidewalk crowd, I held my head high.

Shopping was always followed by another trek through the Virginia suburbs to Cameron Run, an isolated tributary of the Potomac River. Dad backed down a graveled incline to a manhole fifty feet from the water. The clang of steel against steel rang out over the deserted riverbank as he delivered a sharp crowbar blow to the truck's trapdoor. With a roar, a thousand pounds of fetid, lumpy liquid cascaded in a black waterfall and disappeared down the manhole, headed straight to the Potomac River. Dad stood there and laughed. "I'm gettin' rich pumping shit."

In the summer of 1951 we abandoned our one room home off the tavern for a fancy town house in exclusive downtown Alexandria. The Pitt Street home provided a welcomed sanctuary from the chaos of the tavern. I watched Dad prepare a very late tax return that year, showing a gross income of over $50,000. We were climbing what seemed like an endless ladder of riches. Painters and carpenters were always underfoot at the Pitt Street house. We were the only family in the neighborhood with two televisions. Dad installed an elaborate Lionel train set for me in the spare fourth bedroom. I owned two new Schwinn bikes though I could barely ride them. When I tagged along with Dad to Alexandria bars, everyone hailed him as "the man with the Midas touch."

There were a number of tavern jobs that I enjoyed much more than the septic tank truck hustle. It was almost a delight working alongside Raymond, who didn't censor his dirty jokes in front of me. But the real treat was when Dad recruited waitresses to help out with special projects. Not staring at the women in tight shorts and halter tops was almost more than I could manage. One Sunday when Mom took the other children to a playground, I helped Dad and two waitresses paint the kitchen and the rest rooms. Barbara, Dad, and I covered the kitchen. Lois, the beautiful redhead, was in the women's rest room. The four of us were working quietly for about half an hour, when Barbara begged for a beer. We all stopped for a break. I had a couple of Cokes and they had several beers each. Back at work I watched Dad pinch Barbara on the butt twice. The first time he tried to hide it. The second he just winked at me as she giggled.

Lois called out from the bathroom, "Barbara, I'm getting lonely. Why don't you help me?"

"You don't want *me* back there, Lois. You want a man. I'm gonna send Tony back there to take care of you. He's a red-hot Italian lover!"

Dad stepped down from the ladder, placed an arm around Barbara's waist, and announced, "You know, working here with you lovely beauties is the true elixir of life. You make it hard for a man to keep his mind on business. But my dears, I must resist, even if it is difficult in the face of such incredible charms."

"That sure in the hell ain't what you said last Friday night, Tony!" Lois fired back. Then she added, "I've had my fill of you anyway."

Raising her voice, she continued.

"I didn't tell you, Barbara, but Tony gave me a bonus last weekend. Right after closing there on the kitchen chopping block. Then I asked him to loan me twenty dollars. He hemmed and hawed and finally crammed two bills in my purse and told me to take off 'fore his wife came. When I got home I discovered the bastard had stuffed two one-dollar bills in my purse."

Dad retorted, "Lois, my dear, you must be mistaken. Even though it's against my principles to loan money to associates here at the restaurant, I violated that rule and put two tens in your purse."

He paused, then continued, "You know it was dark and we were in a hurry. Maybe the money dropped from your purse while you rushed out. To show you what a good sport I am, since you no longer care to let me sample your wares, I will provide another man who can enjoy your beauty and loveliness, and he comes with money. He has long sought the opportunity to enjoy the sheer bliss of intimacy with you."

"Where is this man, Tony, in New York?"

"No, he's right here in the restaurant, just waiting to be called."

"Hell, send him on back!"

The roar of laughter rang out through the restaurant as Dad pushed me through the kitchen door with two tens stuffed in my shirt pocket. I stood there gawking at the enchanting body that had obsessed me since the night of the burlesque.

While planning a visit to my maternal grandparents I began to discover affluence had its disadvantages. Prisoners of their own success, Mom and Dad felt unable to close the tavern for even a short Christmas holiday. They trusted no one, not even each other, to manage the nightly flow of cash into the tavern. The week before Christmas of 1951, Mike and I stood in Washington's vast Union Station listening to Dad's final instructions. Though we feared making the six-hundred-mile trip to Muncie, Indiana, by ourselves, Dad dazzled us with visions of Christmas gifts and expectant relatives. Still, I protested.

"Come on, Billy, don't be such a baby," he said bitterly. "You're the oldest. Take care of your brother. Understand, Mike? Billy's in charge."

"Yes, Daddy," Mike answered sullenly, as I forced a smile.

Dad thrust a stuffed coin purse toward me that held thirty dollars for food and drinks.

"Okay. Three things. First, don't talk to anyone on the train except the conductor. Second, don't let anyone take your money. If you lose that money, you'll be on your own. Your momma won't be there to take care of you. Third, don't talk with any men when you go to the bathroom, and never, never, ever, let anyone touch your 'thing.' If somebody tries to grab your peewee, I want you to start hollering. Do you understand?"

Our eyes widened as we nodded affirmatively in unison.

"Billy," he said, "this trip is your responsibility. If something goes wrong, it's your fault."

A few hours out of Washington, when I could delay no longer, I reluctantly used the rest room. Then, as we crossed into the Pennsylvania mountains, I dared to order sandwiches and soft drinks from an aisle vendor. He stood impatiently while I struggled to fish the correct change from my coin purse. Finally, he stalked off with an exasperated "I'll be back." A traveler seated across the aisle offered to help. He reached for my coin purse, but I held fast.

"Conductor! Conductor! We're being robbed!" I screamed. All eyes in the car turned toward us. The fellow passenger released his grip on the purse, but I continued to yell for the conductor. He came running. After our seatmate explained that he simply wanted to lend a helping hand, the conductor sought to calm me. There were no more incidents the rest of the trip, but when we arrived in Indiana the conductor made it clear to Grandpa that we would not be permitted to return to Washington alone.

We were always greeted warmly in Muncie, but hardly a day passed without some abrupt silence when I entered a room filled with relatives. The silence indicated to me that aunts, uncles, and even older cousins shared a secret I must not know. Schoolboy sleuth that I was, I tried to discover it at every opportunity. That visit I was certain I had solved the puzzle. While skimming a comic book in Grandma's living room, I spied a recently added snapshot of an elaborately dressed naval officer from among an array of photos on the fireplace mantle. I jumped from the couch and raced to my grandmother's side at the kitchen sink to quiz her about the mystery sailor.

"That's your Uncle Frank," she responded. "Chief petty officer. He's the only one of my children who ever made anything out of himself."

My fascination with military lore was ignited. I wondered aloud when he was coming to Muncie. Grandma snipped, "Not when you're here." She surprised me by seeming to take a perverse pleasure in my bewilderment, and added bitingly, "He never wants to see you kids." That was the first time I was told that someone didn't want to see me. But I was not troubled by her angry tone because I believed I was unraveling the mystery.

"He's mad 'cause my dad makes more money than him!" I concluded smugly.

"Money can't buy everything, Mr. Big Mouth. Anyhow, Frank don't give a damn about your dad's money . . ." She paused, turned off the kitchen faucet, then added in an almost inaudible whisper, "Or your dad."

Sensing the secret was almost within my grasp, I moved closer and tried again.

"I bet he don't like my dad 'cause he's Italian."

"Italian, my fanny," Grandma responded. Squinting through her thick rimless glasses, she snarled, "Frank works with some real Italian boys on his ship. They even showed him how to make genuine spaghetti. That ain't the reason, Mr. Smarty Pants."

"Well, what is it?" I demanded in exasperation.

"I ain't saying!" she hissed, her round pink face turning bright red as she planted her hands on her hips. "If you don't understand it now, you will one of these days."

Though Grandma was cold and secretive, Grandpa was warm and open. My favorite pastime was tagging along as Grandma drove him to work at the Nickel Plate Railroad Yard. Every afternoon like clockwork, we piled into the brand-new maroon Chevy coupe and sped into town. Gravel crackled underneath the car as it glided to a stop next to the huge diesel engine. Grandpa tousled my hair and took the heavy black lunch pail I had carried from the house. Clad in sharply pressed bib overalls with a red cowboy bandanna around his neck, he strode to the huge black-and-yellow locomotive. The crown of his blue railroad man's cap stood stiff against the wind. He paused momentarily beside the engine, scanned the area just like a television gunfighter, jerked his head sideways, and let fly a brown stream of Union Workman tobacco juice. Then with the curl of a finger my grandpa, the engineer, beckoned for me.

I dashed across the yard and scrambled up the ladder behind him. The acrid diesel smell surrounded me as my head passed the cabin floor. I clung white-knuckled to the steel railing as the cab began to vibrate. Grandpa shouted orders to his fireman. He leaned out the side window as we approached the Kilgore Street crossing. Cautiously, I moved toward the open passageway to peer down at the mortals waiting in their tiny tin cars. Soon we rolled past the sea of gravestones in Beech Grove Cemetery. Grandpa cranked the engine to full throttle and motioned for me to step in front of him. I squeezed into the small space between his body and the mysterious, black-faced gauges with white markings. Standing on my tiptoes I surveyed the tracks stretching endlessly before us. I gasped for breath. Grandpa placed his hand on my shoulder, and we faced the onslaught of the wind together, thundering north to Ohio.

That vacation I dreaded the call that ultimately had to be made to Dad. I pleaded with Grandma not to reveal the train incident until I had a chance to talk to him, but she ignored me.

Dad's voice was full of anger. "Damn, Billy, you screwed up. How could you and Mike be so stupid? . . . I'm sure in the hell not gonna come after you. If you hadn't been such a crybaby, none of this would've happened. . . . Here, I'm putting your mother on. She can talk to her little sissy."

"Mom," I asked, "can't you come and get us?"

"Billy," she said, her voice full of stress, "I'll try but it's gonna be awful hard. We've been busy. Sissy and the baby need me here to look after them. They can't take care of themselves. You'll get along all right. You're eight years old."

"Mom," I begged, "please come. We can't do it."

We awoke several days after New Year's 1952 to bad weather. I kept hoping Mom would appear. I even prayed the final morning that Grandma and Grandpa would take us to Virginia, but we found ourselves in the South Walnut Street parking lot of the ABC Coach Lines. At the ticket counter Grandma made arrangements for the driver to help us change buses in Dayton and ask the next driver to make sure we made our Pittsburgh connection.

Snow and ice turned a three-hour trip into five, and I feared we would be late to Dayton. Much to my relief, the transfer went smoothly. When we arrived in Pittsburgh, the Washington bus was late. The driver deposited Mike and me at a bench near the Traveler's Aid booth and left for his next run. As I kept my ear tuned to the fuzzy crackling of the loudspeaker, Mike gave me additional worries.

"Billy, if somebody bothers us, the driver can't come back and help. We'll just have to fight 'em ourselves."

"Mike, how can we fight? We're too little. We need help."

"Who we gonna get? We don't know anybody here."

Finally, our bus was announced over the loudspeaker. Mike was silent as we boarded. I bumped into him as he halted at the top of the steps. Then all of a sudden, he moved deliberately down the aisle, pausing beside an attractive but plainly dressed young woman in her early twenties. With just a second of hesitation he climbed in beside her and motioned me to the seat across the aisle. She looked puzzled.

Mike asked, "Ma'am, can we sit here by you? We have to go all the way to Washington alone 'cause our mom and dad don't love us." Tears welled up in his soft brown eyes as he pleaded. "Will you help us?"

Her mouth dropped open, and with a southern drawl, she responded. "Of course. I'm on my own too."

# Chapter 3

# "Captain of My Soul"

Rental housing was the third and final expansion of the Tony Williams business empire. Dad hatched the idea during a drinking bout with a scrap metal dealer. For about six weeks almost every able-bodied man in Gum Springs was employed to hastily construct five sheet metal cabins behind the tavern.

They were filled with tenants quickly and all seemed to go well for a few months, but early in the summer of 1952, my father, thinking a tenant had skipped town owing us rent, broke down the door of one of the shacks. The lodger was still there—dead. The police arrived, then the coroner. Finally, the undertaker backed his long black hearse to the cabin door and loaded the fellow inside while Mike and I watched with amazement. It was the first corpse I had ever seen. I couldn't tell much about him, but his huge belly puffed up the rubber sheet like a mountain. "He ain't fat, Billy," Raymond said, reading my mind. "Just swolled up. He's been dead almost a week."

That afternoon, Dad, Raymond, and I scoured the shack from top to bottom. While I understood the need for a thorough effort, from the lingering, pungent smell of death, Dad surprised me by stripping the cabin bare. He tossed everything on the pavement: tables, chairs, furniture, rugs, even the bed and bedding and burned them in a huge bonfire. Then he lit a metal-encased candle that filled the cabin with a strange nostril-stinging odor.

"It kills the germs," he said.

Puzzled, I wondered what germs the dead left.

It wasn't until two weeks later that I overheard Harvey and Raymond whispering about why our tenants were fleeing the cabins. Everyone in Gum Springs but me knew the "fat" guy had TB. I had heard all about tuberculosis on television. It killed more Americans than any other disease. There was the belief that you could get it from smoking, even from the air. When I questioned Dad about how he was going to fill the vacancies, it was one of the few times he was at a loss for ideas. I stayed as far away from the cabins as possible until the arrival of Miss Sallie.

The tall, thin, brown-skinned woman in an old-fashioned black dress was just one more person in the endless stream of those who tried to work with Percy. I could tell she was poor from the tattered cardboard suitcase Dad carried from the car. Though I didn't know her, I was concerned as Dad led her to the cabin that my Gum Springs playmates had dubbed "the Dungeon of Death." Halting at the doorway, I wanted to warn her. She took my fear of entering the room as an insult, and roughly brushed past me.

We started off badly and it got worse. Though Percy was hard to please, he actually seemed kind compared to Miss Sallie. When I pressed for a hamburger, she said no without a blink. When Mike sneaked open the kitchen refrigerator for a soda she grabbed him by the ear and marched him out immediately. We made faces behind her back. She caught us, but we didn't care. We knew she was nobody. We owned the tavern! Still, we learned to stay out of her way, and hoped she would be gone by the end of the summer. We were certain her days were numbered because she and Percy argued every afternoon. One day she slapped me when I dropped a bowl of ice cream. That night my mother and father had a fierce argument. Within days, Miss Sallie was gone.

Dad began to drink more heavily than I could ever remember. In fact, he was almost never sober. After a few near accidents on Route 1, I refused to ride in the septic tank truck with him. Mike, loyal as ever, eagerly climbed into the cab. One afternoon as Dad careened around a corner in the Woodley Hills Addition, the passenger door flew open. Mike tumbled to the pavement and broke his collarbone. He was in a shoulder cast for almost six weeks. After that, Mom refused to let any of us ride with Dad. To shield us from the drinking, she secluded us at the Pitt Street house, far away from the tavern. But there was no refuge from the escalating tension between my parents.

My mother's high-pitched wails pierced my dreams. "Agh! Agh!" came the cries. I rubbed my eyes, hoping it was a nightmare. The screams continued. My palms pressed over my ears could not silence the thump of fist against flesh. Trembling, I crept to my door and peeked at my mother, moaning on the bedroom floor. Dad was astride her. His face was contorted with rage. *Pow!* His fist almost disappeared into her cheek. Blood drooled from her mouth. She struggled to push him away. He ripped her nightgown straight down the middle. Her breasts flopped to the side. He grabbed a nipple. His neck muscles bulged as he squeezed it.

"Oooooooh!" she shrieked. He pulled her from the floor. Her face twisted in agony.

"You white bitch. If I ever catch you fuckin' that nigger again, I'm gonna kill you. You understand?" He punched her in the stomach. She spewed blood across the new pink bedspread. He jerked her up.

"Get your white trash ass out of here and clean up," he snarled, and shoved her toward the bathroom. He staggered to the bed and fell across it, fully dressed.

Whimpering, Mom stumbled into the bathroom.

I sneaked back to my bed, not daring to stir until I heard him snoring. The next morning I lay rigid, straining to hear the voices downstairs. There was a man's voice, but it didn't sound like Dad. I slipped out of bed and tiptoed to Mike's bedroom window. As he lay sleeping, I scanned the street for Dad's late-model Cadillac. It was gone. Inching my way to the top of the steps, I strained to recognize the man's voice in the kitchen. "Mary . . . I got the car loaded. . . . The girl is asleep. I'll take the baby. Let's hurry and get out of here."

In panic I descended steps three at a time and burst into the kitchen.

Immediately, I recognized our visitor. Chuck, a white soldier, was a regular at the tavern. Mom's face was bruised and swollen. They both stared at me standing in the doorway in my pajamas.

"Where you going?" I demanded as Mom lifted her suitcase off the floor.

"Billy . . ." She paused.

"Mary," interrupted Chuck, "we gotta get out of here before he comes back and kills ya."

"Mom, ain't we going with you?"

"Yeah," she said, kneeling. "Run upstairs. Get Mike. We got to hurry."

"You gonna wait?"

"Of course. I said I would, didn't I?"

I loped up the stairs. Wrestling jeans over my pajamas, I shouted for Mike. Just as we reached the outside stoop, Dad's car roared up Pitt Street. The Cadillac straddled the curb at a forty-five-degree angle. He leaped out of the car, followed by Raymond from the passenger side. Chuck hastily laid the baby on the back car seat. Mom's grip on the suitcase tightened.

"You lousy son of a bitch, I should . . ." Dad hissed as he strode toward Chuck, fists clenched at his sides.

Raymond grabbed Dad by the arm. "Forget him, Tony, that's not what you came here for."

Dad glared at us from the bottom of the steps for almost a minute. Finally, his face softened. Tears welled in his eyes as the harsh daylight vividly accented my mother's black eye and bruises. Mike and I cowered behind her, clinging to her dress. Fearful he might beat us, our steel army surplus helmets were belted tightly under our chins.

"Tony, I'm going," Mom said. "I can't take it anymore."

"Please, Mary," he said with an earnestness I had never seen before. His shoulders slouched and he slinked up the steps expressing shame for the beatings and drinking. He begged forgiveness, and stood at the doorway looking into the house we had hoped would be a peaceful refuge. "Mary," he cried. All eyes turned to him. "I'm gonna show you how much I love you." And with that —Boom!—he rammed his fist through the plate-glass door. We recoiled in shock as glass shattered all over the steps. He raised his bleeding fist in front of him vowing eternal commitment. As he wrapped it in a handkerchief, we all slowly followed him back into the house.

In July of 1953, Mike and I were on our regular summer holiday in Indiana. Dad arrived unexpectedly one afternoon. Grandpa was on a train run to Ohio. A few angry words passed between Dad and Grandma. Mike and I sensed trouble at home, but Dad revealed nothing as we loaded our suitcases into the trunk of the Cadillac. I knew better than to question him when he was mad, but Mike pestered him about Mom and the other kids. Dad silenced him with a "Shut up, Dummy" as we sped away from Muncie. We fell asleep as he drove through the night.

Dad seemed more relaxed as dawn broke over Route 40. He even cracked a few jokes about the signs we saw along the highway. In Washington, Pennsylvania, he stopped to visit some old friends, Jimmy and Audrey Fisher. While Mike and I wolfed down glazed doughnuts in the kitchen we overheard that Mom had run away again. Since she had left and returned many times we weren't too worried.

A full stomach helped me relax as we began the final leg of our journey home. Near Uniontown, Mike asked if we could stop at the spring. We always loved that spot. High on a mountain ridge, it was a majestic place. It had always been a peaceful interlude on auto trips to and from Indiana. Everyone spoke softly. The entire family had enjoyed the trickle of water down the mountainside. None of us ever argued there. Even Dad seemed soothed by the smooth flowing brook. That morning as we headed to Virginia I yearned for the calmness that came from the spring, and was pleased when Dad stopped.

It was still early morning. We were all alone. As we cupped the cool, inviting water in our hands, Dad remained beside the car frowning and puffing on a cigarette. "Hurry up, boys!" he shouted.

"Come on, Dad, get a drink," Mike coaxed.

We continued to frolic in the water. Dad shouted again. Recognizing the anger in his voice, I moved toward the car. Mike lingered. Dad strode past me.

"Get to the car," he snarled as he jerked Mike away from the water. Mike stumbled and landed on his butt. We watched with pained expressions as Dad straddled the water, unzipped his pants, and urinated in the stream.

Barely a word was spoken during the next three hours as we made our way to Alexandria. I was puzzled to see an official-looking envelope that said NOTICE OF FORECLOSURE lying on top of the mail, but I was too intimidated by Dad's dark mood to seek an explanation. Mom and the kids were gone. Their closets were completely empty. There was no evidence that anyone had ever lived in the house but the three of us.

I glanced at the accumulated newspapers Dad tossed on the table. I found little solace from the headline KOREAN ARMISTICE SIGNED AT PANMUNJOM. My life, which had been so intertwined with the ebb and flow of the Korean War, now began to follow a different path.

We soon retreated to where we began, our previous cramped living quarters at the tavern. A week, then a month passed, but there was no word from our mother. Dad hinted she was hiding in Washington, but Mike and I didn't believe him, certain she would come for us if she were that close. She always had. Dad said something about a divorce, but I wouldn't listen, refusing to believe it had anything to do with us. Mike started wetting the bed and we both began to lose weight. We couldn't understand how our mother could just leave and not return.

When school started in September, my hand shook with doubt as I penciled her name over "Mother" on my enrollment form. Reaching into my book bag, I grabbed an ink pen, and I traced over "Mary Williams" so she couldn't sneak into the school at night and erase her name. Homework kept me occupied, but Mike lost interest in school. Every evening he sat perched on the tavern steps like a motherless bird, eyes darting up and down Route 1, hoping Mom would arrive in the next car drifting into our parking lot.

The waitresses took us shopping and were very kind. But the superficial sweetness was hard for me to tolerate because I knew they just felt sorry for us. I absolutely hated being the object of pity. Dad, soon up to his old games of sexual conquest, reveled in it. He told every woman who walked into the tavern how Mom "stole him blind," then ran off with the "hired help." He introduced each sweetheart to us with "Boys, this is your new momma."

With the Korean peace accord, almost half of Fort Belvoir's soldiers were demobilized virtually overnight. The effect on our business was immediate and devastating. Not that we could have handled our normal crowds anyway, as Dad was always drunk. He no longer had to order me to watch the cash register. I stayed there by choice, because I knew it was critical for our survival. All too soon the crowds dwindled, and the waitresses deserted us for the booming Washington bars catering to the growing government bureaucracy. Since Mom wasn't there to beg Percy to reconsider when he threatened to quit, he soon left for good. Then Mike and I really went hungry. When we begged for dinner Dad tossed us a packet of potato chips from the bar counter display. Soon all the chips, pretzels, candy, Cokes, and pickled pig's feet were gone. Food, beer, and liquor suppliers hounded Dad about delinquent bills. I stood beside him as he pleaded for more time. One by one they all stopped deliveries.

Hoping to "weather this storm" and to maintain the business, Dad landed a job as a security guard on the midnight shift at the Pentagon. Every night he closed the tavern in a flurry at eleven and raced to the Cadillac, now hidden deep in the bowels of Gum Springs to keep it out of the hands of the "repo' man."

One night long after Dad left for work, I awakened to a loud banging from our street-side door. At first I paid little attention. It was common for drunks to pound on our door late into the night. Generally, we just ignored them. Burying my head under the blankets, I prayed the intruders would leave. The door continued to rattle from the incessant banging and a shiver shot down my spine when I heard the handle turn. I bolted upright. Dad had forgotten to lock the door! The stench of smoke and stale beer preceded four white men staggering into the room. I stared at them from my top bunk in disbelief. "Where's your old man?" demanded the beefy-faced leader of the group as he flipped on the lights.

"He's at work. Ain't nobody supposed to be here," I protested lamely.

"Hell, don't worry," he said with a red-faced grin. "I know Tony. We used to chase pussy when you was just a glimmer in his eye. I came by for a beer."

My instinct was to dart to phone the police, but the leader blocked my way. Mike, now awake, yelled to the men as they sauntered into the tavern. "Daddy said we've got to save the beer for customers! You gotta pay!"

"Yeah, we gonna pay. Just like that sonofabitch paid when he gave my old lady the clap," snorted a short, muscular guy who followed the others into the tavern. They took an armful of beer from the cooler and left. My body shook with relief when I heard their car door slam. I leaped out of bed and grabbed a meat cleaver from the kitchen. Mike and I wedged the sofa in front of the outside door and put a dresser across the tavern entryway. I held the meat cleaver in my hand the rest of the night, but I was unable to sleep.

After this, Dad convinced a friend, Sunshine, to watch us at night. Actually, Mike and I watched her from our bunks. We feigned sleep as we heard Sunshine, a beautiful caramel-colored woman, moan and groan beneath her naked Serbian lover, Brownie Valetic, a buddy of Dad's from Midland, Pennsylvania.

Though I began to feel safer at home, I now worried about Dad. He often spoke of foreign spies in the Pentagon. They meant to steal America's military secrets and, according to Dad, would kill anyone who stood in their way. One evening he divulged that a body had been discovered on his shift. Security officers were told to continue their solitary walks through the miles of Pentagon corridors but to contact the duty room every hour.

When Dad missed two calls to the duty room one night, a massive search was undertaken. They checked elevator shafts and Dumpsters. Then they investigated room by room. Soon the entire security force joined the effort. At six o'clock the following morning Dad was found—asleep—in front of a general's empty liquor cabinet. He was fired immediately, another victim of the Cold War.

The tavern business continued to deteriorate and we closed the doors of the Open House Cafe for the last time just before Halloween of 1953. Our final hope was the septic tank business, but Dad crashed the truck into a culvert one night when returning from gambling in Alexandria. Sunshine disappeared like all the others. There was no money for food or clothes. Mike and I wore two khaki outfits bought at a Washington, D.C., army/navy store "fire sale." Dad occasionally put them in the washing machine, but after it broke they were dirty most of the time.

One afternoon following a bout of drinking, one of Dad's cronies offered to take us and our laundry to his house. I distrusted him, but Dad was too drunk to listen to my concerns. Mike and I were driven to a poor white section of Alexandria, off King Street near the railroad station. The area was familiar because a popular movie theater was nearby, but we had never visited any of the dilapidated row houses in the neighborhood.

A musty smell oozed from the yellowed wallpaper as we walked through a narrow hallway into the kitchen. The man motioned us to the kitchen table and tossed us each an apple. We stripped off our clothes, and he loaded the washing machine on the back porch. Naked, we retraced our steps to the foyer and climbed an old staircase. In his bedroom, the man took down a small box of toys from a shelf in his closet. Mike's eyes lit up when he discovered a tiny red fire engine.

As the man led me from the room, Mike was already lost in fantasy.

Sunlight filtered through the bathroom window and a sharp antiseptic smell engulfed us. An old claw-toe bathtub took up most of the room. Soon the water was running, and I sat on the toilet, waiting for the tub to fill. He turned off the faucets, handed me a bar of soap, and motioned for me to climb into the water. While I washed, he began to undress. Soon he was naked. "Scoot up, Billy," he said, "I'm getting in the tub."

I moved forward a bit, unconcerned. Mom would often be naked when we were bathing, and sometimes my younger brother and sister bathed with her. He sat behind me, and began slowly soaping my back. He told me to wet my hair so he could wash it. I felt him move closer to me. When I straightened, he poured shampoo over my head and began vigorously rubbing it. He rubbed so hard it hurt. Shampoo leaked into my eyes and they began to sting.

"My eyes are burning!"

"Rinse your face."

As I leaned over, I felt his hands around my waist pulling me toward him. The water eased the sting in my eyes. But as he pulled me onto his lap, pain shot through me. It became sharper and sharper. I began to cry.

"What's wrong, Billy?"

"It hurts. Something's cuttin' me."

"Oh, don't be a baby, nothing's wrong wit' you."

"My butt hurts," I cried.

He slowly pushed me away. The sharp pain disappeared.

"I think it's time for you to get out of the tub," he said. He reached to the cabinet for a towel. "Here, take this."

I dried myself, but was afraid to touch where it really hurt.

"Hurry up so Mike can get in here."

I never told my father what happened to us. There were only a few brief moments each morning when he was sober.

My tenth birthday passed unnoticed. By Thanksgiving Mike and I were hungry all the time. When Dad had a few dollars we visited a small Italian restaurant near Groveton. Dinner was one big red meatball on a bed of spaghetti and two pieces of white bread with one pat of butter. Mornings were always the same—nothing to eat. Our only hope for food during the day was to be able to buy a school lunch. As soon as I awoke, I badgered Dad for lunch money. Usually he didn't have it. I drank all the water I could to fill my stomach. Solemnly we walked to Route 1 and waited for the bus to Woodley Hills Elementary School.

While we stood at the roadside, Dad confronted early-morning pedestrians who tried to avoid his grizzled, unshaven face. He stood directly in their paths and, after a few brief words, turned and pointed to us. Standing there with dirty faces, shaggy hair, and mud-caked trousers, Mike and I must have been a pathetic sight. As the passersby stared at us, I was embarrassed by how quickly I saw rigid jaws dissolve. Just as the bus arrived, Dad hurried over and handed us each a quarter. Less than a year earlier I carried at least five dollars in my pocket every day. Now I clutched the quarter Dad begged feeling both gratitude and shame.

On January 9, 1954, Dad's fortieth birthday, he drunkenly recited his favorite poem, William Henley's "Invictus."

> Out of the night that covers me,
>   Black as the Pit from pole to pole,
> I thank whatever gods may be
>   For my unconquerable soul.
>
> In the fell clutch of circumstance
>   I have not winced nor cried aloud.
> Under the bludgeonings of chance
>   My head is bloody, but unbowed.
>
> Beyond this place of wrath and tears
>   Looms but the Horror of the shade,
> And yet the menace of the years
>   Finds, and shall find, me unafraid.

It matters not how strait the gate,
    How charged with punishments the scroll,
I am master of my fate:
    Captain of my soul!

Normally Dad shouted the last two lines with dramatic flair. But that day his thin frame shook with emotion as tears streamed down his cheeks. Mike and I shared his desperation and began to cry along with him. I sensed that nothing was going to be the same again. Less than two weeks later, the three of us left Virginia forever.

# Chapter 4

# Rooster

A bright winter morning dawned over western Ohio as I stared out the mud-splattered Greyhound window. My head throbbed from the sleepless eighteen-hour trip. Faded signs drooped alongside U.S. 40. DON'T TAKE THE CURVE—AT 60 PER—WE HATE TO LOSE—A CUSTOMER—BURMA SHAVE. DAYTON 10 MILES announced a white-faced sign with large black letters. My throat ached for water. Mike opened his eyes and fidgeted in his seat to straighten his imitation army fatigue pants, which had twisted around his knees during the long night ride.

"Are we there yet, Billy?" he asked.

"No, Mike. It's three more hours to Muncie."

"As soon as we get to Grandma's, I'm gonna go down to Nye's for Colonial cupcakes and . . ."

As he rambled, I drifted into my own Muncie fantasy. First, I would race up the broad wooden stairs to reclaim my summer bedroom. Then I would search the attic for my uncles' comic books.

Crouching, I squeezed into the tiny attic door. As I pulled the cord, a dim light reflected off the shiny tarpaper ceiling. Focusing my eyes, I discovered two large boxes marked BOOKS. All four of my uncles loved comics, and I was grateful Grandma saved every one. The enticing covers of *Captain America, Submariner,* and *The Phantom* flashed in front of me as I dragged a box to the light.

The smell of mildew enveloped me as I leaned inside it. I snatched a Dick Tracy mystery and helped him solve a crime with Sam Ketcham. Out of the corner of my eye I recognized the purple color panels of *Buck Rogers* and joined him. Perspiration beaded under my shirt. My knees ached from the rough-hewn attic floorboard. Still I hunched over the box. As the Submariner and I broke the ocean's surface, from across the water I heard "Billy . . . Billy."

"Billy!" Dad said sharply as he leaned across the aisle. I looked into his face. The Greyhound's air brakes hissed as it slowed for the junction with State Highway 201. In a somber voice he continued. "Boys, I've got some bad news for you." He paused. We leaned forward, anxiously. The wool of the seat made me itch. "We're not going to stay with Grandpa and Grandma Cook when we get to Muncie."

The gears clunked and the bus shuddered to a stop at an intersection.

"Why not?" I demanded.

"Your mother and I are getting a divorce. We can't stay with them."

Straightening my back, I turned toward him. He tightened his lips. My stomach rumbled with anger. I refused to believe we could not live with Grandpa and Grandma! They would end all the worries about food, clothes, and lunch money. If Dad thought Grandpa and Grandma didn't want us, he was wrong! Reassured, I leaned against the seat. As the bus bumped into gear, I felt a tinge of doubt. He leaned closer and spoke very softly. "There's something else I want to tell you."

"What?" I groaned.

"Remember Miss Sallie who used to work for us in the tavern?"

Dad's lower lip quivered. He looked ill. Had he always looked this unhealthy, I wondered, or was it something that happened on the trip? I felt my face—skin like putty, lips chapped and cracked. Had I changed, too?

"It's hard to tell you boys this." He paused, then slowly added, "But she's really my momma. That means she's your grandmother."

"But that can't be, Dad! She's colored!" I whispered, lest I be overheard by the other white passengers on the bus.

"That's right, Billy," he continued. "She's colored. That makes you part colored, too, and in Muncie you're gonna live with my Aunt Bess. . . ."

I didn't understand Dad. I knew I wasn't colored, and neither was he. My skin was white. All of us are white, I said to myself. But for the first time, I had to admit Dad didn't exactly look white. His deeply tanned skin puzzled me as I sat there trying to classify my own father. Goose bumps covered my arms as I realized that whatever he was, I was. I took a deep breath. I couldn't make any mistakes. I looked closer. His heavy lips and dark brown eyes didn't make him colored, I concluded. His black, wavy hair was different from Negroes' hair, but it was different from most white folks' hair, too. He was darker than most whites, but Mom said he was Italian. That was why my baby brother had such dark skin and curly hair. Mom told us to be proud of our Italian heritage! That's it, I decided. He was Italian. I leaned back against the seat, satisfied. Yet the unsettling image of Miss Sallie flashed before me like a neon sign.

Colored! Colored! Colored!

He continued. "Life is going to be different from now on. In Virginia you were white boys. In Indiana you're going to be colored boys. I want you to remember that you're the same today that you were yesterday. But people in Indiana will treat you differently."

I refused to believe Dad. I looked at Mike. His skin, like mine, was a light, almost pallid, white. He had Dad's deep brown eyes, too, but our hair was straight. Leaning toward Dad, I examined his hands for a sign, a black mark. There was nothing. I knew I was right, but I sensed something was wrong. Fear overcame me as I faced the Ohio countryside and pondered the discovery of my life.

"I don't wanta be colored," Mike whined. "I don't wanta be colored. We can't go swimmin' or skatin'," he said louder. Nearby passengers turned toward us.

"Shut up, Mike." I punched him in the chest. He hit me in the nose. I lunged for him. We tumbled into the aisle. My knee banged against a sharp aluminum edge. The fatigues ripped. I squeezed his neck. His eyes bulged. I squeezed harder. *Whap!* Pain surged from the back of my head. Dad grabbed my shirt collar and shoved me roughly into the seat. Mike clambered in beside me, still sniffling.

"Daddy, we ain't really colored, are we?" he asked quietly.

No! I answered, still refusing to believe. I'm not colored, I'm white! I look white! I've always been white! I go to "whites only" schools, "whites only" movie theaters, and "whites only" swimming pools! I never had heard anything crazier in my life! How could Dad tell us such a mean lie? I glanced across the aisle to where he sat grim-faced and erect, staring straight ahead. I saw my father as I never had seen him before. The veil dropped from his face and features. Before my eyes he was transformed from a swarthy Italian to his true self—a high-yellow mulatto. My father was a Negro! We were colored! After ten years in Virginia on the white side of the color line, I knew what that meant.

Again Dad spoke in a whisper. "You boys are going to have to learn to live with it, and living with it in Muncie won't be easy. But Indiana is only temporary. Once I settle up the business, we'll head to California and start over. We can still be white, but not in Muncie. The town is full of the Ku Klux Klan. Once they know who you are and what you are, they'll do everything humanly possible to keep you 'in your place.' "

The mention of the Klan stirred up frightful memories. At the tavern I heard many stories about beatings, shootings, and murders of blacks, Catholics, and Jews by the Klan. In Virginia Dad was known as a protector of the Gypsies who plied their craft as painters, roofers, and septic tank men up and down U.S. 1. Much to the consternation of the local police and our white neighbors, the Gypsies often camped in our one-acre parking lot while working in the area. One summer we discovered the Klan was angry at us for shielding the Gypsies, but Dad paid little attention until he noticed a group of white men parked across the highway from us several evenings in a row. Late one night, just before closing, a gunshot shattered our front plate glass window. Dad sat up the rest of the night clutching his German Luger pistol. Raymond borrowed a shotgun from a friend in Gum Springs, and Harvey joined the vigil with his trusty baseball bat. I stayed with them until I couldn't hold my eyes open any longer.

Dad said he planned to return to Virginia to tie up loose ends. Soon, we'd all be together. He called us the "Three Musketeers." In the meantime, we'd live with Aunt Bess.

Questions whirled through my mind, but I did not dare to ask them. I feared the answers. Who was Aunt Bess? Was she colored? Would Grandma and Grandpa Cook take us? Were they prejudiced? Suddenly, I recalled Grandma's quip about the "little niggers" on East Jackson Street one afternoon the past summer as she drove

Grandpa to work. But we were different from those kids playing on the street corner. We were her own flesh and blood!

"Dad," I haltingly asked, "if you and Mom get a divorce, will we still be related to Grandpa and Grandma Cook?"

"Sure, Billy, they're your grandparents. They love you too much to forget about you."

The bus pulled into the Dayton terminal. We moved sluggishly to the front. There was a two-hour wait for the ABC Coach Line connection to Muncie. Dad, a step ahead of us, passed through double doors into the cavernous hall. A crackling loudspeaker filled the air. "Hamilton and Cincinnati now boarding at . . ." A crowd converged. A soldier lingered near the doors, kissing his girlfriend good-bye. Earlier, Mike and I would have gaped at them, but now we had too much to ponder. We passed the familiar green Traveler's Aid cubicle. At the lunch counter at the far end of the building we stood quietly while the waitress reached into a glass case for a cold roast beef sandwich. She punched the register keys while Dad split the sandwich in two. It was our first food since Harvey bought us a candy bar at the bus station in Washington the day before. Dad led us to an isolated wooden bench and dropped the small, tattered canvas bag holding all our belongings. "Wait here," he ordered. "I'll be right back."

He strolled across the room as I hungrily ripped a bite from the sandwich. When Dad disappeared through the terminal doors, I panicked. I felt like I was standing alone at the center of the universe. With the bag in one hand and the sandwich in the other, I shouted for Mike. We raced across the concourse, pushing our way past soldiers and sailors. On the sidewalk I looked north, then south—Dad had vanished. I had no idea what to do. Finally, I saw his tall lanky figure enter a tavern a block away. Half dragging and half carrying our bag, I led Mike down the street. Comforted by the knowledge that Dad was inside, we huddled in the tavern doorway.

After devouring the sandwich, Mike and I began our vigil. Every few minutes I peered into the tavern window to check the time on the Schlitz Beer clock. An hour and a half dragged by. We grew cold and restless. Mike kicked beer bottle caps along the sidewalk. Empty bottles lined the bar in front of Dad. I recognized his familiar gestures punctuating a pronouncement on some public event. Drunk! Five minutes passed, then ten. I pressed my face to the cold plate glass window, hoping he would walk outside to scold me.

Just when I was certain we would miss our bus, a heavyset man in a denim jacket approached the doorway. Summoning all my courage, I begged, "Mister, will you tell the man in the brown derby we gotta catch the bus?"

Just five minutes before departure, Dad strode from the tavern and grabbed the bag.

"Come on boys, let's double-time it!"

Mike and I raced behind him, struggling to keep up with his long legs. Though I feared what lay ahead of us, I knew it couldn't be any worse than what we had left behind in Virginia.

The old, barnlike Muncie bus terminal was a familiar sight. To the north stood a four-story department store with sparkling show windows and colorfully dressed mannequins. Trash and litter cluttered the street to the south. The gold-and-black sign of a pawnshop jutted over the sidewalk. Sadly, I recalled our countless visits to Washington pawnshops the past six months when Dad sold our possessions one by one. Televisions, watches, radios, and finally my beautiful Schwinn bikes had been surrendered to keep us alive.

Dad pulled our small bag from the undercarriage and we headed south on Walnut Street. The odor of stale beer and the twang of country music rolled out to greet us as we passed the Tennessee Lounge. I caught a glimpse of unshaven white men in blue chambray shirts and jeans at the bar. We turned a corner and faced yet another sign, this one heralding THE MUNCIE MISSION. Stenciled below in small letters was the message "Lodging for the homeless." A short gray-haired man stared absently from the doorway. Next to the mission was a large white brick bakery. Trays of doughnuts filled the sidewalk display case. I gazed wistfully at them, but noticed they lacked the familiar shiny glaze. Then I saw a note scribbled in the corner: "Day-old bakery goods for sale."

Five sets of railroad tracks ran alongside the bakery. Stretching east and west as far as we could see, they dissected the city. As we plodded eastward on the uneven rail bed, I ransacked my memory, trying to recognize or remember some sight from earlier train trips with Grandpa, yet it all was strange and foreign. Life was so different, so ordinary, down on the tracks. Abandoned warehouses. Windows covered with boards. Overgrown grass sprouted between spur lines. Dad crossed to the south side and passed a large brown

Dague's Coal Yard sign. An eight-foot barbed-wire fence guarded a mountain of shiny black coal. Beyond the coal yard we heard the sound of cars and leaned across a chest-high concrete wall to watch the traffic disappear into the bowels of the Madison Street underpass.

Barbed wire sprouted again on the other side of the underpass. This time it guarded hollowed car bodies, rusted engines, and old oil drums, relics of a gas station storage lot. We came to a weathered brown clapboard house oddly facing the tracks rather than a street. Two evergreen shrubs stood next to the skeletal vines of a grape arbor. Four railroad ties formed steps down the embankment. Dad turned toward the house. Certain this was Aunt Bess's, I hopped onto the wooden plank porch. He grabbed my arm. "That's Miss Lucy's," he said, leading us around the house.

Patches of brown winter grass dotted a muddy backyard. Two wooden barrels full of rainwater with a thin layer of ice on top stood under the rear eaves. Next to them concrete blocks supported a weathered gray plank bench. An ugly ten-by-fifteen-foot shed, completely covered from top to bottom with rough, green-speckled tar paper stood freakishly in the corner of the yard. It puzzled me that anyone would tar-paper a storage shed. Beyond it, a gate opened onto an alley. I skipped ahead. As I reached the gate, I heard, "This way, Billy."

To my surprise Dad stood at the shed. Then I saw a screen door. The peeling green paint blended so well with the ugly tar paper, I hadn't noticed it before. A sagging spring slowly drew the door shut after Mike. I followed him onto a small enclosed porch—four feet square, no windows, just a thin sheet of plywood to ward off the snow. Beer bottles, water-stained cardboard boxes, and trash littered the porch. An ancient icebox with the top door ajar stood in one corner. Outmoded women's bloomers and faded stockings dangled on a rope stretched across the porch. Dad rapped on the door. No answer. I braced myself, praying this was not our new home. It was worse than our rental cabins in Gum Springs. I couldn't bear to think of what it might be like inside.

"Mom must be at work," Dad said.

Mom! I thought in panic. Was this where Miss Sallie lived? How could anyone stay here?

"Let's see what she's got to eat."

Dad fished through the small icebox.

It was empty except for two beers and some gray hamburger patties. Mike and I winced as the sharp odor of spoiled meat wafted toward us. Dad opened a beer bottle and drained it with one long swallow. Then he guzzled a second, tossing the empties into a corner.

"Come on boys. Let's go to Aunt Bess's."

We followed the alley to Monroe Street. As we trudged south, I realized I'd never seen so many black people in Muncie before. What bothered me most, however, was the tattered, down-at-the-heels feel of the neighborhood. The contrast with Grandpa and Grandma Cook's sparkling white two-story home in the new Mayfield Addition was striking. Here, gloomy weather-beaten houses tottered on crumbling foundations. Exposed two-by-fours propped sagging porches. Jagged glass shards were all that remained in many windows. Graffiti-covered plywood sheets partially covered doorways. The yards were small, littered, and unkempt. Across First Street the run-down houses were replaced by a series of flat-roofed two-story concrete block buildings, all a sickly mustard color. There wasn't a blade of grass in sight, just concrete, mud, and gravel.

"This is the Projects, boys," Dad explained. "Colored families live on this side of Madison, and crackers on the other. Stay outta there. If the crackers learn you're colored, they'll beat the hell out of you. You gotta be careful here, too. Coloreds don't like half-breeds either."

An electrical charge surged through my body. Never before had I thought of myself as a "half-breed." TV westerns taught me half-breeds were the meanest people alive. They led wild bands of Indians on rampages, killed defenseless settlers, and slaughtered innocent women and children. Nobody liked the half-breeds—not the whites, not the Indians. A half-breed! Turning it over and over in my mind, I forced my feet to follow Dad up a long hill, barely noticing a sand-and-gravel playground at the edge of the Projects. We skirted it quickly, and Dad opened the gate of a sooty one-story clapboard house. The ancient wooden porch swayed under our weight as the three of us stood expectantly at the door.

A heavy, big-boned woman, almost six feet tall, with light coffee-colored skin, angular features, and long black braids came to the door. She looked more like an Indian than a colored lady. A calf-length dress hung loosely over her thick body and sagging breasts.

The aroma of cooking grease wafted from the house. Peeking from behind her was a thin, dark-brown-skinned girl about my age.

"Boys, this is Aunt Bess," said Dad.

"How you boys doin'?" she said in a slow drawl. Both Mike and I uttered a weak "Fine."

"This is Mary Lou," she said, pulling the girl to her side. She popped quickly back behind her. "Say hi to your cousins, Mary Lou."

Cousins! I winced as a muffled "Hi" floated from behind the large flowered dress.

"Ain't no need to be standin' in the cold. Come on inside and rest your bones," she said, throwing open the door.

Raising my eyes, I stole another glance at Aunt Bess and Mary Lou. Colored! But that didn't make *me* colored, I decided. I didn't look anything like them. I didn't know them, and didn't want to know them.

Secretly, I examined the shabby room. A tattered couch nudged against a wall. Cotton stuffing spilled from the armrest of a faded green brocade chair. There was no television, just an old-fashioned Philco radio almost four feet tall. I turned to the window looking for an escape. Next to it hung a large collage of snapshots almost two feet square. My eyes scanned the dark faces, recognizing no one. Suddenly a photo leaped at me from the corner. White faces. I wondered why they were there. My mouth dropped open as my eyes fastened onto images resembling Mom and Dad. Certain my mind was playing tricks on me, I leaned forward. It *was* Mom and Dad! And Mike and I were right between them! Stepping closer, I recognized the concrete bench in front of the Open Air Theatre. Then I remembered when the picture was taken. Dad made me and Mike walk across U.S. Route 1 barefoot and in our underwear because he was in such a hurry to take that picture. I sank into the faded green chair. Was I really colored?

Aunt Bess's booming voice interrupted my lament. "You boys hungry?" Looking into her brown jowly face, I realized hours had passed since Mike and I shared the roast beef sandwich in Dayton. We nodded eagerly.

"Come on, then," she said. We followed her through a sitting room and into the kitchen. The crisp smell of burning wood filled the air. In front of an old soot-stained stove, she picked up tongs, inserted them into a large circular piece of iron, and expertly slid it across the stove. Flames leaped from the gaping hole. She dropped wood inside, and then with a clank shoved the covering back into place. She motioned us to a window while she sliced corn bread at the kitchen sink.

I stared at the playground we had passed. It was a full block square, mostly taken up by a gritty sand-and-gravel baseball diamond. A ten-foot wire baseball backstop stood in the corner nearest the house. Wire drooped from its top support, leaving a big gaping hole. An empty swimming pool with cracked walls and peeling paint sat in the far corner of the block. Brown weeds sprouted in its crevices.

Aunt Bess placed steaming bowls of navy beans in front of us. When Mom cooked beans I refused to eat them, but in the last six months I had learned to eat anything that was offered. The beans disappeared in minutes. For dessert we devoured strawberry Jell-O mixed with bananas.

When finished, I timidly asked to use the bathroom. "The slop jar's on the back porch, and the toilet's outside. Take the broom, if you go out."

Puzzled, I stared at the corner sink in the dimly lit kitchen. I noticed black holes in the white porcelain where faucets should have been. Some of the houses in Gum Springs didn't have indoor plumbing, but that was different. This was Indiana. Muncie was a big city. It was 1954. I stared again. Paper bags were stacked in the double sinks. I had not misunderstood. She was talking about an outhouse. Heading for the back room, I pondered, "Slop jar?" As I stepped into a cold, enclosed porch I was engulfed by the pungent odor of stale urine. I snatched the broom and stumbled out the back door, transported instantaneously to an urban barnyard. A six-foot mesh fence surrounded the entire area.

Chickens ran in and out of a henhouse. Rabbits scampered behind the wire screen of a hutch. Hay, grain, and farm tools were visible inside a shed. An early morning drizzle had turned the bare earth into a giant mud puddle. Wood plank walkways slick with water, mud, and chicken droppings snaked through the yard. My eyes searched for the toilet, but I couldn't find it. All the buildings blended into a gloomy barnyard gray. Again I wondered: Why the broom?

"Cock-a-doodle-doo!" pierced the air. I whirled to my left. A rooster stood directly between me and what I now recognized as the outhouse. Turning to retreat to the slop jar, I hesitated as I recalled the stench of urine. The rooster scurried toward me, his neck feathers bristled. I tried to wave him off. He came faster, his yellow talons almost a blur. Now only five feet away, I shook the broom at him, but he didn't stop. I poked again. He screeched, beak open, feathers on end. Now he was within striking distance. Dad said we had to fight the whites and the coloreds. He didn't say anything about roosters. I jabbed.

He fell on his side. His fluttering wings showered me with mud and water. I relaxed and whisked him into the mud once more. He screeched, "Nawk! Nawk!" I waved him off, but he kept after me. I grabbed the broom with both hands and waited. When he was three feet away, I swung it like a baseball bat and sent him flying sideways. He began another charge. I turned the hard wood handle toward him. I swung and missed his head, but grazed a yellow talon, spinning him head over heels into the mud once more. I stepped off the wooden walk, sinking into the muck. He frantically sought a grip in the dark water of the yard, trying to flee. I gritted my teeth and raised the broom handle over my head, watching him draw his last breath.

The back door swung open.

"Whoa, boy! Don't ya be killin' my chickens! I'm the only one 'round here that does that!" Shamefully, I looked at Aunt Bess and lowered the broom to my side.

"Just a little tap gets 'em out of the way." She paused. "Look at you. Don't be tracking mud back into the house either. Leave them shoes on the porch. Now go an' do your business."

The rooster and I hobbled away from one another.

An elderly black man sat at the head of the table when I returned to the kitchen. Dad introduced Uncle Osco Pharris. Osco's face beamed as Dad recounted how he had been one of the strongest hands at Broderick's Foundry for thirty years. Dad bragged about him, now pushing sixty, still peerless among the younger men before the flaming open-hearth furnace. Dad raved about Osco's physical prowess for almost half an hour, then asked for a beer.

"Buster, I don't drink no more."

"Don't drink no more?" Dad challenged. "I remember when you used to put away Speck Johnson's corn likker like it was goin' out of style. Hell, you got so drunk I saw you staggering up Monroe

Street with a smile on your face and your dick stickin' straight outta your pants."

"Whoa, Buster. Hold up. Don't you be talking like that in my house."

"Sorry, Osco," said Dad soothingly, "I guess I'm just feeling the need for a little dram myself. Don't suppose you got any in the house for colds, do you?"

Osco shook his head.

"Anyway," Dad continued, unable to conceal his disappointment, "tell me how Wayne and Louise are doing in Cincinnati."

Soon I tired of the stories, walked into the sitting room, and dragged an old rocking chair across the sagging linoleum floor to the warmth of the coal stove.

That night, Mike and I crowded together on the sitting room bed while Dad slept on the living room couch. Mike kicked and squirmed, and I was unable to sleep. As I pushed his leg off me, I realized that we had shared a bed only once, on a vacation to Atlantic City when the hotel had only one room with two double beds.

Lying there in the darkness of the night, I remembered Harvey and Raymond standing behind the Greyhound bus as we waved good-bye. I was almost certain Harvey cried. Maybe it was my own tears. Harvey was too big to cry. As I lay in the strange bed in a strange house, trying to adjust to all the different sounds and smells, I wondered if I would ever see them again. Our lives were changing already. Here in Muncie, Aunt Bess and Uncle Osco called Dad "Buster." In Virginia he had been Tony. I wondered if Mike and I would have different names, too. Would I be Billy, Greg, or "Rooster"?

As I lay there, I was startled by the shuffle of slippers across the creaky linoleum. Rising up on my elbows, I saw Uncle Osco heading toward the back porch. Soon the buzz of urine rang out against the side of the steel slop jar. A minute later I heard a plop. Within seconds the nauseating odor swept over me. I prayed Grandma and Grandpa Cook would come for us as I pulled the covers over my head and tried to will myself to sleep. When it finally came, I was plagued by nightmares. Roosters attacked from all sides and I had no broom.

# Chapter 5 — Learning How to Be Niggers

January 26, 1954, Dad roused us for our first trip to Garfield Elementary School. My biggest worry was that it would be a "colored" school. I did not fear being in classes with black children, but I couldn't shake the memories of the ramshackle school buildings and ancient playground equipment I had seen when accompanying Raymond to collect his nieces and nephews from the all-black Fairfax County schools. It was a great relief to see a new bright-red brick building, and both white and black children milling about the schoolyard.

In the office I peered over Dad's shoulder while he laboriously printed "J. Anthony Williams" in the enrollment form box for "Father." In the blank for occupation he listed "U.S. Army." When he scrawled a "W" in the space for race, I nudged him. He frowned sharply. Rebuked, I joined Mike, who slouched at the door.

The secretary ushered us into the principal's office. A slightly balding man rose from behind a desk stacked high with folders. With little more than a curt "Good morning," he led us from the office. Just down the hall we stopped at Mike's new room. "Lehman," the principal said sternly, "come along." Mike hesitated, hiding behind Dad, his wide brown eyes on the verge of tears. "Go ahead, Mike," Dad said gently, and nudged him forward. As the principal guided Mike through the door, Dad whispered, "Good luck, son. Billy will be waiting on you after school." Mike returned a forlorn nod.

School had been difficult for Mike. He failed the first grade in Virginia, and he was struggling in the second. I knew he wasn't dumb, but I didn't know what was wrong. None of us did. As we stood in the hallway that morning, I hoped Indiana would be better for him. But I worried as he followed the principal to the front of the room, and giggles filtered out to the hallway when his classmates saw the small holes in the seat of his threadbare trousers.

Dad and I were hustled down green concrete steps to the basement. A tall, overweight man with horn-rimmed glasses huffed as he climbed the stairway toward us. His suit nearly burst at the seams. Mr. Hunt, my new fourth grade teacher, perhaps noticing I was tall for my age, asked eagerly, "Do you like basketball?" I searched my mind for something called basketball. In Virginia I played baseball, football, and even volleyball. Suddenly, I remembered a game called "medicine ball." Maybe that was it. The heavy ball was impossible to lift. No one in my gym class enjoyed it. You couldn't throw it, kick it, or run with it. No, I don't like it, I thought. Yet three adults stared intently waiting for an answer. I gulped and muttered, "Yes."

We entered a basement classroom reminiscent of a World War II bunker. Everything was solid concrete except for two small rectangular windows at the very top of the outside wall. From my assigned seat near the back I surveyed my new classmates. A fat boy spilled over the seat in front of me. Two rows over, a girl with horn-rimmed glasses was perfecting the studious look of one in pursuit of the "teacher's pet" prize. I counted five black children around the classroom. Though I had many black playmates in Gum Springs, we never attended school together. I wondered what it would be like. Then I remembered Dad on the bus: "Billy, you're part colored." I wondered if I looked any different. I wondered if anyone else could tell. I wondered if I would have any friends . . . black or white.

Two aisles away near the wall I spied bouncing blond curls and the twinkle of blue eyes gazing at me.

"Get to work!" the teacher shouted from the front of the room.

I lowered my head, desperate to appear busy even though I had no assignment. He lumbered down the aisle toward me. I cringed. Mr. Hunt paused three seats in front of me, beside a brown-haired boy with thick glasses.

"Are you going to take all day, Donald?" He glared.

Silence.

"You've got the right name, Donald, because Donald Dolittle does little." He smiled, congratulating himself on his wit, reached across two students, and thrust a mimeographed math assignment toward me. His sharp tongue made me glad I lied about basketball. Though I solved the long division problems in less than two minutes, I continued to hover over my paper to avoid calling attention to myself. At recess we filed out the rear of the building onto a large shiny blacktop play area complete with swing sets, a jungle gym, monkey bars, and even a sandbox. Students from other classes filled the playground, and I searched for Mike among them. Unable to find him, I drifted toward my new classmates.

"Where you from?" asked Dolittle as we stood in line for a swing. Classmates gathered around as I talked about Virginia and seeing President Eisenhower once when Dad drove us by the White House. Dolittle's eyes glazed as I rambled on about Mount Vernon, but the girl with the blond curls edged closer. Her name was Molly. A head shorter than I, she had the rosiest cheeks I had ever seen. I could hardly take my eyes off her as she introduced her friend, Sally. Tall for a girl, Sally looked me straight in the eye. Her bobbed brown hair swished back and forth as her eyes flitted between Molly and me. For the first time since we stepped off the bus on South Walnut Street twenty four-hours earlier, I dared to smile.

Schoolwork was much easier than it had been in Virginia. That first week I received the teacher's praise several times. What I valued more was the friendship of Molly and Sally. The three of us soon became inseparable. They quizzed me endlessly about Washington. I described the Cherry Blossom Festival and the Lincoln and Jefferson memorials in elaborate detail. They only appeared to lose interest when I babbled at length about seeing the wreckage of the first airplane collision over National Airport.

One afternoon during our second week in Muncie my cousin Mary Lou ran to catch up with Mike and me as we walked to Aunt Bess's. That day was the first time I had seen her on the playground.

She skipped back and forth in front of me as we made our way down Monroe Street, her toothy smile inches from my face, chanting, "Billy likes a white peck! Billy likes a white peck!"

"No, I don't." I spat. "She's just in my class. I can talk to white kids."

She put her hands on her hips and blocked my way.

"I bet she wouldn't talk to you if she knew you was colored."

"Yes she would. Color don't have nothing to do with it!" I protested.

"That's what you think, Mr. Bigshot!"

Ever since we arrived at Garfield, Mary Lou had told anyone who would listen that we were her cousins. I really didn't like it, but when black children asked, "Are you related to Mary Lou?" I didn't deny it. It was only when I saw the revulsion it produced in white kids that I became very nervous.

The next day after lunch at Aunt Bess's, I pulled on my tattered fatigue jacket and headed to school. Opening the gate, I glanced down the hill toward the busy Monroe and Willard Street intersection. No white families lived north of Willard, so normally only various shades of black and brown faces were on the corner. That day was different. Two white faces stood out from the crowd—Molly and Sally. Even from a distance I saw shock register on their faces. They turned toward each other. Molly stared up the hill once more. A final glance, then she darted from the intersection, her blond curls disappearing behind the corner grocery store.

That afternoon Molly and Sally sat in their seats on the far side of the room. As I walked through the door, their heads snapped toward the small window. I slumped at my desk for an endless hour of math problems. When it was time for recess I kept my head down. Mr. Hunt had to order me outside.

On the playground I took a deep breath and moved haltingly toward Molly and Sally, desperately concocting a story about being at Aunt Bess's. I decided to say she was our maid and that Mike and I just ate lunch there. I never had a chance to lie. When the girls saw me approach, they turned their backs to me. I retreated to the safety of the fire escape, feigning indifference. Heads bobbed up and down as they chattered animatedly with other white girls. Some of them stole glances in my direction. I hunched over and hid my face.

After school that afternoon I caught their burning stares once more as I stood alone outside the school door waiting for Mike. The

disgust on their faces made me feel like I had committed some griev-
ous wrong. Mike never came out of the building, and I trudged
home forlorn, feeling the weight of the world on my shoulders. Mike
lay on Aunt Bess's couch with a large white cotton bandage taped
to his forehead. He raised himself up on his elbows and thrust his
oily face toward me.

"I fell off the fire escape during the fire drill. The principal took
me to get stitches. Then he drove me home. He didn't believe we
lived here. He was gonna drive off till Aunt Bess waved him down
and told him we was colored boys."

A month dragged by and Dad did not return from Virginia. I
was furious with him and felt abandoned, and I wasn't alone in my
anger. The mere mention of his name caused Uncle Osco to snarl,
and his bad humor spilled over into the household. When Mike
tracked mud in from the backyard, Aunt Bess gave him a switching.
When I sloshed water while carrying it from the outdoor faucet, she
swatted me with the "rooster" broom. Every day after school I withdrew into my private corner of the sitting room and played with a
small bag of clay. Hours passed while I molded imaginary soldiers
who killed, maimed, bombed, and demolished everything in their
path. Men, women, and children all died; ships sank; towns were
leveled—everything was destroyed.

One afternoon Aunt Bess tired of me being underfoot and ordered me outside. I sat at the edge of the playground. Mike was
playing football with boys from the Projects. I smiled as he streaked
across the gravel field with the ball tucked under his arm. A
chocolate-skinned boy in a blue cotton cowboy suit complete with
fringed pant legs gave chase. He grabbed Mike's arm and jerked
him to the ground. Mike slid across the gravel as the ball bounced
crazily into the street. I leaped to my feet. Mike lay motionless for
several seconds, then finally pushed himself up from the hard
ground.

"What'd you knock me down for?" he demanded.

"This is tackle. We get you down any way we can," the boy
growled in response. "It ain't two-handed touch like you crackers
play."

"Tell him, Reggie," crowed a boy I recognized from Garfield
School.

Mike brushed the gravel from his clothes and nodded. From then on, every time Reggie's team ran in Mike's direction, he fiercely blocked Mike. Even when runners headed in the opposite direction, Reggie swung at Mike. Finally, red-faced and exasperated, Mike lunged at his attacker. Reggie punched him in the face. Mike fell backward. The other boys surrounded them, shouting, "Whip him! Kick his butt, Reggie! Kill that cracker!" I raced to Aunt Bess's for help.

"Aunt Bess, Aunt Bess, some colored boys is beatin' up Mike!" She sauntered to the window overlooking the playground. "Come on! Come on! Mike needs help!" I shouted, tugging at her apron.

"Let go, boy." She pushed me away. "You better get on over there and help him. He's your brother. You the one gotta take care of him."

I hesitated.

"Whatcha waitin' for, boy? Do you wanna fight me or them? Git!" she shouted one final time, and reached for the buggy whip in the corner near the stove.

Tears filled my eyes as I realized no one was going to help Mike. Not Mom, not Dad, not Aunt Bess. We were on our own. I ran through the house and leaped off the porch. As I reached the crowd, Mike lay on the ground shielding his face. Blood seeped between his fingers as he twisted and turned, trying to dodge the hail of fists. Reggie grinned at the laughing crowd. "Guess I showed that cracker. . . ." I pushed through the boys and grabbed him by the neck, pulling him off Mike. He tumbled backward on the gravel. I kneed him in the stomach. A fist to the mouth. Then all over his head, the same way he hit Mike. Soon his nose bled. The crowd fell silent. "That white mothafucka's kicking Reggie's ass," I heard. "Let's get him."

The sound of shoes shuffling across the gravel distracted me. Then a crack filled the air. With my hands gripped around Reggie's neck, I looked over my shoulder. Aunt Bess was lashing her buggy whip.

"Don't you all bother him!" she shouted. "If you do, I'm gonna put this here whip across your little black butts!"

"Miss Bessie, that white boy's gonna kill Reggie!" protested one boy.

"They ain't no white boys," responded Aunt Bess. "They niggers just like you. They got the same right to be here! Come on, Billy, git Mike and let's go on back to the house."

I left Reggie holding his nose and pulled Mike to his feet. There was yet another long rip in the sleeve of his army fire sale jacket. We followed Aunt Bess across the gravel playground. Maybe, I thought, there is somebody in the world who cares about us.

The next Saturday morning a tall, golden-skinned boy of sixteen arrived at the house. Aunt Bess called Mike and me into the living room and said, "Boys, this is your brother Jimmy."

As I surveyed the young stranger, I tried to absorb Aunt Bess's startling pronouncement. Neither Mom nor Dad had ever mentioned him. Yet his prominent nose and dark brown eyes bore a remarkable resemblance to Dad. He also had Dad's lanky build. In fact, he looked more like our father than either Mike or I. I wondered why we had never heard of him before. But if Jimmy had been forgotten he was not unfriendly.

"Glad to meet you, brother Billy," Jimmy said, cheerfully extending his hand.

Jimmy, a drummer for the Muncie Central High School Bearcats band, wore black pants, a long wool coat with brass buttons, and a purple-and-white cape. He was on the way to a high school pep rally and invited us along. As a result of my teacher's obsession with basketball, I learned a lot about it. In fact, our class spent more time discussing Muncie basketball teams than any other subject. Although there were two high schools in Muncie, only Central counted when it came to basketball. Central had won four state championships and was the odds-on favorite to capture a fifth in March 1954. The Muncie Fieldhouse, where the Bearcats played, seated over seven thousand people and was packed for every game. Folks waited years to buy season tickets. The Bearcats were ultimately derailed that year by a team from a tiny Indiana town called Milan. Later, the saga of Milan's march to the state championship and final victory over Muncie Central was the basis for the popular movie *Hoosiers*.

That morning Jimmy urged us to go to the rally and then "to Whitely and see Uncle Sam and Aunt Ceola."

The new names and places were strange and unfamiliar, but Mike and I eagerly followed Jimmy downtown. Purple-and-white team posters were prominently displayed in every window, and purple-and-white banners stretched high across South Walnut Street. Names of Bearcat team members like Jimmy Barnes, "Big

John" Casterlow, and George Burks were whispered as if they were gods. In spite of the huge crowd gathered at the fieldhouse, and a boisterous pep rally, basketball still held little interest for me, and I was glad when we left the gathering.

Broadway curved northeast away from downtown Muncie to McCulloch Park. Directly east of the park was Whitely, the home of Muncie's second-largest concentration of blacks. Bounded on the north by Centennial Road, on the south by the White River, and on the east by the Nickel Plate Railroad tracks, it was isolated from the rest of Muncie. The tracks edged along the eastern border of Whitely for almost twenty blocks without one street connecting it with the adjacent white areas.

Jimmy led us to a small grocery store at the corner of Lowell and Penn. The sign over the door said SAM WHEELER'S GROCERIES, THE COUNTRY STORE THAT'S GOING TO TOWN. The store shelves were crammed with canned goods, breads, cookies, and potato chips. A near empty glass meat case stretched across the rear of the wooden-floored room. Behind it stood two large glass-doored freezers. A light golden-skinned woman in her mid-forties stood at the check-out counter. Jimmy introduced her as Aunt Ceola.

"Hi, boys," she said in a cheerful voice. "I'm so glad to see you. Jimmy's been talking about you all week." She reached under the counter and handed Mike and me each a candy bar.

We gushed thanks and ripped off the wrappers. She turned behind the counter and drew back a cloth curtain that opened onto a small living area. I heard a television from within.

"Boys, you all come on out here. I got somebody I want you to meet."

Two dark-brown-skinned boys our age walked from the room. Though the older boy and I were the same height, he outweighed me by at least thirty pounds. His thick shoulders and full, square face resembled those of a boxer. The younger boy was about the same size and weight as Mike.

Aunt Ceola explained that the boys were related to her and to Jimmy and, therefore, probably to us. It all sounded so complicated, but the boys seemed to accept our relationship without question.

"Why don't you run up to Longfellow and play some ball?" said Aunt Ceola. "Boys, show Mike and Billy the playground."

Recalling my last playground fight, I mumbled softly, "I don't wanna go."

Jimmy, no doubt sensing my fear, accompanied us.

Longfellow School playground was almost a mirror image of Madison Street—mostly sand and gravel. All of the children were black. That is, none of them were white. There was every imaginable hue of brown, ranging from deep chocolate to the color of the speckled light brown eggs we found in Aunt Bess's henhouse. And now two palefaces—Mike and me.

As we stood at the edge of the basketball court, an unusually short light-brown-skinned boy approached us. Though his skin color fit in with the rest of the boys, he seemed a bit out of place. All at once I realized that his hair was different. It was the same as Mike's and mine—long, dark, and straight. I towered over him by at least six inches, but he stood squarely in front of me and demanded, "What you white boys doing here?"

I was ready to quip, "None of your business, Shorty," when Jimmy interjected.

"They're my brothers, Pancho! Don't mess with them or I'll kick your little Mexican butt back across the street. Anyway, what you bothering them for? They're your cousins, too."

I tried to conceal my amazement, wondering how many more surprises the day would hold.

"No way," protested Pancho. "I'm Mexican John Vargas's boy. We don't have no crackers."

"Yeah, but Ruth Vargas used to be a Williams, which makes us cousins with all the Vargases."

Pancho shrugged his shoulders, tapped the basketball, and said, "Let's play ball!"

With the growing list of honey, brown, and chocolate relatives, it was becoming harder and harder to perceive myself as white. Yet I knew I also had two white grandparents, three white uncles, two white aunts and a houseful of white cousins. They were less than one mile away, just across the Nickel Plate Railroad steel barrier that separated Whitely from white Muncie. Not one of them had come for us.

That evening while I was doing homework, I overheard Aunt Bess and Uncle Osco arguing in the kitchen.

"Them boys gonna eat me out of house and home if Buster don't get here soon," Osco complained. "And they fight with Mary Lou all the time. I don't care what you say. I'm gonna get shed of them 'fore they drive us to the poorhouse." I held my breath, wondering what he meant.

"Osco," replied Aunt Bess, "them boys is family. We can't just turn 'em out."

"Well, we ain't the only family they got. Sallie Ann's they grandmother, and she ain't even been up here to see after 'em. They got white folks, too. If'n they still here by next weekend, you gonna give 'em to the orphanage."

I couldn't sleep that night, and my stomach ached all the next day. That afternoon as Mike and I sat alone on the concrete ledge surrounding the playground, I told him what I'd overheard.

In a weak voice he said, "Billy, I'm scared. We won't know anybody at the orphanage. Do you think we'd stay together?"

"Not if one of us got adopted. We might never see each other again, and we'd never find Mom and Dad."

A miserable week followed. Mike came down with a cold, and my stomach continued to ache. We hoped for Mom or Dad, or our white aunts or uncles, or even Jimmy to appear, but we had no visitors. The dreaded Sunday of Uncle Osco's ultimatum arrived. Miss Sallie was summoned. There was no warm greeting for us from the woman we now called Grandma Sallie. She remained the stern, angry woman we remembered from our past life in Virginia. She huddled with Aunt Bess and Uncle Osco in the living room. Mike and I listened intently from the kitchen door.

"Osco, I ain't got no room for them little peckawoods in my shack."

"I ain't got no room up here either. We too crowded."

"How am I supposed to take care of 'em? I work all day at the drive-in. I can't cook. I only got a hot plate."

"Look, Sallie Ann, these your grandchildren. You either take 'em or Bessie's gonna give 'em to the welfare people tomorrow morning."

"Damn that Buster," said Grandma. "I'm always cleaning up his shit. Why don't he grow up? You'd think a Howard University nigger be smarter."

She paused, and then exhaled. "All right. I'll come and get 'em next Saturday."

"No, Sallie!" Osco shouted. The rocker slid across the floor as he stood abruptly. "You gotta take 'em now."

She started to argue, then sighed. "All right. Pack their bags, Bessie."

Aunt Bess walked into the kitchen, her eyes downcast. We looked at her, hoping for a reprieve. She shook her head. Stretching to a shelf above the sink, she grabbed two brown paper sacks and handed one to each of us. Uncle Osco fled to his bedroom, Aunt Bess and Mary Lou stayed in the refuge of the kitchen. We moved silently to the sitting room and stuffed all our worldly belongings into the bags. Grandma Sallie stood in the doorway, crossing and uncrossing her arms impatiently. We followed Grandma through the now-vacant living room. There were no good-byes. Clutching the grocery sacks, we walked the four blocks through the Projects to 601½ Railroad Street.

What I had mistaken for a tool shed in January was now our home. Three tiny rooms. Crammed into the narrow kitchen were a two-person table and an ancient potbellied stove. A two-burner hot plate was on a counter next to a cold water faucet. There was no sink or drain. Dirty water was tossed into the yard. Squeezed into the room next to the kitchen were Grandma's bed, a couch, and a dresser. Her house did have one advantage over Aunt Bess's—an indoor toilet in the tiny, windowless back room—but there was no sink, tub, or shower. Crammed next to the toilet was a wooden army folding cot—our bed. Mike curled up at one end, with me at the other.

We soon discovered that Grandma, like Dad, was an alcoholic. She had no appetite. Whatever food she needed she nibbled while cooking at the Madison and Kirby drive-in. Every evening after school we lingered at the kitchen window overlooking the alley, waiting for her to trudge up the hill behind the service station. To keep warm we turned on the hot plate and rubbed our hands over it. We had to make sure it was off and the burner was cool when she arrived so she wouldn't complain about her electric bill. Once I tried to start a fire in the potbellied stove, but only succeeded in filling the shack with smoke. Most evenings Mike and I huddled together for warmth until she arrived.

There was little to do at Grandma's. We spent countless hours pouring over the contents of an old shoebox that contained the memorabilia of our father. It was full of photographs and love letters to him. I was disappointed not to find any pictures of my mother.

Dad's youthful face beamed from photos taken in exciting places like the Boardwalk of Atlantic City and Times Square, New York. He sported stylish clothes, and invariably had a beautiful woman on his arm.

I read and reread the letters to him. A judge's daughter from Arkansas explained how she would love him forever, but marriage was out of the question. She had discovered he was colored. Dr. Alain Locke of Howard University expressed profound sorrow that Dad felt he must pass into the "white world." I pored over and over the mementos of Dad's past for clues, hoping to understand what had happened to my father and to our family.

As I touched and searched the photographs, a multitude of feelings were evoked by them. Mike, Sissy, the baby, and I had been let down. More than let down, we had been betrayed . . . why? The handsome smiling face staring back at me showed so much promise. What had gone wrong? Every day I looked at the photos and letters. If I'd had a bad day on the playground or at school I felt hatred for both Mom and Dad. Then I'd feel remorse for my feelings and just beg God to let me see them again.

When Grandma appeared at the crest of the hill, Mike and I raced from the cold shack to rummage through her purse for the two frozen hamburger patties and the handful of french fries she stole while alone in the drive-in's basement kitchen. Grandma Sallie was a woman of few words. She had unique ways of conveying the rules of the house. She had absolutely no tolerance for complaints. Once when she placed our hamburger patties and fries before us, Mike clamored, "Greg has more french fries than me." My grandmother swiftly and silently picked up Mike's plate and scraped half his fries onto mine. Mike's mouth dropped open in bewilderment. As I wolfed down our evening meal, I was grateful my grandmother was willing to steal to feed us. I felt shame when I recalled how much I had hated her in Virginia.

Every day after school we stopped at Aunt Bess's. If Uncle Osco wasn't there she quickly whisked us to the kitchen, where we gobbled the remains of navy beans and biscuits left over from breakfast, rushing to finish before Osco returned. If he was home, she shook her head no when answering the door. Even as she put her finger to her lips, she slipped us a piece of corn bread or some cold biscuits in a bag. We stepped quietly off the porch and gulped the food down on the sidewalk, making sure we didn't have anything in our hands as we passed the kitchen window and waved to Uncle Osco on our way to the playground. On Saturdays, Aunt Bess bought groceries at the Park & Shop Supermarket on South Walnut Street. On the way home, she paused near the playground ledge where Mike and I often played by ourselves. After a quick glance to the house to make sure Uncle Osco wasn't peeking out the kitchen window, she reached into the bag and handed us a loaf of bread or a quart of milk and ordered us to take it straight to Grandma's. We scurried through the Projects with our bounty.

Grandma complained bitterly about how much Mike and I ate, and about what we cost her in heat and electricity. If I forgot to turn off the kitchen light after studying, she grumbled about it for over an hour. If I threw a piece of coal in the potbellied stove without permission, her shrill voice filled the room until we were asleep.

Late one evening while I finished my homework, Grandma and Mike left the house together. When they returned later, Mike averted his eyes, and his whole body quivered. That night as we lay on the cot, I asked Mike where they had been.

"Grandma made me steal coal from Dague's."

"You're lying. They got fences all around the place."

"I crawled under the fence."

"Mike, if the police caught you they'd send you to reform school."

"She's gonna make you steal next time, Billy. She said so."

"I ain't gonna," I said, lying back on the hard canvas cot.

Later that week Grandma took me to the coal yard after dinner. We picked up coal that had fallen off the railroad cars. When I balked at crawling under the fence, she said, "You little peckawood! Get your butt under there and get that coal. We gonna freeze if you don't."

"I don't care, Grandma," I said, shivering in the late winter night. "I ain't gonna go to jail. You can beat me if you want to, but I just can't steal."

"Don't nobody want to beat your narrow behind," she said in exasperation. She glared at me for a moment and then sniffed, "Get on the other side of this bucket. Help me carry it back to the house."

Luckily, the weather soon turned warmer and our late-night trips to the coal yard ended. However, the spring brought little change in our daily routine.

Night after night I lay on the cot, consoling myself with the belief that my parents were just testing us. They wanted to give us a taste of how hard life could be. Relentlessly, I clung to the dream that one day Mom, Dad, Sissy, and the baby would arrive in our Cadillac. Mike and I would step into it and return to the good days we knew in Virginia.

Late the Friday night before Easter 1954, Grandma Sallie shook us awake.

"Wake up boys, your daddy's here! 'Bout time he gave his poor old mother some relief! Thinks I don't have anything better to do than take care of his little peckawoods."

Dad stood silhouetted in the doorway.

"Where you been, Buster? I been lookin' after these boys for almost two months."

"Momma, you know I've been in Virginia trying to salvage the business. Aunt Bess promised she'd keep the boys until I returned. I didn't even ask you because I didn't want to impose."

"You may not of asked me, but I had to take your boys before Bessie and Osco gave them to the orphanage. And don't be giving me no words like *savage* and *inpose*. Tell that to your white friends. Just because you went to college don't mean you a big shot nigger 'round here."

Sitting up in bed, I rubbed my eyes.

"Get dressed, boys," Dad said grimly. "Let's go outside and talk."

Sullenly, I pulled on my pants and shoes, glad to see him after his lengthy absence, but angry that he had deserted us for so long. I moved silently through the shack past Grandma, now back under the covers beside her boyfriend, Joe. I could just make out the green luminous dial of the clock on her dresser—four a.m. We walked through the alley to Kirby and Monroe. Dad dropped to the curb and motioned for us to join him. Mike scooted as close as possible. Hesitating, I moved to the far side of Mike.

The street lamp cast a sharp cold light on our hunched figures. Dad's clothes were different from those he'd bought in Washington department stores. His gabardine suit was dull and oil stained. Buttons were missing, and there was a small tear on the shoulder. His white shirt had a frayed collar. Only a dark brown fedora angled across his forehead was a reminder of better days.

Dazed and uncertain, Mike and I slouched over the curb, elbows resting on our knees. The fatigue pants we'd bought so long ago in Washington were completely tattered and stained. Our shoes were too small for us and had worn-down heels and holes in the bottoms. Perhaps embarrassed by his long absence, Dad delivered an order like a drill sergeant.

"Sit up straight, boys! Don't hunch over, it's bad for your posture." We straightened our backs and turned expectantly toward him.

"Didn't think I'd see you boys tonight. Aunt Bess told me she'd keep you till I came back. Were you bad?"

"No, Daddy, we weren't bad," answered Mike.

"What in the hell happened, Billy?" he said, challenging me again as if I were to blame for everything that had occurred in our lives. Still, for some reason I felt a strong sense of responsibility for the family, and tried to explain what I really couldn't understand.

"When you didn't come back like you said, Uncle Osco got mad. He told Aunt Bess he wasn't gonna take care of a no-'count nigger's half-breed boys. He said that the best thing to do was to send us to an orphanage, and that was what he was gonna do if you didn't come back within a week, so Grandma Sallie took us."

The chill of the concrete penetrated my thin pants and gave me goose bumps. I began to fidget and moved closer to Mike. Dad began again. "I just don't understand it. Aunt Bess knows Momma doesn't have any place fit to keep you. And Momma doesn't have any sense either. Look at her, in there laying up in bed with Joe Turnipseed. . . ."

Dad reached into his pocket and drew out a bottle of Wild Irish Rose. He slowly screwed the cap off the bottle and took a long swallow of wine. We recoiled as he exhaled a pungent breath.

"Boys, I thought I was going to work out something with the business, but the bank foreclosed and we lost everything, the tavern, the Pitt Street house, the Cadillac. We don't have shit."

He swung the bottle straight up and guzzled down the contents. Then he rolled the bottle across the sidewalk into the night shadows.

"I did see your momma, though. She's living in Washington with that black bastard she ran off with. I found out where she was and called to see the children. When I went over there, him and two other mothafuckers acted like they wanted to fight. Shit, if it had been my Golden Glove days I would have whipped all three of them by myself."

"Is she coming to see us?"

"I don't know, Mike. She didn't say anything about it. She asked how you boys were doing. . . . Know what I told her?"

"What'd you say, Daddy?" asked Mike, leaning forward, full of hope.

"I told her you were in Muncie, learning how to be niggers!"

# Chapter 6

# Bob and Weave

Dad was different. His spirit was broken. The fun, energy, and vitality of the man we'd known in Virginia was gone. For the first few days after his return to Muncie he never removed his hat. When he did I was shocked. His thick, wavy hair had vanished. His head was covered with ugly-looking sores and scabs. Though he never seemed to worry, I suddenly realized he had not weathered the changes in our lives any better than we had. His unsightly appearance kept him around the house, but rather than resting, he drank constantly.

The relationship between Dad and Grandma was a complex, tangled web of love and hate, mutual dependency on alcohol and on one another. Grandma was still bitter over being treated as a maid instead of being welcomed as family. She often delighted in Dad's failure as a white man in Virginia and his current dependence on her. She particularly relished the failure of his marriage. She alternately called him a "lazy nigger" and "the smartest man in Muncie." They fought incessantly, and relied on alcohol and a constant stream of drinking companions to protect them from themselves and each other.

Our initial joy over Dad's return soon evaporated as Mike and I realized there would be no change in our lives. When drunk, Dad made grandiose plans. When sober, he was morose and uncommunicative. He dwelled incessantly on the loss of the business and wallowed in bitter resentment toward our mother.

When Dad sobered up with the help of white men from Alcoholics Anonymous, we allowed our hopes to soar. Grandma resisted Dad's abstinence because his first mission was to drag her on the wagon as well. With his sobriety in AA we saw some of his zest for life return as well as his administrative zeal. He assigned Mike the daily task of cleaning the porch and yard of bottles and other debris. I was to teach Grandma to read and write. She had no formal education and signed her name with an X. I had no idea where to start or what to do. After a few dismal lessons during which I tried to have Grandma read from my fourth grade book, we mutually agreed to quit. When Dad discovered we had given up, he complained, but never undertook the job himself.

Although Grandma was unable to read or write, I discovered that she had no handicap when it came to counting money. One afternoon she sent me on an errand to Nasty Momma's, the corner grocery store, owned by an elderly white woman. After buying a can of pork and beans for our dinner, I sneaked a nickel for a candy bar, and quickly gobbled it down to hide any incriminating evidence. I had barely handed Grandma her change when she discovered the shortage. The price of my treat was a very harsh spanking.

The punishment might have been unusually harsh because Grandma had not been drinking for a few weeks. Tension ruled the household when they were both sober, but sobriety never lasted long and chaos soon resumed. Every evening there was a steady flow of visitors to Grandma's. Men and women drifted in and out of the shack to gamble and drink. Anyone with a bottle was welcome. I staked out the corner next to the potbellied stove and tackled my schoolwork, but the shouting and arguing made it hard to concentrate. Mike didn't even bother to study. He sat alongside Dad absorbing the nightly monologues and bawdy jokes.

Joe Turnipseed received most of Grandma's attention. He was always the first to arrive. She scurried around the small room whisking everyone off her bed, except Joe. She made sure he always got a sip when the wine was passed. A hod carrier, Joe shouldered mortar and bricks every working day of his adult life, and it showed. Even though sixty years old, he had thick arms, a muscular torso, and a shiny bald head. He would sip wine and nod off to sleep, falling across Grandma's bed. Though he never talked much, occasionally he tossed us a couple of dimes to race to Nasty Momma's for ice cream bars.

One night as the wine bottle reached Grandma, she removed the handkerchief always stuffed in her brassiere and daintily swabbed the lip of the bottle.

"Momma, why you wiping that off?" asked Dad. "We all niggers here."

Grandma retorted curtly, "I ain't no nigger. I'm a Indian!"

Dad turned to the crowd. "I bet you all don't know what tribe Momma belongs to."

All eyes turned expectantly toward him.

"She's a Monig." He paused. "More nigger than Indian!"

The shack vibrated as the crowd erupted with laughter. Grandma's face hardened. "My daddy was Shan Higginbottom. He was an Indian from Bristol. He was just a little bit colored. Momma was the only one that was really colored."

"It didn't make no difference in Kentucky whether you was Indian or colored," Dad said. "They still ran you out of town for having a white man's baby!"

Grandma rose from beside Joe on the bed and stalked toward Dad. Trembling, she shook her long, bony finger in his face, "James, you may be the smartest man in Muncie. But you evil! If you keep playin' the dozen with me you gonna find your yellow ass out on the street!"

Inching forward on my chair, I braced for another, perhaps final, insult. A sinister smile crossed Dad's face. Then his eyes clouded.

"Aw, Momma, you know I love you. But you gotta laugh at things. Remember how Granddaddy Shan said we had to laugh at the peckawoods to keep from crying."

The memory of Shan always softened Grandma's face, and Dad told yet another adventure with his grandfather during his teenage years. I was never able to determine the exact nature of Shan's heritage—Indian or black, or a combination of the two. What was clear was that he was adored and revered by Grandma. The closest that Dad came to being in real trouble with her was saying or even inferring something derogatory about Shan Higginbottom. However, Aunt Lucy, Shan's sister-in-law, who at the time we arrived in Muncie was in her eighties and living in the Projects, called Shan the "meanest man that ever lived."

The most reliable report I received on Shan did come from Aunt Lucy. She allowed that while he was mostly black, he did have a bit of Indian blood in him, probably Cherokee since he was from somewhere in eastern Tennessee. Grandma had eight brothers and sisters. Kentucky was a hard place to make a living, and over half of her family migrated to Indiana. Aunt Bess, the oldest, was the first to arrive in Muncie. Then came her brothers Galen and Herschel. Grandma chose to stay in Kentucky to be near her father. Dad's birth changed that.

My father's father lived in a fine antebellum house in the rolling hills of Bowling Green. He was a man of wealth and leisure, a true son of the South. My grandmother worked for his wealthy white family for less than a year before she became pregnant by the young master of the household. Immediately, she was fired from her job. After my father's birth, his light skin was a daily reminder in turn-of-the-century Bowling Green of the forbidden and unforgivable star-crossed union between black and white. Hostile stares on the streets and murmurs in the stores about her "white nigger" baby were followed by relentless demands from both whites and blacks to flee that racially torn town. Yet my illiterate grandmother managed to withstand the attacks. She drew strength from her ability to challenge the prized racial purity of the city, parading her "white" baby in a shabby, wooden cart she pulled while shopping downtown. Her determination was reinforced by her stubborn father, Shan Higginbottom. Tall, dark, and sinewy, he delighted in confounding racial lines. He proudly strode through the streets of Bowling Green with his brown skin and long, braided hair defying classification as either colored or Indian. My grandmother battled efforts to exile her from Kentucky for almost a year. Her fierce will evaporated early one summer morning when an older brother's mutilated body was discovered lashed to a railroad track. The murder was never solved. Grandma believed "he was killed because he was colored," and feared for the safety of her young son. Despite never having been farther away from Bowling Green than Russellville in neighboring Logan County, my grandmother boarded a bus to Muncie, Indiana.

Though Dad revealed our family history in a matter-of-fact way, I was intrigued. At first I didn't believe him. I had been around drunks long enough to discount half of what they said, but many family members ultimately made their way to our shack and confirmed Dad's stories.

Some nights I felt sorrier for Dad than I did for myself. His searing pain was most evident when he revealed the one occasion he saw his father. Flushed with the success of a year at Howard University, and certain he was bound to achieve all his life goals, he passed through Bowling Green with a college roommate. They were on the way to his roommate's hometown, the all-black Boley, Oklahoma, for a brief summer visit. Though Dad made countless trips to Bowling Green during his teenage years, he had never seen his father. Determined finally to meet him face-to-face, he purchased several magazines from a downtown drugstore, planning to masquerade as a salesman, then at just the perfect moment reveal his true identity. But as he stood on his father's porch in the summer of 1937, he could not say "I am your son." I don't know whether it was pride, spite, or anger, that sealed his lips. I always believed Dad hated the white part of his heritage, which had rejected him so fully and completely. He fled Bowling Green that afternoon to return only once more, thirteen years later, to bury the only father he had ever known, Shan Higginbottom.

The nightly crowds huddled at Grandma's relished Dad's stories about how he tricked the white man. Every time the white man was exposed as a fool, laughter rang out through the shack. The victories were small and inconsequential, but I realized the telling and retelling served the valuable purpose of soothing wounded souls. Grandma bragged about stealing food from her employer every single day. Dad related how, when passing for white in Virginia, he became the first "spook" president of the whites-only Forty-and-eighth American Legion Post. He even convinced the legionnaires to buy an old bus that, unbeknownst to them, had been discarded by a black singing group, the Sweethearts of Rhythm. In fact, the women had lived in the bus when denied lodging at white southern hotels while touring the country during World War II. Dad always loved to describe how he lured the white southern boys into dice games when he was in the army. "Easier than taking candy from a baby," he'd say with a wink.

Dad grew somber when he narrated the story of how, as a teenager, he masqueraded as white and sneaked into Marion, Indiana, thirty miles from Muncie, site of the last hanging in the north,

August 7, 1930. He infiltrated the festive white crowd milling around the courthouse lawn where two black teenagers hung long after being beaten, kicked and drug from jail. Four thousand white citizens had stormed the jail and applauded as the youths were killed. Dad shared the horror of Indiana's lynching with Muncie's black community. It was as if he had walked into hell and come out with a report on it.

Then there was the nightly recitation of lost ambition. Dad became morose when he recounted failed dreams of becoming a lawyer. But he would brighten as he quipped, "I've got me a big shot lawyer in the making. He's sitting over there gettin' coal dust on his books. He's gonna be the man I wanted to be. Right, Counselor?"

All eyes in the room turned toward me. I never wanted to say anything at all. I preferred the role of silent spectator, but every night Dad challenged me. He expected me to avoid his failures and right all the wrongs done to my family and the entire Negro race. It was a tough order for a ten-year-old boy. Even though Mike sat beside me, I was the one chosen. He singled me out to claim the dream and the destiny that had eluded him. If he didn't fully convince me of my potential, he seemed to persuade his drinking cronies.

One man would interject, "Greg, don't forget where you came from when you livin' high on the hog." Then another would add, "That boy's serious as a heart attack, he's gonna make it, and he ain't gonna forget nobody." Then a doubter would snipe, "Man, that boy ain't gonna think about all you niggers when he's sittin' up on the white folks' hill."

The skeptics always forced me from my chair, books tumbling to the floor, to proclaim, "Yes, I will." I have no idea what Dad or the other drunks crowded into 601½ Railroad Street saw in me. But night after night, after the Higginbottom family history was recounted and all the misdeeds of the white man were cussed and discussed, the drunks predicted my future. As I began to acquire a reputation for being a serious, straight A student, my dreams were reinforced in the neighborhood as well. Even Aunt Bess joined the chorus when I stopped by to beg a bit to eat. "Billy," she'd say, stretching the prize toward me, "you gonna let me come visit you in the White House?"

"Of course, Aunt Bess. I'll even send a car for you," always got a wink and a biscuit. The drunken women who hung around Grandma's joined the refrain about my future by cackling, "That boy sure is blessed." As I trudged to the cot beside the toilet I shared with Mike, I did not feel blessed, but I earnestly hoped life would get better.

Finally, around midnight, visitors would begin to leave and Dad stretched out on the couch across the room from Grandma's bed. Often after-hours rapping on the door shook the little shed and woke us all. If the caller had a bottle, the door swung wide open. Most of our visitors were black, but from time to time white men from Shed Town, Muncie's low-income white area, showed up at Grandma's. Orville was one of them. In his mid-forties, Orville had a pale-gray concrete block face with a vivid white scar across his left cheek. I was terrified by his wine-induced memories of youthful knife fights and rapes of young Tennessee girls at knifepoint. One night Dad complained that Orville didn't bring any wine. Mike and I peered around the cloth curtain that separated the toilet from the rest of the shack. Orville shouted, "Buster, don't give me any shit, as much of my wine as you've drunk. Now give me a drink before I cut your balls off!"

Terrified, I grabbed the wall to steady myself. Then I heard Dad.

"Now look, you old peckawood, you're a guest in my house. You don't come in here and ride roughshod over everyone. If you can't conduct yourself with decency and honor, get the hell out of here. Or I'll throw your ass out. I used to be in the Golden Gloves, and if you fuck with me, it's gonna be *Bing! Bing! Bing!* Down the alley!" Dad crouched in a fighter's stance.

"Well, let's just see how good you fight with a knife stuck up your asshole," Orville hissed. Dad popped him in the nose. Blood squirted everywhere. Orville fumbled for the knife in his pocket. Dad smacked him again. His face turning crimson, Orville lunged at Dad, knocking him into the stove. The chimney pipe crashed to the floor. Soon they thrashed about the room.

Joe, in bed with Grandma, tossed the covers back. The room shrank as he leaped out of bed nude, his hod carrier muscles elongated by the motion of the single hanging light bulb. Two steps brought Joe into the kitchen, and he pulled Dad and Orville apart, holding them by the napes of their necks like two kittens.

"Look you all, I don't want you messin' up Sallie's house! If you want to fight, get on out in the alley. If you keep scufflin', you boys gonna have to whoop me too! Now sit down an' drink your wine like you got some sense."

Both men gave Joe a hang-dog look, then they dropped their heads like two children and mumbled, "He started it." They glared at one another for a moment. Finally, Dad shoved the bottle across the table to Orville. I thanked God Joe was in the house that night.

The next afternoon Mike and I trekked downtown to the unemployment office with Dad. As we made our way along the railroad tracks, I asked, "Daddy, why can't we go back to Virginia? I'm afraid of all the fightin' and cussin'."

"Billy, can't you understand, there ain't shit to go back to? I thought we'd just be here a while, and I'd be able to hustle money for California, but everybody in Muncie knows I'm colored and won't give me work."

He stumbled over a stone on the track bed, then looked up. "People in Indiana never let you forget you're a nigger! Look at Momma. She's been cooking at the drive-in for damn near fifteen years. She can't even walk in the front door. They treat her like a kid when she's the oldest woman there. All they can say to her is 'Hi, Sallie Ann.' " He mimicked them with a high falsetto voice. He grimaced and added bitterly, "I should shoot out their tires some night."

We reached the Dague Coal Yard crossing. "But Dad," I protested, "what about all the fighting? You might get hurt. What's gonna happen then?"

"I guess you'd just have to go to an orphanage if Mom can't take care of you."

"I don't want her to take care of me."

"I don't want to go to an orphanage," said Mike.

"Maybe Uncle Osco was right. It might be better for you both. Think about it, boys. In an orphanage you'd have a decent place to sleep, clean clothes, and not have to go to school hungry. Remember the movie where Father Flanagan took in orphans at Boys' Town? Life could turn out much better for you there. Plus, if I can get you out of Muncie, you won't have to be colored. I'm telling you, boys, it ain't easy being a nigger."

Mike grabbed Dad's coat. He began sobbing. "Daddy, please don't send us away! We promise to be good."

Dad placed his hand on Mike's shoulder. "Boys, you shouldn't be here. It's not safe at Mom's and you fight every day on the playground 'cause you look white. Think about the orphanage. It would free me up to get back on my feet. Maybe if I can be on my own for a while, something will break for me. Later I can come and get you. . . ."

Tears rolled down Mike's face.

"You promised we were going to stay together!" I charged. He touched my shoulder, but I jerked back.

"Come on, boys, stop crying, be big soldiers. My boys don't cry." Then with a sigh he added, "You're not going to the orphanage, and I'm not going anywhere either, at least not for now. I'm broke."

Still troubled, I asked him where we would live since it wasn't safe at Grandma's.

"You have to accept it. I don't have a job. And Mom can't afford anything else. Hell, she doesn't make fifty cents an hour. I never said Muncie was going to be easy."

Then in his crowing barroom tone he continued, "Billy, all this will pale into insignificance. One of these days when you're a big-time lawyer, people won't believe you lived at Six-oh-one and a half Railroad Street and didn't have a pot to piss in. But in the meantime, it's going to be 'dog eat dog.' You have to learn to bob and weave. The only consolation I can give you is that this isn't forever. We'll be on our feet one day.

"Anyway, I don't want to hear you complain. I'm doing the best I can, and if you don't like it you can go live with your mother! If you can find that white bitch!"

The harshness of Dad's words shocked me. I was angry at my mother for abandoning us, but not ready to bar her totally from our lives. Though we hadn't heard from her in almost a year, labeling her a "white bitch" pushed her over the line and banished her totally from our lives.

Just then we heard the whistle of a passenger train. We stepped off the tracks and stood with our backs against the siding of an abandoned warehouse. The screech of steel wheels slicing against the groaning tracks shut out the rest of the world. Lighted coach windows blinked past us. I gazed at the passengers, so isolated and peaceful, lounging in their seats, with their heads resting against sparkling white cotton cloths. Already robbed of so many dreams, could I believe Dad when he said that one day Muncie would be just a vague memory? Was it idle boasting, or was there a small kernel of truth in his words? He was a master at drawing tantalizing visions that never materialized.

Though only ten years old, I faced one of the hardest choices of my life: to dream or to despair. Too young to realize the odds against any one of us ever walking away from those tracks and changing the circumstances of our lives, I chose to dream.

# Chapter 7

# "Saved"

"Hello, Dora," said Grandma to the heavyset, dark-brown-skinned woman who strolled through the alley gate.

"Billy, move your things out of the way."

I swept my hand across the concrete walkway for the four remaining jacks. Then I joined Mike on the plank bench. Dora Terry's presence puzzled me. She didn't fit in with our regular crowd. I'd never seen her smoke, drink, cuss, or fight. In fact, she belonged to Reverend Sanders's Christ Temple Pentecostal Church, a true evangelical mission. The only talk about church at Grandma's was how black preachers were getting "rich and fat" spreading the Gospel among Muncie's gullible believers. If she was there to convert the "sinners" I didn't think she would have much success. She was looking for Dad, but he was at Bob's Tavern.

Turning to Mike and me, she said, "How you boys doing?"

"Fine, thank you, Miss Dora," we answered in unison.

"Billy, you wanna spend the night? It's your turn." Mike had been invited the previous week and had described a hot dinner in minute detail. I'd do almost anything to avoid sleeping next to the toilet. Almost a week earlier, a stumbling drunk trying to negotiate his way out of our bathroom after using the toilet fell on Mike and me and broke the cot. Dad had not yet fulfilled his promise to fix it. We were sleeping on the floor.

"Sallie, do you think Buster'd mind if Billy spends the night with me?"

"No, Dora, I know he won't mind."

"Billy, get your pajamas and let's go on up to the house."

Looking straight into her eyes, it took all the honesty I could muster to say, "I don't have none, Miss Dora."

"Come on then," she said, looking at me like I was a lost puppy. "Help me carry this bag. Mr. Merle didn't eat half the things I cooked for dinner."

My arms tightened around the paper sack as we headed to Monroe Street.

Miss Dora's long, plain black cotton dress blew softly in the wind. Slowing my pace to hers, I realized how short she was. At five feet tall, I was almost eye to eye with her. We walked north on Kirby Avenue to her house. Flowers circled her gray wooden-frame home. The yard was mowed and the bushes neatly trimmed. A swing swayed gently on the porch. As she opened the door, a linoleum floor gleamed in the sunlight. Her living room was almost as large as Grandma's entire shack. The aged furniture showed signs of meticulous attention, with vases and lamps placed on white lace doilies. Carefully, I followed her through the dining room into the kitchen, fearful of inhaling lest I break something.

My eyes were glued to the bag of food as she reached deep inside it. First, she extracted an almost full quart bottle of creamy milk, then two large slices of yellow cake with chocolate frosting. Three freshly baked, golden-crusted dinner rolls were followed by two crisp fried chicken legs. Last was a small glass bowl heaped full of mashed potatoes.

She set a plate on the table in front of me, then hesitantly suggested, "Why don't you wash your face and hands, Billy?"

Embarrassed that it hadn't occurred to me, I rose from the chair and walked to the kitchen sink.

"Not there."

"I'm sorry, Miss Dora, where's your washbasin?"

She looked at me and chuckled. "I don't have a washbasin. Use the bathroom sink. It's right off the dining room."

Walking into the bathroom, I felt like a fool. We had only been in Muncie six months, and I'd already forgotten normal people had sinks, bathtubs, and commodes, not outdoor privies and cold-water spigots. The white porcelain bathtub stirred memories of our Alexandria town house. I was shocked by my image in the mirror. My face was so thin and dirty I hardly recognized myself. The water turned scummy and gray as I scrubbed and scrubbed with strong-smelling hard-water castile soap.

The aroma of crisp chicken was barely savored before I swallowed it. The pure white mashed potatoes melted in my mouth. The crusty rolls vanished in two bites. I was licking chocolate off my fingers before I realized the cake was gone.

As I looked up to draw a breath, Miss Dora shook her head with a sympathetic smile. She daintily stripped a small piece of meat from the other chicken leg as I basked in the delicious feeling of having eaten a real meal.

Though she was fifty-two at the time she came into my life, Miss Dora had been in Muncie since she was sixteen. She arrived with an eighth grade education from Grady, Arkansas, as the wife of Pete Terry, one of Muncie's gambling and bootleg legends. Pete had an after-hours joint in Muncie and operated it until he died in the late forties. Though much younger, Dad was one of Pete's gambling protégés.

After dinner, I heard more about Miss Dora's days as the wife of a small-time hustler and, surprisingly, about my own family.

"I met your momma in those sportin' days. Her daddy used to drink and gamble, and she came with him once in a while. She was pretty, but not much more than a girl. Nobody could understand why Buster married her. Buster was one of Muncie's first colored boys to go to Howard University. Everybody was proud of him. He was handsome and smart! Who-ee! He knew almost everything. All of us knew he was gonna be somebody. Your momma was cute, but most people thought Buster was marrying 'neath himself, even if she was white. It sure's created hard times for him, but if you make your bed hard, you just have to turn over that much more often.

"What bothers me is that you boys didn't do nothing wrong, but you the ones payin'."

Outside, dusk had settled and the streetlights flicked on. Soon, drunks would begin to gather at Grandma's. Miss Dora rose and said, "Come on, Billy, it's time for bed."

Time for bed? I gulped. It couldn't be past eight o'clock.

"Dad don't make me go to bed till late," I said.

You could miss half your life going to bed so early, I thought. Think of all the excitement and radio programs after eight o'clock!

"Come on," she said. "A growing boy needs his rest."

Dejectedly, I followed her through the house. We entered a narrow room next to hers. It was bare except for a single cast-iron bed. She opened a closet and removed bedding. Then she asked, "Do you boys ever see your momma's people?"

"No ma'am, we ain't heard from them since we got here. I guess they don't know where we are."

"Those white folks know where you boys is."

"Well, how come we ain't seen 'em?"

"White people just don't like to come down to the colored section. A lot of them is scared, and others just don't want nothing to do with us."

"Then why don't they tell us to come and see them?"

"Sometimes people is just too busy for children. They have jobs and burdens, and then they just forget."

Springs squeaked as I turned toward the wall, trying to figure out if she was right. They squeaked again as I rolled onto my back. I shifted to the middle of the bed and they squeaked once more.

"Try to be still, Billy," I heard through the open door connecting the two bedrooms.

Lying in the center of the bed, motionless, it seemed like hours before I fell asleep. I dreamed of my mother. She and my younger brother and sister were in a small boat on a large lake. I stood on shore as they pulled away. She kept saying something to me, but I couldn't understand it. I leaned closer to hear. My foot slipped into the water. All I could make out was "Good-bye" and I began to cry. When I realized it meant forever, I couldn't stop the river of tears.

"Billy! Billy, you all right?"

"Huh?" I said as I came out of a deep sleep and saw Miss Dora standing over me in her nightgown.

"You were crying out for Mike. Are you okay?"

"Yes'm."

"Have you boys been apart since you come to Muncie?"

"Not much."

"You must be missing him," she said. "That's why you crying. Go on back to sleep, Billy." She walked into her room. I lay quietly, trying to drift off once again. Then I looked through the open door and saw Miss Dora kneeling by the side of her bed. Raising up on my arms carefully to avoid making the bed squeak, I could just barely hear her praying.

"Lord, please give me strength. I need Your guidance. It's too much for an old widow woman, but I got to do something."

The next morning while we ate oatmeal Miss Dora suddenly asked, "Billy, would you and Mike like living here with me?"

I almost choked. "Yes ma'am. Do you really mean it?"

"I'll have to see if it's okay with Buster."

"It won't be no problem with Daddy, Miss Dora."

Later, I learned the purpose of the overnight visits was to help her decide which one of us to take. She felt she could stretch her weekly twenty-five-dollar salary as a domestic to feed and clothe one of us, but two would be impossible. In the end, however, she decided we could not be separated and that she had to try to save us both.

Playing in the alley the next afternoon, I overheard Miss Dora and Dad talking in the yard.

"No, you can't move in with the boys," she said emphatically.

"Come on, Dora, I can't be separated from them."

"If you was worried about that, you'd get a job and a decent place to live, instead of running 'round with all your no-'count friends and drinking and gambling."

"Well, Pete made his money gambling."

"But he kept his home life separate. You didn't see no drunks hanging 'round my house then, and you ain't gonna see none now. The boys can come and live with me, but you gonna hafta stay in the alley."

"Why don't you let me come on up? You must be wanting a man since Pete died. You remember how you used to give me a little piece when I was just out of high school?"

"Buster, sometimes I think all that drinking affected your brain. That was twenty years ago. I'm a church woman now."

"Now, you don't do everything the church says. You dye your hair. I bet you even use a little bit of makeup if the truth be told," Dad said with a laugh.

"I don't use no makeup, and if I keeps out the gray a bit that's my own business."

"Well, what if I won't let the boys leave Momma's?"

"I just can't believe you wouldn't let them better themselves when they have a chance."

He paused for a moment and I feared our future was in jeopardy. If he stood in our way, I would never forgive him. Walking to the gate, I stood quietly, still hidden from view, waiting for his decision.

"You're a good woman, Dora. I appreciate this. When I get a job, I'll give you something for taking care of them."

"I ain't taking them in to make no money. I got enough to live on, but the boys need clothes and food. You got to help me."

"I'm trying to find a job. If I get one, I'll give you half of my check. If I can't find work maybe we can get them on welfare."

The summer of 1954 Mike and I moved into Miss Dora's. She opened the door of the attic. Narrow wooden steps rose almost vertically to an open landing. They looked even steeper when I saw no railing.

"Go on up, boys. I can't climb the stairs. Billy, you take the front room. Mike, the one facing Vine."

With my grocery bag suitcase in one arm and the other braced against the wall, I followed Mike. The wall was cool to the touch, but at the top we were overcome by hot stale air. The only place I could stand upright in the V-shaped attic was in the exact middle of the room. I opened a small window. Mike wrestled with another one, and a light breeze began to move through the attic. Mike said it was "hotter than hell." "Shut up," I whispered desperately. "Do you want her to hear you complaining?"

"Dag! Can't I say anything at all?"

"No, you can't. If you do we'll have to go back to Grandma's."

An ancient chipped dresser stood in the corner of my room. Carefully, I placed all my clothes inside the top drawer. Then I sat on the bed. The mattress sagged deeply in the middle, but I didn't care. I had a room of my own! Looking around, I noticed the coal furnace chimney, separating my room from the rest of the attic. Then I realized there were no heat registers. Maybe if I moved my bed next to the chimney I would be warm during the winter.

That evening Mike and I were in the middle of a game of jacks on the kitchen steps when Miss Dora called us to dinner.

"Can't we finish the game?" Mike protested.

"No, come on in here now."

"I don't want to," Mike said.

"I said come in here now. When I call you I expect you to come. I'm not gonna be waiting on you."

Mike followed me into the kitchen and slammed the door.

"Don't be jerking the door just 'cause you mad."

"Yes ma'am," Mike responded. I vowed to be on my best behavior, hoping that I might stay if Mike had to go.

That night Miss Dora again brought fried chicken leftovers from Postal's home, where she worked. Throughout the prayer I kept my eyes on the lone chicken breast perched atop two legs. "Amen" was hardly out of her mouth before my arm shot across the table to snatch the chicken breast off the plate.

A firm hand grabbed my wrist.

"There's two rules I want you to learn while you live with me. First, I don't like no boardinghouse reach. We may not have a lot to eat, but you'll always get a share. Second, when we have chicken, the breast is for me, and legs and wings is for you boys. Do you understand that?"

"Yes ma'am. I'm sorry. I didn't mean to make you mad."

Her dark brown face widened into a smile. "I ain't mad. I just want you to know what I like and what I don't like. That way we can live together easy."

For almost a month Miss Dora didn't give us a key to the house. She feared we would let Dad and his drunken buddies gather there. Each evening after school Mike and I waited for her on the colored side of the railroad tracks. Sometimes just before six o'clock we crossed the tracks and raced to Madison and Charles, directly across from Postal's house.

One day, after waiting till six-thirty, we even crossed Madison Street and knocked on the front door. Old man Postal, a retired newspaper printer, rose from his chair and hobbled to the door of his enclosed porch. Suffering from lead poisoning, his skin was several shades paler than the white pajamas he wore, and his long thin white hair stuck out wildly in all directions. He looked like a blue-veined ghost. An impish smile crossed his face as he ushered us inside.

"Dorie!" he shouted to the kitchen. "Your pickaninnies are here!" He burst into a high-pitched laugh.

Miss Dora stormed onto the porch.

"Don't you be calling them boys pickaninnies! That's slavery talk. My momma and daddy didn't like it, and I don't either. I ain't gonna stand for it."

Mike and I stood quietly in the foyer, waiting for Postal to respond. Was he going to fire her? I hadn't seen many colored people talk back to whites. I looked into Postal's light blue eyes and saw the smile drain from his face. Miss Dora stood with hands on her hips.

He dropped his head.

"Now Dorie, you know I was just kidding. I didn't mean any harm by it."

Miss Dora's frown softened. "I know you didn't, Mr. Merle, but you gotta be careful what you say. Things like that hurts people. This ain't slavery times no more."

He recovered with a chuckle. "Yes it is. I been a slave to Momma, the newspaper, and you for twenty years!"

"Get out of here with that talk." She laughed. "Come on, boys, let's get back to the kitchen."

We always called her Miss Dora. I'm not sure why. That's what Dad called her, and maybe he told us to do the same. Or I might have called her Miss Dora because she was not my birth mother and I simply couldn't bring myself to call her Mom. Perhaps my reluctance was a manifestation of my own prejudice. The stares of white bystanders made me uneasy as we shopped together in downtown Muncie. My face would redden with embarrassment when they gawked at me as if I was violating some law or tradition. No doubt, I allowed my emotions to be controlled by what I thought some nameless, faceless, white person would think if he overheard me call her Momma.

Whites weren't the only ones who felt we didn't belong with Miss Dora. Her late husband's sister, Nell, made her views clear during a visit from Pittsburgh. She sat on the porch with Miss Dora while I played in the yard within earshot. Nell prattled loudly as if I was of no importance.

"Dora, you wasting your time trying to take care of them boys."

I heard a sharp intake of breath from Miss Dora. Embarrassed, I tried not to look up from my stick soldiers. As I heard the scratch of metal against wood, I stole a quick glance. Miss Dora inched forward in her chair toward the swing, which groaned under Nell's weight.

"I like them and they need some help," she whispered. "You should'a seen how they was living down there in the alley, amongst all them no-'count thieves and hustlers. I almost cried when I walked through the gate at Sallie's and saw Buster and her, both stretched out on the ground, dead drunk! The boys was just sitting there on a plank bench waiting for them to wake up."

"It ain't your responsibility, Dora. I don't care if you is religious. They got a daddy, a grandma, and a whole lotta white and colored folks that could be taking care of 'em if they had a mind to. Their white folks don't even come by to see 'em. You should be tired of taking care of ungrateful crackers. You done it all your life. Soon as these boys get grown they gonna plumb forget about you. They gonna run away and be white boys, and you'll never hear from 'em again."

Nell made me so mad I wanted to leap on the porch and strangle her to death. Even then I knew Miss Dora was making a tremendous sacrifice for us and my gratitude was immense.

"Nell," she said, as she moved even closer to the swing, "I didn't take those boys in expecting they was gonna take care of me in my old age. You don't know them. They good boys and they need a home just like other people, and I got one for them."

"Dora . . ." Nell began to whine. The metal chair banged against the wall as Miss Dora stood abruptly. She leaned over until she was nose-to-nose with Nell.

"I won't have you low-ratin' them anymore. They my boys, and I'm gonna take care of them as long as the Lord gives me strength."

Dad did find a job at the Whitely Car Wash for a short while. Every Friday afternoon—payday—Mike and I tried to intercept him before he reached the dice game at Watson Tell's. When unsuccessful, we made the trek to Watson's two-room shack in an alley off Willard Street behind the used car lot. One afternoon while Mike rapped on Watson's door, I stuck my nose against the screen, peering inside for Dad. We hoped Watson would answer, but it was Katie, or "Aunt Katie," as Dad demanded we call her, who waddled to us. She positioned her short, rotund figure to block our view.

"What'cha boys want?" she slurred.

Peering through the screen, I could see that her wig was lop-sided, revealing black stubble on her dark-brown scalp. The blast of wine breath confirmed she would be difficult.

"We got to see Daddy, Aunt Katie," Mike pleaded. "Miss Dora needs him." Mike pulled the screen door handle, but it wouldn't budge. Katie held the hook.

"I don't like you boys here when the mens is gambling. This is business. Now go on and play. I'll tell Buster you came by."

"Please, Aunt Katie, can't we come in?" I begged. "It's important. Miss Dora said we had to talk to him."

"Go on now," she said. "Your daddy will be home later."

Miss Dora told us to bring Dad home, and we were determined to do it. We did have one advantage over Katie. From where we stood we could see heavily traveled Willard Street and she could not.

"Mike," I whispered loudly, nodding toward the street, "is that a patrol car?" He glanced quickly toward Willard. For an instant he was puzzled; then he understood.

"Yeah, Billy, it's the cops."

"Aunt Katie," I said, feigning panic, "you'd better let us in before the police wonder what we're doing behind the car lot."

"I sure hope they don't hear the gambling when they drive up here," Mike added earnestly.

"Shit," she said. "Come on in, but don't'cha be bothering the men. You all hear me?"

"Yes ma'am," we said, and rushed past her to the back room.

"Mothafucka, give me my money!" rang out as we neared the gamblers. Five men crouched on their hands and knees in a circle, dollar bills tightly clutched in their fists. Dimes, quarters, and nickels lay on the dirty brown linoleum floor in front of them. The money changed hands and a bottle of cheap wine made its way around the room. When it reached Dad, all eyes turned toward him expectantly. "Get a good taste, Buster! I'm gonna whip your ass," hollered Lucius. "Yeah!" came a chorus of murmurs from all sides. When I saw Dad lift the bottle to his lips, I knew I had to work fast.

"Come on, Dad, let's go home," I said. "Miss Dora's waiting. You promised to go to the grocery." He looked up from the dice he had just rolled across the floor. The point was nine.

"You boys head on home and tell Miss Dora I'll be there in a little bit," he said, and reached for the dice. "Now take off." He gripped the dice in his right fist and shook them.

Over the rattle of plastic I said, "Dad, if you don't come she's gonna be mad. You promised."

Sighing in exasperation, he lowered his clenched fist to his side. He turned toward us. I sensed he was weakening and hoped we could get him out while he still had some money.

Lucius rose up on his haunches. His bloodshot eyes narrowed in anger. "Buster," he growled, "don't think you gonna take off after you done beat me out of my twenty dollars. You gotta give me a chance to get my money back 'fore you go. Now, your point's nine."

I held my tongue, fearful of Lucius's rage.

Dad, too, sensed he was helpless to leave the room. He turned to us.

"Here, boys, each of you take a quarter and go buy some ice cream. Tell Miss Dora I'll be along soon."

I took the money, and then said, "Dad, what about some grocery money?"

He reached into his pocket and withdrew a ten-dollar bill. Lucius stepped into the circle, his brown face turning two shades darker. He towered over us.

"Buster, get them boys outta here! We trying to shoot some bones, man! Don't be giving 'way my money. Leroy done took yours, now I want mines back."

Dad laid the ten-dollar bill on the floor in front of him. "Fadin' all bets," he said. We retreated to the sofa. He rolled seven.

"Looks like that Howard University nigger ain't so slick after all," chuckled Lucius as he snatched the money in front of Dad.

Once again we had to rely on Miss Dora. Out of her twenty-five dollars weekly salary, she paid for gas and electricity, bought coal, fed and clothed Mike and me. Despite Dad's constant promises, he gave nothing.

We finally received a letter summoning us to the Welfare Department. Miss Dora stood at the dark-brown wooden counter while Mike and I sat on a bench that ran the length of the front room. A pimply-faced white man in a short-sleeved shirt stood behind the counter chomping on a candy bar. As he approached Miss Dora, he glanced at Mike and me. Then he bombarded her with questions.

"What you doin' with two white boys?

"Where's their mother?

"Why doesn't their daddy work?

"How much money do you make?

"Isn't twenty-five dollars enough to live on?

"Do all you people think there's free money up here?

"Why don't you sell your house to take care of them?"

Feeling a mixture of rage and shame, I stood next to her. My fists clenched below the counter, and I wished I could kill the man. Miss Dora didn't seek anything for herself. She was willing to be degraded for our benefit. Finally, the clerk disappeared behind a partition. Forty-five minutes later he returned with a check. He slid it quickly onto the counter, carefully avoiding Miss Dora's touch.

Outside the office she showed it to me. I couldn't believe my eyes. Humiliated for a mere five dollars and fifty cents! It was supposed to feed and clothe Mike and me for one week. Mike wanted to return and throw the check in the welfare man's face. For once I agreed with him. Finally, Miss Dora persuaded us that five-fifty was better than nothing, and we walked the six blocks to the supermarket at the South Walnut Street railroad crossing.

The unpleasant aroma of disinfectant filled the aisles. As Miss Dora shopped, I tried to keep a running total to make sure we didn't go over the five-fifty. Two of my favorite treats, strawberries and doughnuts, found their way into the shopping cart.

The cashier, an attractive young girl, tallied the groceries as we placed them on the counter. She announced loudly, "That comes to six dollars and ten cents."

I looked toward the front door, hoping Dad would suddenly appear with sixty cents.

Miss Dora said, "I'm sorry, ma'am, but we only have this check for five-fifty."

The clerk grimaced as Miss Dora handed the check to her. In a high-pitched nasal voice she said, "You shoulda got your welfare approved before gettin' in line. Now I gotta get the manager to clear my register."

"I'm sorry. This is our first welfare money."

"It's too late now. Remember it next time. There's a lot of customers waitin'. Whadda you want to put back?"

I turned to conceal my disappointment as Miss Dora pushed aside the fruit and doughnuts.

The following week we returned to the welfare office. We waited for almost an hour. Finally, the same administrator approached. He said simply, "No check!" The five dollars and fifty cents of the previous week was the first and last welfare money we ever received.

We had barely stepped into the courthouse yard when I exploded.

"How come they can't give us any money? You'd think we asked for all the money they got!"

"Take it easy," responded Miss Dora. "I guess the welfare people just ain't giving out money when children's daddies can work."

"But our daddy ain't taking care of us."

White passersby stopped and stared at us, but I no longer cared. I looked to the only mother I had for an answer.

"I don't know the rules," Miss Dora said. "All I know is we don't get it."

"Well, what are we gonna do? How we gonna buy food?"

Miss Dora took my hand and gently guided me down the street.

"You got to stop worrying so much, Billy. You startin' to make me nervous. The Lord has brought us this far, and He is gonna help us find a way. We gonna make it."

A calmness came over me as I stood there and let her faith envelop me. At that moment, I realized that our struggle had become her struggle.

Directly across the street from Miss Dora's in the downstairs of a two-story clapboard house was Roach's Cafe. Though it wasn't much to look at, the years of segregated restaurants in Indiana gave it somewhat of a celebrity status. Amon Roach, owner and operator of the café, often proclaimed that he served "many of the greats from the black experience" as they passed through Muncie—Bill Doggett, Goose Tatum, and even Lawyer Chavis from Indianapolis. Roach's was about the only decent place in Muncie where they could eat since the white restaurants wouldn't serve blacks.

On the rare Saturday nights when Mike and I had enough spare change from collecting pop bottles in the neighborhood, we would have a treat from Roach's. A dark-brown-skinned man with short gray hair, Mr. Roach wore wire-rimmed glasses. Dressed in a black bow tie and a long white cotton apron stretching from his chest to his knees, he was perpetual motion inside the restaurant. He always greeted me with a booming voice.

"What can I get you, young man?"

"I want to look at the board a minute, Mr. Roach."

"Well, you better hurry up. That skillet's hot and ready to pop."

He scrutinized me sternly for a few seconds. I stared at the menu chalked on the small blackboard behind the counter:

Chit'lin Dinner ..................... 1.75
Chicken Dinner ...................... .95
Barbecue Ribs ...................... 1.00
Corn Bread ........................... .10
Sweet Potatoes ...................... .20
Collards .............................. .30
Pig Feet .............................. .75
Pork Chops ......................... 1.55
Ham Dinner ........................ 1.45
Fish Sandwich ....................... .35
Sweet Potato Pie ................... .25
Neck Bones .......................... .75
Apple Pie ............................. .25

While reading, I slithered onto a stool. Roach shot me a scowl. He knew I wanted a carry-out order and the stools were only for sit-down customers. Self-consciously I stood. The sharp, tangy smell of barbecue made my mouth water, but I never had barbecue money. I counted my change once more to make sure.

"You made up your mind yet, boy?"

"Yes sir," I responded slowly, hoping to prolong my stay. "I want three fried fish sandwiches, one plain, one with mustard, and one with ketchup, two pieces of apple pie, and one slice of that sweet potato pie."

"I thought that's what you wanted," he said as I handed him the exact change. "Don't be bashful in here, just speak up when you come in."

Ten minutes later Mr. Roach walked out of the kitchen with three greasy wax-paper bundles and placed them in a small brown bag. He took the pies from the glass case on the counter, cut three pieces, wrapped them, then piled them on top of the fish. Carefully placing my hand on the bottom of the bag in case too much oil seeped through, I ran back across Kirby Avenue.

Mike, Miss Dora, and I sat on the porch and enjoyed our feast as we watched the Saturday-night revelers appear on the street. Men dressed in neatly pressed suits passed, followed by women in high heels and tight flowered dresses. Most were on the way to Bob's

Tavern. On Saturday nights even Miss Dora stayed up late—until ten p.m.! She always left the porch with a warning:

"Boys, when that bell rings tomorrow morning, I want you both sitting in Sunday school. I don't want you in bed, or getting ready, or on the way. You be there for Sunday school, or you'll be sitting in church all day with me."

Miss Dora attended choir practice on Tuesday, Bible class on Thursday, and church all day Sunday. When she wasn't at church, the sisters dropped by the house to visit. In Virginia we had spent so little time in church that at first I was fascinated by all the praying and singing at Christ Temple. Soon, though, the long, long hours turned Sunday into a day to dread.

Every Sunday morning, dressed in our rummage sale suits, Mike and I set off to Grandma's for offering money. We hoped Dad would be asleep, because then we could rustle through his pants for loose change or gather pennies left on the floor from the night's final effort to buy wine. Otherwise, we had to beg for offering money on the street.

The Saturday night crowd, their suits and dresses now rumpled, lined the street in front of the Dew Drop Inn. The women, with makeup faded from the long night, wobbled on their high heels. Many sat on the concrete steps waiting for the doors to open for coffee. We knew most of them, either from Grandma's or from standing outside Bob's Tavern with Dad. Everyone knew we were on the way to church. They hailed us with a half-serious "Pray for me, boys!" Sometimes the women would give us coins for the collection plate, and Miss Dora said we better put them in it.

The bell almost always began ringing just as we turned the Pershing Street corner, and we raced the last fifty feet. A signboard nailed to the exterior wall announced:

CHRIST TEMPLE
Apostolic Faith Church

BISHOP OSCAR E. SANDERS, PASTOR

Services
Sunday School 9:30 A.M.
Church 11:00 A.M.
Evening Meeting 7:00 P.M.

Doors closed behind us. Carpeted steps led up to a large room with rows of wood-backed pews. Men, women, and children were scattered throughout the room. Pomade hair oil glistened in the light filtering through the stained-glass windows. The men wore dark suits, white shirts, and dark ties. Women dressed conservatively as well, although an occasional muted print appeared in the sea of gray and black dresses.

Brother Anderson, one of the deacons, was our teacher. He had flawless shiny skin the color of black ink, and his muscular body bulged in the tight suit he wore. He stood erect with head high and shoulders back. It wasn't his suit or physique that was most impressive. It was his wide and open face; his eyes always stared straight into you. You sensed you had better look directly at him, and listen. Brother Anderson wasn't the type of person with whom you laughed and joked. Though I could always get a smile on the street, inside the church he was serious business.

Many of the boys from the Madison Street playground—Theotis, Alan, Ed, Roger, Randy, Larry, and Theopolius—were in my Sunday school class. It had taken about six months, and many scuffles and arguments, before they grudgingly accepted Mike and me as part of the neighborhood life. All of us alternated reading the Sunday school lesson printed on loose-leaf colored paper. Then Brother Anderson quizzed us. Most of the boys had spent long hours in Sunday school and knew the stories. Ed was knowledgeable about almost every biblical reference. It was a rare morning when he wasn't waving his hand trying to attract Brother Anderson's attention. At Garfield School, he was shy and quiet. He never volunteered. Even when our Garfield teacher coaxed him to participate, he said nothing. Yet in church he was outgoing and self-assured.

Sunday school ended with a final hymn, a report from Sister Truitt on the amount of the offering, and a few parting words from Bishop Sanders. As we stood one Sunday, Bishop Sanders selected a girl from my Garfield class to recite a verse from memory. Painted on the mural behind the pulpit was part of Psalm Nine:

> I will praise the LORD with my whole heart;
> I will tell all Thy marvelous works.

As she said, "I will praise the Lord . . ." the Bishop's hand shot up for her to stop. His bass voice filled the huge room. "Kids nowadays don't even try to learn the Good Book!" Chastened, she made a last-ditch effort to please him by quoting the shortest verse in the Bible, "Jesus wept."

Bishop Sanders shook his head. "He sure did weep when he heard you. Listen to you, not even trying to learn the Lord's words, makin' a mockery of your Sunday school lessons, and you was born free, too." The bishop scanned all of the children for another victim. His eyes locked on me and I began to sweat. Then I relaxed as his eyes passed on to other prey. Just then Ed shoved the Sunday school lesson into my hand. Puzzled, I looked at him, but he pointed to the verse for the day. Sensing an urgency in his face, I looked down and read it, just as I heard the bishop say, "Gregory, why don't you give us a verse?" I raised my head and recited,

> "He is despised and rejected of men,
> a man of sorrow, acquainted with grief."
> [Isaiah 53:3 (K.J.V.)]

For a brief moment I allowed myself to feel despised, rejected, and abandoned. Yet that feeling vanished as I felt a growing sense of belonging, and turned to Ed with a grateful smile.

After Sunday school, Mike and I followed the other boys toward the door. As we headed down the outside aisle, hoping to escape a hot Sunday afternoon in the rock-hard wooden seats, we caught sight of Miss Dora and her beckoning finger. She pointed to the empty space beside her. "Church," she said. Dejectedly, we sat down.

There was a ten-minute hymn, followed by announcements and reports about sick and lame church members. Then visitors stood and introduced themselves. Bishop Sanders's call for the offering was preceded by a sternly delivered warning that he hated to hear the clink of coins in the plastic collection plates. He glared at me when I slowed the process by placing my money in the plate coin by coin.

While the deacons retired to the office to count the offering, the women of the choir began another hymn. The tempo picked up and everyone joined the singing. The sounds of the choir, piano, tambourines, and the entire congregation swelled around us. Everyone was up, moving to the music. Even the bishop swayed and stomped behind the pulpit. As the hymn reached its crescendo, loud wails of

"Thank you, Jesus," "Amen," and "Praise the Lord" filled the room. When the music ended, most remained standing, to "testify." Many asked the Lord to look after sick friends and family. Others gave thanks to God for leading the way to a religious life. Some shook with emotion, their words tumbling together. A babble of strange sounds filled the temple. Church members threw their hands in the air and trembled in front of their seats. Others moved into the aisle and danced toward the pulpit in a trancelike state. Deacons scurried to block the steps to avoid injuries.

Though I watched it happen Sunday after Sunday, I doubted that people could really speak in tongues. Then that afternoon I was startled to see Miss Dora rise from her seat. Eyes closed, her body swayed gently from side to side as she chanted a strange language. At that moment, I knew speaking in tongues was authentic. Miss Dora had far too much integrity to fake anything. This openness, however, was hard for me to accept. My survival depended on my ability to conceal my emotions; I sought to reveal nothing about how I felt. In fact, I struggled not to feel anything too deeply. Yet Miss Dora and the brothers and sisters of Christ Temple surrendered total control to God, and didn't worry about what others might think or do to them for their thoughts or beliefs.

Testifying continued for almost half an hour. It was hard not to be drawn into the swirl of emotion. Tears came to my eyes as men and women recounted how the Lord rescued them from lives of crime, gambling, and the "street life." Finally, when it seemed that all emotions were drained, Bishop Sanders glided into the sermon. That day it was on "faith." As he began his sermon, I felt as if he were speaking directly to me.

"And I say to you, each and every one of you sitting out there, you have to believe! Believe what the Good Book tells you. You must have faith that God exists!"

He paused for a moment of reflection and added, "Even during our simple daily tasks, we need faith. Just last week I was buying a refrigerator, and when I opened the door I saw the light come on. I asked the salesman, 'Does that light stay on all the time?' He said, 'No, it goes off when the door shuts.' Well, how was I to believe that, when I see the light is on even when the door is open just a tiny bit? I'll tell you how I believe. I believe because I have faith! I have faith that the light goes off when the refrigerator door is shut!

I have faith in the written Gospel of the Lord! And I have faith in God!''

Bishop Sanders followed with a "fire and brimstone" message, warning those who didn't repent that they would spend an eternity with the devil. He reinforced his message with the admonition "Sinners are on the express bus to Hell!" Silence filled the church as he softly began the "Call to the Altar," a last chance for sinners to be saved.

His pace quickened. He traveled the length and breadth of the pulpit, back and forth. He scanned the congregation for a soul to be saved. His eyes fastened on me. With his piercing look, and the loudest tone he could muster, his voice filled the temple.

"When you gonna give up that good-timing and playing, and walk in God's shadow? Who knows how much time you have to make this decision? You could walk out of this church today and be run over by a truck! Your soul would be lost forever!"

In almost a whisper, he added, "You have a chance to decide where you will spend eternity. Don't turn your back on God. There's nothing out there that's worth losing your soul for. Come join us." Still staring at me fiercely, he threw his arms open. "We reach out to you. We are waiting." He leaned over the edge of the platform, thrusting his hand well into the second row of seats. I shrank back. "Take the first step to salvation. Get up from that soft, easy chair. Come down to the altar and give your life to God."

I hunched down in the seat, trying to be inconspicuous, wrestling with my conscience. Maybe he was right about spending eternity in Hell if I wasn't saved. But would the church require me to give up my most precious goal? Suddenly I felt a powerful force on my shoulder. My heart jumped to my throat. I resisted, but the force became heavier and stronger. I couldn't move. Was it God or the devil?

I spun around to see sweat dripping from the face of Brother Anderson. Leaning forward, his hand lay heavy on my shoulder.

"Gregory, it's time to think about getting saved. It's the only way to salvation."

Miss Dora, placidly sitting beside me, nodded in agreement. I dropped my head, avoiding eye contact with the bishop. After an interminable few seconds, he moved to the other side of the platform and looked for another lost soul to save. The Call ended and

I sighed with enormous relief, realizing I could postpone my decision once again.

After services we walked next door to the church dining hall for the monthly dinner. Elders sat at the head table with the bishop at the center. Adjacent to them was the choir, some members still in their robes. A third front table was for the ushers. Large families had their own special places. The rest of us filled the rear of the room. The food was tasty, but Miss Dora warned us not to return for seconds. There were too many people to feed.

After dinner I noticed Bishop Sanders momentarily alone. He stood at the door, toothpick in hand, plucking remnants of the chicken dinner from his teeth. I wanted to join the church, but there was one dream I couldn't surrender. Could he help me?

In a fumbling manner I put the question to him. Then I stood meekly, waiting for an answer.

He laughed. "Sonny, don't you know that it's easier for a camel to go through the eye of a needle than it is for a lawyer to enter the Kingdom of Heaven?"

Unwilling to give up my dream of becoming a lawyer, I turned away from him. Yet his sermon cycled over and over in my mind during our walk home with Miss Dora. My faith grew as I looked at her and believed life would get better, that there was a reason for everything, and that the Lord brought us to her to help us find our way.

# Chapter 8

# Hustling

Although Miss Dora provided a home and refuge from the chaos and danger at Grandma Sallie's, Mike and I quickly realized we had to work to survive. Miss Dora's twenty-five-dollar weekly salary barely paid for coal at sixteen dollars a half ton. Dad rarely contributed, although he was always on the lookout for jobs—for us. I began to learn a lot of very early lessons about how people lived at the margins of society, and especially what I would have to do to survive.

My first job was as a "coal hustler" for a local drug dealer nicknamed "Grass." My task was to make sure that the coal scuttles in his house were always filled so he didn't have to trek to the backyard shed in the middle of the night. I was with him just a short time before he became a guest of the state of Indiana in one of its correctional facilities. I didn't like the job anyway. It wasn't the danger of being around a drug dealer and his pals as much as the fact that I had to pay my father a commission on the three dollars a week I earned. Dad argued for half since he arranged the work, but I convinced him to accept only fifty cents. Though it was no laughing matter then, today I chuckle at how persuasive Dad could be. He actually had me feeling guilty that I gave him so little for his "finder's fee." At the beginning I was angry that he didn't try harder to find work for himself and support us the way he had in Virginia. But the first lesson I learned was that my anger had no effect on him, and more important, it didn't keep me from going to bed hungry. Mike and I resigned ourselves to the fact that we were on our own. As we made our way to our jobs, we often passed Dad on the street corners sharing jokes and wine with his buddies. It was infuriating as we passed to hear him brag to his companions, "My boys know how to hustle."

Mike had a much more interesting first job than I did. He was the "broom boy" at "Uncle Highball's" gambling joint. Every evening before the crap games started, he trotted to the small dingy room Highball rented in a shabby two-story walk-up. Mike swept the scarred linoleum floor before the regulars arrived. One of Uncle Highball's white girlfriends didn't like Mike around the gambling so she managed to get him fired. She took over the job, but one evening, a bit tipsy from too much bootleg whiskey, she was unable to balance her three-hundred-pound frame on the staircase. Fortunately, there were just a few bruises on her after she bumped down the steps and through the screen door, but her ankle was broken. Highball sent a numbers runner to bring Mike back to work. Later, Highball had a losing streak with the gamblers. Bad luck, and some kind of ailment, forced him to close his joint. The last time I saw Highball, he was propped up in bed. His girlfriend was nursing him back to health with pig's feet and Thunderbird wine.

Highball's bad luck and Grass's incarceration did not end our need for work. During the summer of 1954, Dad lined up a farming job for me with a relative named James Grider. Uncle Jim, in his mid-sixties, was one of Muncie's few black farmers. He owned a tiny, thirty-five-acre plot of land north of Muncie near Albany. He raised chickens and pigs, and grew corn, okra, and collard greens. Every Saturday morning he peddled chickens and produce in Muncie's black neighborhoods.

As Uncle Jim described the backbreaking hoeing, planting, and plucking and cutting chickens, my interest dwindled. But Dad, always a visionary, especially when it involved someone else's time or money, saw it as an opportunity for free chickens, garden vegetables, and even a little cash. Aware of Dad's views on commissions, I probably wouldn't have taken the job, but just about that time Miss Dora had to have the roof patched. We were barely existing on half a bowl of oatmeal in the morning and Postal's leftovers in the evening.

That first Friday, Uncle Jim picked me up at lunchtime. We stopped at every small-town diner between Muncie and Albany dumping rotten meat, fruit, potato rinds, and all types of stinking garbage into large oil drums lashed on the back of his truck. I tried to brace the cans as we raced over the country roads. It all went smoothly until Uncle Jim plunged pell-mell down a dip, sending me a foot in the air. I managed to keep the drums in place, but was drenched with slimy garbage.

Uncle Jim had an extra work shirt in the cab, but by late afternoon when we arrived at a small-town café, I was reeking of garbage. While I wrestled a can to the alley, a middle-aged white man appeared at the rear door. From his long, casual chat with Uncle Jim I guessed he was the owner. My body tensed when I heard the man ask: "Who's that white boy?"

Uncle Jim said I was his nephew.

"He's the whitest colored boy I ever seen. Are you sure he wasn't just caught in the wrong net?" The owner chuckled.

I wanted to smash his face with the can when I lugged it back to the diner, and caught him gaping at me. His sharply pressed long white apron reminded me of the Ku Klux Klan leader I saw on Uncle Osco's new television following the 1954 Supreme Court decision outlawing segregated schools. That beefy-faced, white-robed Klansman stood in front of a burning cross, railing against black and white children learning together. He claimed that the Supreme Court was encouraging "race-mixing" and the only result would be the "bestial mongrel mulatto, the dreg of human society." In the refuge of Uncle Osco's sitting room, I had laughed at the pale, jowly southerner. In a white sheet and pointed hat, he looked more like the "dreg of society" than anybody I knew. Yet his nasal repetition of "mongrel mulatto" finally hit like a thunderbolt. He was talking about me. I was the Klan's worst nightmare. I was what the violence directed against integration was all about. I was what they hated and wanted to destroy. And that was the biggest puzzle in the world to me because I had absolutely nothing.

The café owner had a different idea. He didn't want to destroy me, he wanted to exhibit me. While I lugged garbage from his rear door, he hovered there beckoning me inside. There were people he wanted me to meet, he coaxed. He tried to engage me in conversation. "Gonna be a pig farmer like your uncle?" he asked with a chuckle.

"I'm gonna be a lawyer," I quipped.

His face reddened with laughter. "You gonna have to shovel a lot of shit to make that happen. Come on, these folks really want to see you. We all wanna see Muncie's first colored lawyer. I even got a piece of pie for you."

I knew he was insulting me, but I was tempted by the pie. When I noticed Uncle Jim frowning, I mumbled "No thanks." Soon the café owner was miles behind, and I was overcome by feelings of self-pity, confusion, and anger. As Uncle Jim turned down a gravel lane, I concentrated more on keeping the garbage off me than on fantasizing about dumping it on the man who had ridiculed my dream.

As the truck slowed, a strange form sprouted on the horizon. Uncle Jim pulled to a stop, and I realized it was the unfinished foundation of a house protruding three feet above the ground. The black tar paper sides and top gave it a sinister aura. It was Uncle Jim's home.

"Boy, I'm sorry about that ol' white man," he said as we carried groceries to the house. "He don't know shit. I learned a long time ago that you just have to laugh at white folks or they'll drive you crazy. Forgit 'bout him. We gonna have us a helluva dinner."

The strong scent of herbs and spices enveloped me as I stepped into the basement living area. Sunlight filtered through several tiny windows and cast a warm glow over the room. Ball Dome jars filled with apples, peaches, and tomatoes lined shelves above the sink. An easy chair, a well-worn couch, and *Farmer's Almanac*s scattered about the room gave it a coziness that contrasted with its stark exterior. Soon the aroma of sizzling pork chops and fresh biscuits filled the air. We sat down to one of the best dinners I had eaten in a very long time. As I swallowed my second piece of apple pie, I decided that if I could eat like this every day, I'd do anything to keep the job. Just as I was ready to stretch out on the couch and let the food digest, Uncle Jim said, "Let's head to the barn."

Actually, it was more like a shed than a barn. While it had the usual gray weathered wood of farm buildings, I was disappointed that it was only one story and didn't have a hayloft. Inside Uncle Jim rolled a huge oil drum next to a scarred wooden table. I filled it with water while he built a fire underneath. Once the water was boiling, I brought chickens from the coop.

The meat cleaver glistened in the air. *Whap!* It slashed down— and through a chicken's neck. It stuck into the wooden tabletop. Uncle Jim jerked the cleaver from the wood and gave one more short stroke, severing the remaining tendons. The noise level rose to a crescendo. It was as though the chickens collectively sensed their fate. My eyes fixed on the pool of blood standing on the table. My body tingled with goose bumps. Unfazed, Uncle Jim deftly swept the cleaver across the tabletop, knocking the head into a can. Blood squirted from the headless cavity as he dropped the chicken onto the floor. It fluttered around the room. "Give me 'nother one, boy," he ordered, and I woodenly handed him another struggling chicken. Hypnotized by the slaughter, I jumped as I felt a bump against my leg. A headless chicken bled over my shoe. "Come on, Billy, get busy," Uncle Jim shouted over his shoulder. I began to dunk chickens into the bubbling water. A short scalding loosened the feathers, and I fished the carcass out with a steel hook. The plucking began. Soon feathers completely covered the floor, the table, and us. Once denuded, the chickens were hacked again and Uncle Jim reached deep inside for the entrails. The pile of livers, gizzards, and hearts grew in front of me as I struggled to dig out sand and grit with my fingernails. After cleaning more gizzards than I could count, I stole a glance at Uncle Jim's watch. It was well after midnight, but I dared not let him know that I was struggling to keep going. He leaned over and squinted at the gizzard in my hand.

"That's it, boy. I'm gonna make a farmer out of you yet. I know you want to be a lawyer just like your daddy did. But hell, I never wanted to be a farmer either. I wanted to be a soldier."

In the early morning hours, Uncle Jim recounted his experiences during the "Great War." World War II seemed distant, but World War I was almost beyond my comprehension. Nonetheless, that night, I learned he was among the first "Negroes" from Muncie to join the army, did basic training at Camp Dodge, Iowa, and joined the 367th Infantry—which, like all Negro units, had only white commissioned officers—in France. He fought up and down the trenches and in the Argonne. He was even promoted to sergeant. All the officers claimed that he was a good soldier. When Uncle Jim told his captain he wanted to make a career out of the army, the white man pumped his hand like an old friend. But when he expressed his desire to be stationed in France, the captain became angry and said, "All you colored boys want is white women. I thought you were different. Every one of you darkies is gonna be on the first boat home as soon as this war is over." Uncle Jim said, "I decided then and there to get out of the army. I had hoped to stay in France because I realized it was how life was supposed to be. I could go wherever I pleased, eat in any restaurant I could afford, and walk through villages without fear of being beaten, lynched, or called a nigger." As I listened to Uncle Jim, I decided to be more careful about sharing my own dreams.

At seven a.m. we arrived in the Muncie Projects at Second and Monroe. The black women stood curbside. A larger second group waited at First and Vine. Uncle Jim took orders and made change at the foot of the truck. I bagged the apples, tomatoes, corn, okra, string beans, and chickens. The hottest-selling item was greens, and by the third stop I was beginning to learn the difference between collard and mustard greens. The women shouted at me if I reached into the wrong box. They could tell the difference from six feet away.

Some of my buddies passed by on the way to the Madison Street playground. They called me "Farmer Greg" and began a chorus of "Old McDonald Had a Farm." I wasn't that embarrassed by their teasing, especially later when two of them asked if Uncle Jim needed any extra help.

After the Projects we traveled to Five Points, then to Industry, and finally to Whitely, where it seemed we stopped at almost every corner. We finished at seven p.m. Miss Dora stood at the doorway. Her dark brown face widened with a grin as Uncle Jim counted out three one-dollar bills, and handed me a chicken and a huge armful of greens. At dinner I recounted the last thirty-six hours and gave Miss Dora two dollars. When I trudged upstairs to bed she began cutting the chicken into pieces and soaking the greens. A feast was planned for Sunday. Miss Dora even promised me a breast. I drifted off to a satisfying dream of devouring crispy fried chicken.

Soon Uncle Jim asked me to work more. It was a hard three days of lugging garbage, feeding hogs, weeding the garden, and killing chickens late into Friday night. Saturdays seemed to last forever. At the height of the harvest season Mike was recruited. He didn't like the idea, but when I described Uncle Jim's breakfast of fried eggs, potatoes, bacon, and crunchy toast, he reluctantly joined us. Everything went smoothly for the first couple of weeks, then one afternoon Mike dropped a dozen eggs as he ran out of the henhouse, broke a limb off an apple tree, and kicked Uncle Jim's cherished cat when it rubbed up against him. We tussled over the steel hook when it was time to scald the chickens, but I finally managed to wrest it from him. Mike didn't like cleaning gizzards, so Uncle Jim had him load greens into the crates for Saturday morning. Mike kept mixing the collard and mustard together. By then I was an expert, so I walked over to help him. Totally unprovoked, Mike hit me. I stumbled, knocking the crates onto the floor. I grabbed him in a headlock, and we fell together, crushing greens beneath us. Uncle Jim sent Mike to bed and threatened to fire him. Mike defiantly proclaimed, "I ain't gonna walk through all that pig shit again anyway, I'm gonna go make me some real money gambling." Mike did little gambling but was beginning to mimic Dad's bravado as well as his disdain for regular work. I hoped to keep my job on the farm, even if Mike quit, but on Saturday evening, Uncle Jim fired us both. I was angrier at Mike for causing me to lose that job than at Uncle Jim for firing me. I learned that it was impossible for Mike and me to work together without one of us getting in the way of the other.

While we worked on the farm, Dad did odd jobs washing windows and mopping floors in downtown Muncie. Although forty, he was also an occasional "shoe shine boy" at Nick "The Greek's" Shoe Repair and Cleaners on South Walnut Street. Nick had a four-chair stand and a lower-middle-class white clientele. After we were fired by Uncle Jim, I cut lawns on Saturday mornings, and Mike worked alongside Dad at Nick's. Afternoons, I visited them downtown.

The shop door bells announced my entrance. Nick, head down, slammed the steam presser's scorched brown pads together, flattening the pants stretched between them. A clank of a foot pedal, and steam filled the air. A dim fluorescent fixture provided most of the light in the long narrow room. Everyone was lost in the rhythm of the work. Tall and broad-shouldered, Mike looked much older than his nine years. Not only was everyone busy working, they were all silent—except Dad.

"Nick!" he shouted over the hiss and clang of the presser. "Did I ever tell you about the time I passed for Greek in Atlantic City? Man, I was king of the Boardwalk. I had a tailored white suit, suede shoes, and a diamond ring set in solid gold. All the women knew me as Jimmy Willmatis, 'the Greek Adonis.'

"Since I was passing for Greek, I had to find a Greek roommate, and I ended up with one of your compatriots. Dimitrius never took a bath. He said when he was a boy on Chios, his father made him pledge not to bathe because it destroyed precious bodily fluids. He stank to high heaven! Was that the custom in the old country, Nick?"

Nick shot Dad a withering scowl. Dad chuckled, winked at me, and beckoned me closer. The customer's face was hidden behind the *Muncie Star*. Dad reached for an open can of polish and ran two fingers over the top, coating them with brown wax. It took three applications to soften the cheap leather. Then with two brushes from under the chair a gloss formed as he began to slowly alternate strokes across the toes and down the sides.

He grabbed a long cotton polishing rag from the "V" in the shoe last. With a flourish he popped it and brought it down on the toe. His hands flashed up and down. The customer now laid the paper in his lap. The rag went *poppity, pop, pop! Pop pop!* Dad looked up at the customer and shouted,

> "I'm happy Jack,
> The world's greatest bootblack!
> I was born in the wilderness,
> Suckled by a boar,
> Got four rows of jaw teeth,
> And always room for more!"

He released one end of the rag and the final pop became a bang.

The finishing touch was the application of sole dressing. Dad dipped an old toothbrush into a bottle of brown liquid. Without spilling a drop on the floor, he guided it around the sole of the shoe like an artist with a sable brush. As it dried, he stepped back from the stand and bowed. Even in the ill-lit room, the shoes gleamed. The performance elicited a whistle of appreciation from the customer, and—as he stepped down from the stand—a tip. When Dad reached out to accept the dime, I felt that he had sold himself cheap.

It seemed I was the only one in the family worried about positions of superiority and inferiority. Dad never talked much about it, saying he didn't sacrifice the "privileges of manhood and right by accepting the small token of appreciation for a job well done." Mike had only one goal, to make as much money as possible in the shortest amount of time. Since Mike worked only for tips, he learned to avoid the nontippers, or "frogs," as he called them. There was one particular frog who not only expected a perfect shine but complained if he didn't receive it. One Saturday Mike was the only person working the stand when the frog appeared. Mike refused to shine his shoes. Nick fired him on the spot, and when Dad and his buddy "Pinchin' Bug" returned from lunch both of them were fired for complaining about Mike's dismissal.

The next day, Dad built a small wooden shoe shine box for Mike to use on downtown street corners. Sensing that he would have a good chance of attracting customers if he worked near Nick's, Mike boldly claimed the corner of Walnut and Charles, three doors from the shop. I can still remember Mike's pitch.

"Shoe shine, shoe shine!

"Step right up!

"No need to wait at Nick's!"

Mike waved the *Muncie Star* and shouted, "Read the news while you wait! McCarthy says Communists Infiltrate CIA!"

Mike's sparkling brown eyes were so appealing, it was almost impossible not to linger for a moment. If a potential customer paused ever so slightly, Mike thrust the paper into the customer's hands and slid the shoe box in front of him. When asked the price, Mike responded with his final gambit, again as Dad had instructed, "Sir, there exists no fixed price for the shine. I only ask that you give me whatever you feel my services merit."

Mike soon became serious competition for Nick and the other downtown shoe shine parlors. The parlor owners gained a sympathetic ear from the local police as they received their free shines. The patrolmen agreed to rid downtown of the pint-sized menace, Mike Williams. But Mike was learning to be elusive, and when he saw the cops headed in his direction he rapidly gathered brushes, polish, and newspaper and disappeared into the Saturday morning crowds.

After being fired by Nick, Dad and Pinchin' Bug started a new scheme and began spending mornings and afternoons scouting the trash behind meat and produce stores. They operated mostly on the smell test. If you could stand to hold it to your nose for ten seconds it was probably okay. I made the rounds with them, but I was too squeamish, especially when they'd dive back into the garbage for food too pungent for my taste. Dad did have a knack for making a great fruit salad out of throw-aways he salvaged from the trash. But we always disagreed on the meat. As it turned out I wasn't the only one at odds with him on that score.

One morning as we were scavenging behind the meat market the police rolled up behind us and flipped on their red lights.

"Buster, you ain't selling that meat. You know it's against the law."

"Of course," answered Dad, "I know it's against the law. I don't sell it. I don't even eat it. Me and Pinchin' Bug give it to the dogs." He tossed some gray hamburger meat to his dogs, Babe and Thunder, who hadn't eaten meat in weeks.

Dad *was*, of course, selling the meat to local cafés, establishments which I learned to give a wide berth.

There was one "hustle" absolutely essential to our survival—the rummage sales. When I was ten they were truly embarrassing and humiliating for me. Held in small rented rooms of run-down, mostly vacant brick buildings near Seymour and Mulberry, they were on the main walking route downtown. As Mike and I stood in line with Dad and several dozen women waiting for the doors to open we saw many of our Garfield classmates. I tried to be as inconspicuous as possible, but boys from the Projects often passed and laughed at me waiting in line for the chance to buy secondhand underwear, socks, and ill-fitting old-fashioned shoes. One afternoon on the playground I struggled to explain the initials "WW" sewn on my jeans in bright red stitches. I said my true name was Gregory William Williams rather than admit that I had found the jeans at the rummage sale that very morning.

Muncie's rummage sales did have a bit of an egalitarian flavor about them. It was one of the few times poor whites and blacks mingled together. The women scurried from one sale to another, even sharing gossip and advising one another on what items looked most well cared for.

While Mike and I tolerated the rummage sales, my father absolutely adored them. In all our years in Muncie, I can't recall a time when he didn't have an ample supply of suits and ties. My buddies who reveled in his salty street corner tales wondered how he could dress so sharply when everyone in the neighborhood knew he didn't have a job. The answer was the rummage sales. Dad bought shirts for fifteen cents and "modern" (less than ten years old) suits for under two dollars.

Our arrival at the rummage sales usually generated an audible groan from the clerks. Dad was on a first-name basis with all of them. Although they painstakingly priced the clothes, he saw the figures scrawled on the white adhesive tape as nothing more than a starting point for negotiation. To me the merchandise was old, shabby, and undesirable, but Dad was as arrogant and happy as he had been in Washington's department stores. I generally stood alone just inside the front door looking at books pretending I had just stumbled onto the rummage sale by mistake.

As soon as Dad found one of his famous "treasures," he took it to the woman in charge, made an elaborate bow, kissed her hand, called her "Princess Charming," and asked for a price reduction. When flattery failed, he stood in the middle of the crowded room almost nose to nose with her, and began, "Madam, I realize you've placed a reasonable price on this shirt, but my funds are limited, and I'm simply trying to provide clothing for my sons." Then he'd shout for us to stand beside him in our worn garments to emphasize his point. He would plead, "I'd appreciate your reconsidering the price."

Anyone could see that the shirt he held in front of him was much more likely to fit him than either one of us, but details were of little importance to Dad. I really felt sorry for the clerks. Though they tried to elude him with a firm shake of their heads, "No" usually just energized him. He dogged the women across the room, reciting in a deep bass voice every flaw of the shirt—a rip here, a stain there, a missing button, a frayed collar. Then he would again challenge the price.

One morning while Dad cornered a poor clerk, I tried to slink away, but he jerked me beside him, as if he needed a ragged modern-day Oliver Twist next to him. I prayed for invisibility, and cursed my fate for having such a crazy man for a father. My heart went out to the poor white woman, who had not expected to run into the Buster Williams "bulldozer" when she came out that Saturday morning to lend a hand to the poor. Dad managed to chop the price twenty cents.

Without savoring his victory, Dad embarked on his second goal: never to leave a rummage sale without receiving something free.

That morning, his eyes rested on a large console radio gathering dust in the corner. It was not old enough to be an antique, nor new enough to be worth anything, and the case badly needed repair. My instincts told me there would be no way he could ever get the clerk to give it to him. Dad began his pitch: "Excuse me, but does that radio work? I can't check it because the plug is missing."

"I don't know, Buster. Frank knows, but he's not here."

"Well, it's been here several weeks now so I imagine it doesn't work."

"You might be right." She tried to slip away, but Dad trailed her like a tenacious puppy.

"Since you haven't been able to sell it, why don't you let me have it? I like to tinker. I might be able to fix it and gain some use out of it."

"Buster," she said, turning toward him, her face beginning to show her exasperation, "the price tag says five dollars."

"I know what the price tag says," he said, his voice echoing throughout the room, "and I also know that you haven't been able to sell it."

Dad continued at full volume. "Clear your inventory, madam. Moving merchandise is the name of the game. It cultivates repeat business and a satisfied clientele. Actually, I'm willing to do you a favor and take it off your hands free and clear, no questions asked."

At the mention of "free" *all* eyes in the room fastened on them. Now I knew Dad was going to lose. There was no way she could give it to him, because everyone else would expect something as well. Just as I was about to savor Dad's defeat, I saw an uneasy look on her face. Come on, come on! I wanted to shout. Don't let him beat you! Finally, she responded wearily, almost in tears. "I don't feel like arguing with you, Buster. Take the radio and get out of here!"

"Thank you, Doris," he said, bowing to her. "Your generosity is exceeded only by your charm and good looks!"

Before giving her a chance to change her mind, and just when I was in the middle of my usual prayer for the power to disappear, Dad shouted, "Come on, boys! Double time! Billy, Mike! Get the radio! I'll get the door."

Dad moved like lightning when we hustled that radio out of the shop. He had a silly grin on his face, just like he had hit the jackpot. Mike and I carried it half a block down the street before he let us stop and rest. It was much heavier than we expected. There was no way we could carry it the eight blocks home, even if Dad helped—an unlikely prospect. While Mike and I tried to catch our breath, Dad scanned the street for a friend in a car. We sat curbside for almost twenty minutes with only strangers passing. It looked like he would have to leave the radio on the sidewalk. Serves him right, I thought, always begging and bulldozing.

Finally, a police car driven by a white officer turned the corner and moved slowly down the block toward us. Dad gazed intently at the driver for a moment, then charged into the middle of the street, waving his arms as if there had been a murder. When the car stopped Dad hustled to the driver's side. The officer rolled down the window and said with a chuckle, "What's going on, Buster?"

I couldn't believe it. It seemed like everyone in Muncie knew Dad.

The officer continued in a sarcastic tone, "Somebody trying to rob you?"

"Damn, you know nobody messes with an old prizefighter like me. Hell, I'd have them all over the street—*bing! bing! bing!*—before they opened their mouths."

Then shifting to an earnest tone, he continued softly, "Me and the boys just spent our last five dollars buying this radio for my elderly mother so she can have some listening enjoyment at night. Now, I don't have money for a cab. Can we throw it in the trunk of your car?"

"Buster, you know it's against regulations. The sergeant will bust my ass if he catches me giving you a ride."

"Come on, be a sport. Remember that new jacket I found for you at the rummage sale? Remember when I took your shoes home and gave 'em an army spit shine?"

Realizing Dad was prepared to drone on interminably about past debts, the officer simply held up his hand and said, "Fuck it, Buster. I'll open the trunk."

Two days later I walked into Grandma's and Dad handed me three crisp one-dollar bills.

"What's that for, Dad?"

"I sold the radio."

"How'd you sell it? It didn't even work."

"There was a loose connection in the back. I fixed it and sold it for ten dollars to one of the hillbillies at Super Par Gas Station down the alley. I got three each for you and Mike, and I kept four since I was the negotiator on both ends. See what you can do if you're alert?"

That was the first time a commission came my way from Dad.

I continued going to the sales with Dad and Mike until I discovered they were stealing. Outside, halting in the middle of the sidewalk, I stammered, "I . . . can't believe you, Dad. Stealing from a rummage sale! How low can you get? What if you'd gotten arrested?"

"Billy, I'm not stealing. I'm liberating. This is redistribution of wealth in its most basic and fundamental form. If the white folks won't give it to you when you offer a fair and just price, then you have the right to take it. It's a simple transfer of wealth to oppressed people."

I told Miss Dora about the stealing. Rarely did I see her so mad. She marched to Postal's every morning to do an honest day's work though she barely received survival wages. Even though we went to bed many nights with just enough food to stop our stomachs from growling, she never stole from Postal. She only brought home what was left over from his table. She could never tolerate lying, cheating, or stealing. She lit into Dad the next time she saw him, but that didn't deter him. I knew he would make me join him unless I had another job. I found two jobs, one delivering newspapers and another busting clods for Uncle Osco in his garden. Dad didn't like not having me at his side on Saturday mornings, but agreed to excuse me if I would give him a paper—free.

# Chapter 9

# Politics and Race

My father's greatest gift to me was to instill the ability to dream and visualize a future of my own making. Perhaps that was his greatest weakness as well. He was the consummate dreamer, always beguiled by one scheme or another that he was convinced would be *the one* to bring him fame, and money. Politics was one of those "absolutely foolproof" schemes he promised would put us all on "easy street." Early one summer morning of 1954 Dad stood in front of Miss Dora's. I was surprised to see him. Just two weeks earlier she had chased him away from her doorstep when he arrived drunk while she was entertaining two sisters from Christ Temple Church. She threw a washtub of water on him when he gyrated his hips at the women. But irrepressible as always, he was now back on the sidewalk and crowed up to the attic that he was reclaiming his "political heritage with the Republican party." Miss Dora, the realist, scoffed at his grandiose ideas, but Mike and I tagged along to the Delaware County Republican Headquarters.

The storefront window was plastered with elephant cutouts and red, white, and blue streamers. A dozen workers scurried about the room as we entered. Several waved to Dad and a few approached us. After some small talk we met the local boss. Whatever a political leader was supposed to look like, he didn't fit the mold. He lacked the slicked-back hair and the large bow tie of Thomas Dewey I remembered from watching television in Virginia. His heavy muscular frame seemed more suited to bib overalls than a suit.

Dad thrust a page of yellow legal-size paper covered with his careful printing into the hand of the Chairman, who nodded approvingly as he scanned Dad's suggestions for a new campaign brochure. Dad beamed with delight as the Chairman threw his arm over his shoulder and escorted him behind a cloth partition to the party's inner sanctum. Mike and I followed a young secretary to a refrigerator at the rear of the room where she handed us each an ice cream sandwich. When Dad and the Chairman reappeared, disappointment clouded my father's face.

"I was hoping for something full-time," he said to the party leader standing beside him.

The man shook his head and responded, "Sorry. But soon the Democrats will be out on their asses. Do all you can for us now, and I'll take care of you then, Buster."

For the next several weeks pages from yellow legal pads littered Grandma's floor. She didn't have much use for the Republicans. Every time Dad raved about them, she countered with stories from her early days in Muncie when the Klan was strong and had infiltrated the Republican party. The Klan openly paraded in Muncie during the 1920s. Once a Republican party leader astride his white stallion during a Klan parade threatened Grandma with a beating if she didn't salute a Confederate flag. She was so terrified she peed on herself. In 1954, that very same Klansman was one of Muncie's most prominent citizens, revered by many residents as a patriarch of the Republican party.

After her diatribe against the Republicans, Dad looked up at me from across the kitchen table. "Mom don't know a damn thing about politics. She's just a country girl from Kentucky. The Republicans are different today," said Dad. "They're the party of Wendell Willkie."

He retrieved a shoe box from under Grandma's bed and thrust a yellowed stack of papers into my hands.

"I wrote this before you were born, back in the days when I was gonna be somebody. That speech stole the Muncie election. Too bad Willkie didn't have me in his national campaign."

I sat down and read.

*October 1940*

*Mr. Chairman, Ladies and Gentlemen: It is indeed a pleasure to be with you again politically. Most of you here know me well and are acquainted with my venturesome political career which has carried me as high as the first Negro Democratic candidate for state representative from Muncie. Then too, there are those among you who remember how I began my political career as a Republican back in the 20th precinct, ringing door bells and hauling voters to the polls on election day. Now, thank God, I'm back home with the Republicans—I'm here to stay and all hell can't move me.*

*I want you to know that I wasn't paid to come back to the Republican party. But I was paid to leave the Democratic party— How was I paid?—I was paid by broken promises, like any other Negro who gave them their support.*

*I'm a Republican because it is the party that has never deviated from its tradition of justice, fairness, and equality to all, regardless of race, color, or creed. These principles have come down through the years from President Lincoln, and now they are to be championed by a new Lincoln in the person of our own Hoosier— Wendell Willkie. As a young lawyer in Ohio, even before he had a notion that he would occupy public office, he showed how he stood —by striking at every type of intolerance that came in his way. In Akron, Ohio, Willkie played a leading part in opposing the Ku Klux Klan. As a delegate from that state in 1924, he fought for the nomination of Al Smith over the Klan-backed McAdoo.*

*My friends, the New Deal has been a complete failure. The New Deal has done little to end color discrimination, but a great deal to prolong it. It had a wonderful opportunity to show America how the Negro ought to be treated, but it bowed to the will of the reactionary South. Today more than ever, when Negroes are anxious to fight for their country—we realize that discrimination has continued in the Army, Navy, Marine Corps, and Coast Guard, and not a word of condemnation has come from the White House, although President Roosevelt is commander-in-chief of these services. For the Negro, the New Deal has been the Old Deal in New Clothes, with powers almost as great as those of Hitler and Mussolini. The Democratic administration winked at discrimination in the NRA, FHA, WPA, and CCC. Worse, it helped spread Jim Crowism over the country.*

> *America amidst the confusion of rising and falling nations,*
> *when liberty and freedom are on the gibbet of crucifixion, needs a*
> *man like Willkie for President. A man who believes that, "Out of*
> *one blood, God made all races to dwell on the face of the earth."*

Several afternoons a week Mike and I accompanied Dad to Republican Headquarters. He conferred with party officials about his ideas while we gorged ourselves on the abundant supply of soft drinks and ice cream sandwiches. One afternoon when my head throbbed from the chill of four ice cream sandwiches in ten minutes, Dad appeared from behind the partition. He beamed as he flashed a glossy black-and-white printing of "his" brochure.

"This is going to be distributed countywide! There's more than five thousand copies," he said, pointing to pamphlets bundled in manila paper and stacked along the wall. "Never underestimate the power of the written word." He smiled, then said, "Man, I haven't felt so good since I broke with the Democrats."

The three of us climbed into a large black Buick with the party leader and visited precinct headquarters scattered around the county. We helped unload the stacks of pamphlets. At every stop white party members pumped Dad's hand and congratulated him on the brochure. One elderly man even called him "Shakespeare." Though Dad bubbled with enthusiasm about how important he was to the Republican party, I was skeptical until I saw the reaction to that first brochure, then a second. By that time I too reveled in the adulation as we strolled into campaign headquarters, seeing ourselves as an integral part of the plan to reshape Muncie, Delaware County, and eventually Indiana.

To help tide us over until the Republicans recaptured all the local partronage positions, Dad lined up odd jobs for Saturday mornings. We painted garages, cut grass, and cleaned offices for Republican party leaders. One Saturday as we crossed the University Avenue bridge over White River and entered Muncie's exclusive residential area near Ball State Teachers College, I asked Dad how he could endure such menial work. It was hard for me to understand how he could be the equal and maybe even the superior of a white man on Friday, but his lackey on Saturday. He looked straight at me. "Billy, I don't sacrifice the privileges of manhood and right by cleaning toilets and saying 'Yes sir' and 'No sir' to these Johnny-comelatelies. I'm trying to work myself back into a position of sobriety and influence. One of these days I'll be back on my feet and I can tell these peckawoods to kiss my ass. You have to kiss asses a long time before you can kick 'em! . . . Man, after the elections I'm gonna be somebody." The idea of "payback" had a lot of appeal for me. To some extent that may be a factor that kept me going in Muncie. That there might one day be a time of reckoning.

One Saturday we toiled for Judge Carson, a high-ranking Republican officeholder. The judge, short and square-faced, snapped out terse orders. Mike and I raked while Dad mowed the grass. After four hours, Mrs. Carson leaned out her rear screen door and announced that lunch was ready.

The aroma of simmering beef stew wafted through the air of the immaculate kitchen. Mrs. Carson stood in front of an open refrigerator. I spied two full quart bottles of milk and was hopeful I could have my fill. She ushered us to a small dark-brown wooden booth tucked in the corner of the room. As we wedged into the booth I smiled at her, trying to show my appreciation for lunch, but she remained impassive as she placed silverware and a butter dish in front of us. Then she opened a loaf of bread, counted exactly three slices, and placed them on an empty saucer. The taciturn judge strode past us into the large dining room off the kitchen and sat at the head of a long mahogany table covered with a white lace cloth. Mrs. Carson silently placed three almost-full bowls in front of us. Without responding to our chorus of "Thank you" she retreated through the dining room door, closing the door behind her.

Another giftless Christmas was eased by Dad's promise of new winter coats once the Republicans took power. Many Democrats were about to find themselves jobless. When Dad reported for duty, he learned his much praised writing skills had earned him a City Hall job—as a janitor. The pay was fifty dollars and fifty cents a week. I was consumed by bitterness. Even at a young age I recognized that he was a talented speaker and writer. Everyone in the party had pressed him for ideas and assistance, and with the dream of reward he had given willingly of himself. Yet it was clear he had bartered away his most precious comodity—his mind—for a pittance.

Yet, the only sad face around Grandma's that week was mine. Dad remained optimistic. "Hell yes, I'm disappointed," he said, "but it's a start. They have to take care of a lot of people, and I just came back to Muncie. Once they realize how important I am, they'll give me something else."

Mike and I quickly became familiar faces at City Hall. While Dad cleaned the courtroom and offices, we played cops-and-robbers in the Police Department's temporary detention cells, hide-and-seek in the City Council chambers, and baseball in the parking lot. We also were unpaid volunteers for the city. Mike swept and cleaned the drinking fountains. I fished soggy cigars and cigarette butts from sand-filled corridor ashtrays. Mike and I struggled to carry the heavy galvanized bucket down the hall without spilling water as Dad whipped the mop back and forth across the black-and-white linoleum tile. Dad worked with absolute concentration until the mayor, a city judge, or council member crossed our path. He would then pause to engage them in the latest political gossip. Most lingered, swapping yarns. The patronage system created plenty of intriguing gossip. The husband of an important campaign worker had been promoted overnight from patrolman to police captain, ahead of at least twenty-five more senior and experienced officers. There was a scandal when a department head hired his nearly illiterate brother as his second-in-command. I think many of the politicians lingered to chat because Dad knew their views on the issues and often patterned his thoughts after theirs. He was so low on the political totem pole that no one ever seemed to notice that he often stood on both sides of most issues. When Dad perceived that the officeholder was impatient to leave, he would sustain his attention by turning to Mike and me and describing in acute and agonizing detail the person's pivotal role in Muncie's political history. He had the ability to make almost anyone appear as a true statesman. It was a rare person who did not puff up with self-importance when Dad showered him with lavish praise and flattery.

For six months Dad managed to control his drinking, and even began to give Miss Dora money to help with our care. He also continued the odd jobs on weekends. One Saturday he and I worked the entire day and late into the night helping Judge Carson renovate an old office as the judge prepared to resume his law practice following retirement from the bench. Though the judge was leaving office, Dad said he was still a powerhouse in the community and a good man to know. It was well after midnight when we began our walk home. Just as we neared Main and Madison, a plain green

Ford slowed to the curb beside us. I immediately recognized it as a police detective's car. Ambrose Settles, one of Muncie's two black detectives, was driving. He roughly gestured for us to stop in front of the Muncie Club, the exclusive domain of leading white businessmen.

"What do you want, Ambrose?" Dad shouted into the open police car window. "We're on our way home. We just finished at Judge Carson's."

Ambrose stepped out of the car and slammed the door. He was over six feet tall and weighed at least two hundred and fifty pounds. The buttons on his shirt strained to contain his massive chest as he waddled toward us. His forearms were larger than my thighs.

"I don't give a damn if you been working for the Chief of Police. I want to talk to you about that Willard Street burglary."

"I don't know anything about it. You've known me all your life. I went to school with you and Keg. You know I'm not a thief."

"My brother ain't got shit to do with this. I know you, Buster. You're too scared to steal, but I know you had something to do with it."

He grabbed Dad by the arm, shoved him toward the Muncie Club. "Get your ass up against the wall!" he shouted, making Dad spread-eagle, hands against the bricks.

Ambrose kicked Dad's feet apart and he scratched wildly to maintain his balance.

"Let's see what you got on you," said Ambrose, jabbing him in the kidneys. Dad let out an "Oof!" Ambrose moved his hands slowly down the outside of Dad's pants, then up the inside of his legs. Suddenly, his right hand closed to a fist as it passed the knee and rammed dead center in the crotch. Dad jumped straight into the air.

"Damn, Ambrose! You know I ain't carrying nothing! If you weren't such an Amos-and-Andy detective, you'd know I didn't have shit to do with that burglary." He glared defiantly, but Ambrose smacked him in the face, spun him around, and whacked him across the back of the head. Jerking Dad's arms together, Ambrose snatched handcuffs from his belt.

"Shut up, Buster! I'm arresting you on suspicion."

"Suspicion of what, Ambrose? You're supposed to have some evidence. You just mad 'cause the Republicans didn't promote you. I'm gonna get the judge on the phone tonight. You think you can run roughshod over me. I'm not an old backwoods nigger. I'm a city employee. I know my rights . . ."

"You ain't shit but a funky-assed janitor. If you say one more word to me, I'm gonna kick your ass right here on the street. I'm arresting you on suspicion of burglary, and the law says I can keep you in jail seven days before I charge you. Now be still so I can handcuff you."

Ambrose shoved him to the squad car. As he opened the door, Dad asked, "What about my son, Ambrose? How's he going to get home? There's a curfew and you know these streets aren't safe."

"He can walk like everybody else, and you better hope a patrol car doesn't pick him up, because then we'll have two half-breed niggers in jail." Turning to me, Ambrose roared, "Now git on home, boy." I fled down the street trying to hold back the tears.

Dad did not commit the burglary, but he knew the fellows who did. The previous week they had been at Grandma's daily, begging him to find a buyer for the stolen calculators and office equipment. I sensed Dad enjoyed the drama and danger of trying to fence the stolen goods for extra cash. However, for seven long days the excitement of criminal life was replaced by the reality of jail. Neither Judge Carson nor any of Dad's City Hall "friends" intervened. Within hours of his release he fled to Louisville, Kentucky, the home of my grandmother's sister, Aunt Roxie. If anyone asked, we were to say we didn't know where he was or when he would return. No one was ever arrested for the Willard Street burglary.

Though Dad sent Miss Dora a letter with a small money order every couple of weeks, Mike and I felt abandoned. One late summer afternoon as we aimlessly window-shopped outside of Woolworth's on South Walnut Street, Mike began wildly pointing and shouting.

"That's Mom, Billy! That's Mom!"

At the corner of Jackson and Walnut beside Morton Standt Jewelers, a tall, slender, auburn-haired woman opened the door of a blue Packard. In the distance she looked so much like our mother that my heart began to pound wildly. Mike pushed through the crowd, jostling an old man who spun toward him with a scowl. Mike fell to the sidewalk, but scrambled to his feet and raced after the car, his thin black coat flapping behind him. Just as we were half a block away, the Packard turned east on Jackson Street. We rounded the corner and continued the chase, but by Mulberry the car was out of reach.

In front of the Wysor Theater we bent over, breathless, holding our stomachs.

Mike gasped, "Billy, that was Mom! I know it was!"

He wanted so much to believe it. I said, "Mike, I don't think so. It looked like her, but that woman was too tall. Mom was shorter."

"No she wasn't, Billy. Mom was tall. Don't you remember?"

"Yeah, I remember," I said as I realized how fuzzy her features were in my mind. "Just think about it, Mike. If Mom really was in Muncie, she would come to see us. Wouldn't she?"

He looked at me for a minute. He wanted to believe I was right, but he wasn't sure. Neither was I.

With Dad in Louisville, the longing for our mother became even more acute. We felt we could not share our feelings of loss with anyone. We didn't dare mention Mom to Miss Dora, fearful she might consider us ungrateful for all she had done. She considered us "her boys" and we didn't want to hurt her by admitting we still yearned for our mother.

One afternoon while Mike and I sat at Miss Dora's kitchen table playing checkers, a car horn sounded from Kirby Avenue. A few minutes later, Miss Dora appeared in the kitchen entryway and said, "Boys, there's an old white woman out front honking her horn. It's probably your grandma. Go on out and check."

Mike and I bolted upright.

"Why don't she knock on the door and come in like normal people?" Mike challenged.

"I don't know. You'll have to ask her. You know how scared white people get down here. Now go see her."

As we stood at the front door, we recognized the now faded maroon Chevy coupe from our summer visits so long ago. It *was* Grandma Cook! We walked slowly down the steps. Although we lived less than ten minutes from her house, we had not seen her once since our arrival in Muncie almost a year and a half earlier.

Grandma's pale white face peeked from behind the steering wheel. We stood at the car door while she glanced up and down the sidewalk. She slowly leaned across the front seat and released the lock. A musty smell greeted us as Mike climbed into the back and I settled into the front. Immediately Mike leaned toward our grandmother. She recoiled, pressing herself against the door.

"Have you talked to Momma?"

"I spoke with her last week."

"When is she gonna come and see us?"

"I don't know. Move back, Mike. I can hear you without you trying to sit in my lap. She's working two jobs and don't get much time off."

I leaned toward her. "How are Sissy and Tony Junior doing?"

"Okay, I guess," she said in a nonchalant voice. "We only talked a short while." Grandma continued to peek warily in the rearview mirror.

"Has Momma been to Muncie?" I asked, wondering about the woman Mike had seen on the street.

"That ain't for me to say."

"Has she been to Muncie?"

"Like I said, Billy, it ain't for me to say. That's her business. Now don't ask me any more about it."

I searched her pinched face. Her tight lips revealed no more, but I knew. My breath became short. I couldn't believe our mother had traveled six hundred miles and hadn't tried to see us. I struggled to hold back the tears. Raising my eyes to Grandma, I searched for sympathy.

"Stop that sniveling, Billy."

Stifling my emotions, I vowed not to let her know how much it hurt. I would never let anyone know. I wanted to kill my mother, my grandmother, and everyone white. I turned to Mike to urge him to leave the car. I could see that he had not realized the bitter truth. He believed Mom cared about us.

"Where's Momma living?" asked Mike, pulling himself over the back seat.

"In Washington, D.C."

"Can I have her address so I can write her?"

"Don't be stupid. You know I can't tell you where she's living."

"Why not?"

"She doesn't want Tony to get her address."

"I won't give Dad the address. He's not even in Muncie. He's in Louisville. I just want to find out about Sissy and Little Tony."

"No!" she said angrily. "I won't give you her address and have Tony pestering her and the children."

"If we can't write her, is she going to write us?" Mike challenged.

"She said she'll write me, and I'll tell you what I hear from her."

"Grandma, tell Momma I want her address!"

She spun around in her seat and glared at Mike.

"Don't tell me what to do! I don't carry messages for niggers! Now get out of the car. I'll see you when I got something to tell you."

Mike fell back like he had been stabbed. Our grandmother grabbed the steering wheel. Somehow we crawled out of the car. In the kitchen, we managed haltingly to tell Miss Dora what had happened. She placed her arms around us. We buried our faces in her bosom and released long and sorrowful wails and sobs that had been submerged since our mother abandoned us in July 1953.

"Boys, sometimes life is just plain hard. Most children don't have the trouble you've had, but God has some purpose in all this. You just have to walk on through it. I'm always here with you."

My mother's youngest sister was the only member of my mother's family who ever reached out to us. She and her husband lived less than six blocks away in a run-down white area near Five Points. At that time they had two small babies, and the four of them crowded together in a tiny efficiency apartment. My uncle worked off and on at the General Motors plant, and my aunt did washing and ironing to help make ends meet. An ironing table stretched almost the entire length of the living room, and it was always piled high with clothes. During our visits Mike and I learned the "secret" family history that had been hidden from us during our early trips to Muncie.

My mother was the bright star of the family. She earned school prizes and awards while the rest of her brothers and sisters struggled through or dropped out of school. Pinning their hopes for a college graduate on her, the family saved enough money to enroll her in a boarding school near Tipton. The more success Mom had in school, the more Grandma pushed her. It wasn't school for the sake of learning that motivated Grandma, it was keeping up with her in-laws. Several of Grandpa's relatives were college educated. One was even a superintendent of schools in a district north of Fort Wayne, and Grandma Cook was always ashamed of her own meager education. My mother crushed her hopes for revenge against those relatives, first by becoming pregnant, second by dropping out of school, but most of all by marrying a "nigger."

As soon as my grandmother heard of the marriage, she stripped my mother's room of awards and photographs. My grandmother announced that my mother ceased to exist. My birth and the birth of my brothers and sister were greeted with silence.

Year after year Mom and Dad traveled to Muncie, hoping to be accepted. It was difficult to pierce the barrier erected by my grandmother, but first a sister, then a brother, agreed to see "Mary's kids." Finally one summer, even Grandpa slipped away for a clandestine meeting with his daughter and his grandchildren. When he saw Mike, Sissy, and me for the first time, his husky body began to shake. Without a word to anyone, he donned his engineer's cap, drove home, and summoned my grandmother to the kitchen table. In a soft but unyielding voice, he said, "I don't care what Mary's done. It's time to let her bring her babies home."

My grandmother was speechless. It was one of the few times during the marriage when he defied her. She did not challenge him. Grandpa returned that afternoon and took Mike, Sissy, and me to meet our grandmother. I was six years old.

As I listened to my own painful history in the small tenement apartment, I only had one question. Why didn't Grandpa come for us now? My aunt grew somber. "He's dying of cancer," she whispered, and I realized the charade was over at last.

A few afternoons later I walked through Grandma Sallie's door and noticed a newspaper tucked in a bag of groceries on the table. Though Grandma was unable to read or write, she sometimes made an elaborate gesture of buying a paper to impress her neighbors. She often asked me to read it to her. She preferred articles about our neighborhood, but it was rare to find anything about Negroes in the Muncie paper. At one time it carried a social column called "The Colored Circle," but that had been discontinued. I sat at the kitchen table while Grandma rested on her bed. As she removed her shoes and began to rub her feet, I scanned the paper. In disbelief I read aloud of a fourteen-year-old black Chicago youth murdered while visiting relatives in Money, Mississippi. Apparently, he had whistled at a white woman. Kidnappers broke into his relatives' house in the middle of the night and abducted Emmett Till at gunpoint. Searchers later discovered his body in the Tallahatchie River. The youth had been shot in the head, lynched, and had a seventy-pound cotton gin fan tied around his body.

Laying the paper on the table, I turned to face Grandma, hoping she would tell me that nothing like Emmett Till's death could really happen in America.

"Billy, you don't know nothing about peckawoods. That's the reason I was always scared about Buster being in Virginia. They might have found him out and lynched him."

"Nobody would've bothered Dad," I insisted. "He owned a restaurant and tavern and made a lot of money."

"It don't make no difference what he owned. He was still a nigger, and if they found him out, he would'a been a dead nigger. You better watch out too, boy, and not mess around wit' no white girls. It was the ruination of your daddy. I bet them killers don't get a day. Anybody that growed up in the South know they ain't going to jail. And probably wouldn't, even if they done it here."

White men were charged with Emmett Till's murder and tried in front of an all-white jury. In September 1955, I read the news of the acquittal to Grandma as she sat in her kitchen.

"Maybe now you'll believe I know about politics, Billy," she said as she soaked her feet in a metal washtub after a long day cooking in the basement of the drive-in.

# Chapter 10

# The Color Line

Late summer of 1955, Mike and I coaxed Miss Dora to make a trip to Louisville to visit Dad. We did even more "hustling" than usual—taking every job imaginable to save for the bus tickets. We even managed to work briefly side by side to detassle Uncle Jim's corn. Aunt Roxie lived in the heart of Louisville's black ghetto at 1602 West Chestnut. Dad introduced us to kids our age, and we quickly became friends while swimming and playing basketball at the all-black Shepard Park playground. Though it had a lot of similarities to Muncie's Madison Street playground, there were two big differences. First, it had a usable swimming pool, which I absolutely loved, and second, girls as well as boys played on the basketball court. The girls were some of the best players I had ever seen. It made such an impression on me that after Louisville I could never understand why Indiana didn't have girls' basketball teams.

Aunt Roxie's bubbling enthusiasm about life contrasted sharply with Grandma's cold demeanor. Aunt Roxie told me I would never forget her age, fifty-five, because she was born in 1900, but she acted more like twenty-five. We loved her boyfriend, her neighbors, and her church. I was in heaven when we barbecued ribs in a park along the Ohio River. I promised my new buddies, and Aunt Roxie, that

I would return to Louisville every summer for a visit. It was a care-free and happy time, marred only by the news that Dad would stay in Louisville indefinitely because he had found regular work at Manpower, Inc. It was with great sadness that I carried our bags to Aunt Roxie's boyfriend's car for the trip to the Louisville bus station.

As we climbed into the car, the sky began to darken. Rain was pounding on the windshield when we reached the heavy downtown traffic. At the bus station, Mike and I scrambled for the shelter of the terminal. Standing inside, I held the door open for Miss Dora as she carefully picked her way through the sidewalk puddles. The staccato beat of rain bore down on the roof and echoed in the cavernous room. Out the rear door rain cascaded over the huge buses. No one ventured outside, even though a three-foot overhang provided some protection. A voice crackled over the loudspeaker, announcing a delay in the departure of the bus to Indianapolis.

Dad, as always, had our final instructions. "Boys, I want you to be good and mind Miss Dora," he said, leaning over to hug Mike, then me. Just as Dad handed Miss Dora forty dollars, a scrawny young white man in a gray uniform and hardbill cap stuck his head over Mike's shoulder. He looked at Dad, then in a slow southern drawl said, "You all supposed to be in the colored waiting room. It's on the other side of the buildin'. You gonna hafta go on over there."

His words made no sense to me, but as I turned to the benches and counters behind us, it was instantly clear. There were only white faces in the room, and all of them seemed to be glowering at us.

"You can't stay here," insisted the white man. "The boys can if they wanta, but you two gotta go."

"They're my sons," said Dad, anger rising in his voice. His fists quivered by his sides. I began to fear for our safety.

"Come on, Buster, let's go," said Miss Dora, gently tugging his sleeve. Unmoved, he locked eyes with the attendant. Silently, I prayed he would listen to her. Finally, he snatched our bags and we filed out the rear door. There under the overhang as the rain poured down, I saw the sign we'd missed two weeks earlier on our arrival in Louisville: COLORED WAITING ROOM. For almost a minute we froze in absolute silence. We couldn't bring ourselves to follow the attendant's order. Frowning, he motioned us away from the doorway, but we huddled under the overhang with our backs to him. Rain splashed on the pavement and splattered over our shoes as we drew tighter and tighter together against the building. The memory of a fun-filled two weeks slowly dissolved in tears and rain.

Mike dashed for the bus door as soon as it swung open. He hopped into the seat behind the driver. I slid beside him. Miss Dora, following two white women, slowly climbed the steps.

"Come on, boys, let's move back."

"I want to sit here," Mike challenged as the white women stared.

"We ain't supposed to. Now take this sack and git on back like I said."

We moved to the very last row. Rain streamed down the window in crooked patterns. Outside, Dad remained with his back pressed against the station wall, staring into the distance. I didn't even try to catch his attention by waving good-bye. The aroma of Aunt Roxie's fried chicken dinner floated up from the box on my lap as we pulled out of the station, but I had lost my appetite.

The Madison Street YMCA—or, as it was known throughout Muncie, "the colored Y"—was across Third Street from Aunt Bess's. It occupied an entire square block, with a small indoor game area and an outdoor playground consisting of a sand-and-gravel baseball diamond, an earthen basketball court, and a condemned swimming pool. City health officials closed the pool shortly after World War II, yet it sat empty and abandoned for twenty years, usurping over a quarter of the outdoor playing space. Even at age eleven I felt cheated out of a decent park. The downtown—or "white"—Y had a game room that dwarfed ours, as well as a swimming pool, a gymnasium, and an indoor track.

Mike always mixed easily with the Madison Street playground boys, shooting pool, throwing horseshoes, and playing softball. Generally, I joined him, but often when he was elsewhere, I stood alone in the shade of the Quonset hut, waiting for the basketball court to empty. Then I'd race inside for a ball. Being alone meant I had less explaining to do about myself.

Roy Buley, the playground director, dished out pool cues, paddles, and basketballs like a mother bird feeding a nest of hungry chicks. A chocolate brown, rotund man, and a former football star, Mr. Buley was never without a corny joke and a friendly smile. One afternoon as I approached the counter he held the basketball under one arm and stretched the other across the counter.

"Two out of three," he said, wiggling his right thumb in the air. A self-styled "thumbologist," he grabbed my hand and we locked thumbs. Struggling, I pushed and pushed to bend his thumb. But he flipped it from side to side. Three deft fakes, and then my thumb was flat against the counter. He released me. Then pinned me again.

"You need to practice, Greg, you're not concentrating," he said, tossing me the basketball with a chuckle. I dashed for the dirt court.

I raced up and down for almost an hour, totally absorbed in my fantasy of becoming a Muncie Bearcat basketball star. Rain did not deter me. Even when the dirt changed to mud I continued to play, oblivious to my mud-splattered clothes, face, and hands. Looking toward the building, I saw several youngsters staring out the window facing the basketball court, laughing. Only a heavy downpour and Mr. Buley's insistent gestures from the window drew me inside.

Totally saturated, I stood quietly against the wall and waited to play Ping-Pong with Mike. Just as Mike and I stepped to the table, Jerry Deveraux, one of my Garfield classmates, jumped in front of me.

"It ain't your turn, Jerry," I said.

"Get outta here, I'm playing." He grabbed a paddle from the table. "Come on, Charles, let's play!" he shouted across the room. Charles drifted over to us.

I jerked the paddle from Jerry. "Give me that!" he said, shoving me against the wall.

"No!" I shouted, pushing him into the sharp corner of the green plywood table.

"Ow! Gimme that, you white mothafucker, or I'll kick your ass!"

"I ain't white!" I said, smacking him with the paddle. His eyes widened. I dropped the paddle and charged headfirst, butting him backward and sprawling on top of him.

"I ain't white! I ain't white!" I pounded him again and again in the chest.

Within seconds Mr. Buley dragged me to my feet, his face contorted in a frown. "Stay here and cool off," he said. "When the rain stops, get outside. Jerry, you come here. . . ."

Tired and out of breath, we sat in opposite corners of the small room glaring at each other. Mike stood beside me. As soon as the rain lessened, I headed for the door. Just as I stepped onto the wooden porch, Mike shouted, "Greg, watch out!" It was too late. Jerry hit me in the back of the head. Spinning around, I grabbed him by the neck. Soon we straddled the rough plank steps trying to choke each other to death. Mr. Buley weaved through the crowd at the door and again separated us.

"Look, if you two can't straighten up you're not going to be allowed on the playground for a month. Greg, go home now. Jerry, stay inside until I say you can leave."

The sun was setting as I walked down Second Street. Mothers perched on Project stoops bounced diapered babies on their knees. I lingered at the edge of the Projects at First and Monroe. Two men staggered from the bootlegger "Speck" Johnson's house, a two-story gray clapboard home. One man pulled a bottle from the plain brown bag he carried as they climbed into a rusty Ford pickup. After quick swallows they sped toward Madison Street. Thirty seconds later Speck shuffled from the side door and dropped into a metal chair under his large catalpa tree. He sat alone, holding a paper sack, and took a long draw from the bottle inside. Usually he waved when I passed, but today there was no recognition. I wanted to talk. He was the only person in the neighborhood who was whiter than me. Dad said a skin disease had turned him from dark brown to a stark colorless white. Even his eyebrows were white. Only a few small splotches of brown remained. I wanted to know what happened. How long had he been white? Did people call him "white" all the time? Did it make him angry? I wanted to know so much, but I lacked the courage to approach him. I walked on, leaving him to his bottle and his solitude.

The Pooles lived next to Speck. The freshly painted home was a marked contrast to the nearby Projects. Their well-manicured yard featured neatly trimmed bushes, a flower garden, and fancy wrought-iron tables. Apparently, Mr. Poole made good money as a bartender at the all-white Muncie Businessmen's Club, or at least I thought so, eyeing the shiny late-model Buick parked in front of his house. But as Dad said, "Money can't make you white." Fancy areas of Muncie were off-limits to blacks. Only much later in the mid-sixties did the more exclusive suburbs of Muncie open to a trickle of black families, and even then there were incidents of harassment and cross burning.

Earlier that summer Mr. Poole hired me as a caddie. He and his close friend, Jack Mann, one of Muncie's few black police officers, were avid golfers. Jack graduated from Central High School in 1932 with Dad. The first black to play on the Muncie Central Bearcats, he led them to a state basketball championship. Now he and Mr. Poole were weekend golfers—out of town. Muncie's private clubs were closed to blacks. Some concern had been voiced about discrimination when Muncie opened its first club and excluded Jews. When a new course opened it admitted Jews but excluded Negroes. Neither Jack's achievements nor Poole's daily contact with Muncie's white elite was enough for either to make the roster at Muncie's country clubs. They golfed at the public course in New Castle, fifteen miles away.

Across from the Pooles', two boys fired rocks at birds in an elm tree. Willie, a Garfield School playmate, hailed me. I joined him and a new boy, Brian Settles, in a game of hide-and-seek. Twenty minutes of futile chasing was enough to bore us all, and we talked on the curb until Willie's mother called him to dinner. Brian invited me to watch TV. Since we didn't have one at Miss Dora's, I eagerly accepted. He lived in a modest one-story two-bedroom house, directly across from the Pooles. We had been watching television for almost an hour when Mrs. Settles and Brian's sister, Vicki, arrived home.

Mrs. Settles knew Dad. I wondered if they had met at Bob's Tavern. When I learned she was a children's librarian I was embarrassed about my assumption. Apparently, Mrs. Settles and Dad attended classes together at Ball State in the 1930s. She graduated and Dad quit. She remembered Dad had wanted to be a lawyer, and wasn't surprised that I had taken up that dream. Mrs. Settles seemed impressed that I read three books a week because Dad said lawyers had to read a lot.

"Did you hear that?" she needled Brian, who was engrossed in a TV western. "Greg reads three books a week. I've been trying to get Brian to read. You know, if you boys like, I can bring books home for you."

My interest in reading led to a dinner invitation from Mrs. Settles. Her golden pork chops, thick mashed potatoes, and German chocolate cake sealed my interest in eating there as often as possible.

Mrs. Settles had received her B.A. and M.A. from Ball State. When she graduated, she, like so many other blacks in Muncie, was unable to break the racial barriers in the Muncie public schools.

There were only a handful of black teachers in the school system despite the fact that blacks comprised over ten percent of Muncie's population, and Ball State Teachers College graduated many highly qualified black teachers every year. Refused employment in Muncie's public schools, Mrs. Settles was relegated to cleaning houses just steps away from where she had taken her college classes. The afternoon she interviewed at the library she kept her hands under the table to hide the soot in her fingernails from her morning job of cleaning a white family's fireplace. Once I became a regular at the Settles household she constantly reinforced the importance of an education to me and the other boys from the Projects, who gathered on her porch in the evenings, sharing our goals and aspirations. Though our dreams were huge and our expectations high—given the reality of our circumstances—not once did Mrs. Settles discourage us or tell us that we could not sculpt our own lives. She encouraged us with her wisdom and books from the library. She fed us, body and soul.

Brian and I soon became inseparable. We swam at an old rock quarry, fished for carp and catfish in the White River, and spent hours playing basketball on the Madison Street playground. When my old foe Jerry Devereaux shouted "Here come the white boys" as we stepped onto the basketball court, I was relieved to be in the company of Brian. I knew I had at least one friend who accepted me as I was.

One crisp Saturday morning in the fall of 1955 I stopped to pick up Brian on the way to flag football practice. Mrs. Settles was sweeping the front porch. Brian walked through the door carrying his trombone case.

Puzzled, I asked, "Brian, what'cha doing with the trombone? We're playing football."

His face fell. Mrs. Settles glared at him. "Brian Settles! You told me you had a music lesson!"

*Whap!* She smacked him with the broom. "You know we have work to do around here! You're just like your daddy. I can't get you to do a damn thing. And you wanta be a used-up ballplayer just like him." She whacked him on the head again. He raised his hands to protect himself, which made her even angrier. Retreating to the sidewalk, I wasn't sure whether to run, cry, or double over with laughter. Finally, Mrs. Settles, exhausted and out of breath, ordered

Brian inside to dust and vacuum. I slithered away. Later that afternoon, I stood outside Brian's bedroom window, and apologized. Only when he began to ask what happened at practice did I know we were still friends. When he mentioned the morning squabble, it was all I could do to stifle a chuckle. I said, "Your momma sure bopped you on the head."

Brian grimaced, "Yeah, I didn't deserve that. I clean, mop, vacuum, and even cook. Sometimes she just loses control."

There was a pause. Brian leaned closer to the screen separating us. "I'll tell you a secret, Greg."

I stepped closer to the window.

"She really ain't my mother and Keg ain't my father either . . . I'm adopted." He lowered his head and continued in a whisper. "Nobody knows it around here, but my daddy was colored and my momma was white. Momma got me from an orphanage in Lincoln, Nebraska."

I was stunned by the revelation. Brian's golden skin and brown curly hair matched that of Mrs. Settles, so he never had to justify his color as I did. But for the first time I began to understand why his face reddened when Jerry hailed "the white boys" as we joined our Project playmates. Though I continued to endure barbed teasing about my white relatives, I began to take some solace in the belief that there were many more members of the black community who wanted to ignore white relatives than one might imagine. Denial of their full heritage was due less to anger and prejudice toward their white families than the total and absolute rejection of their existence by them.

That fall my main interest in school continued to be reading. At least once a week my sixth grade teacher, Miss Newman, took our class to the Maring Branch Library, a block from Garfield School. It was always difficult to decide which books to select. Classics like *Treasure Island, Kidnapped, Oliver Twist*, and *The Count of Monte Cristo* filled many hours as I sat in my attic bedroom. I lost myself in countless biographies, and was inspired by the lives of Abraham Lincoln, Ben Franklin, and George Washington Carver. Every night I was transported far away from Muncie. One Thursday as the class crowded around the Maring Branch Library checkout desk, Miss Newman surprised me by drawing attention to my selections. "Children, do you see what interesting books Gregory has chosen today?

Some of you boys might especially like this new one he found on helicopters. Good choices, Gregory." It was obvious Miss Newman liked me. Earlier in the year she had nominated me for captain of the safety patrol. I lost to the quarterback of our football team, but I was grateful for her confidence in me.

Two weeks before the end of the school year Miss Newman stopped me in the hall. "You know, Gregory," she said, peering over her half glasses, "we have a nice graduation ceremony for sixth graders. It's a time to recognize the class and to announce awards and honors. The most coveted prize," she continued, "is a medal awarded to the student with the best academic record and all-around school participation. I know one young man who deserves the award, and I'm certain will receive it," she said with a twinkle in her eye. "Please make sure your father is at the ceremony. I'm sure he'll like it."

That evening I dashed to Grandma's to brag that I would receive the award. Everything was getting better. Just that month Dad had returned from Louisville, and was working on a regular basis at the cannery. Still drinking, however, he sat in the middle of a group guzzling wine. When I blurted out Miss Newman's message, he rose from the couch and patted me on the shoulder.

"Son, I'm so proud of you. One of these days you're gonna be somebody. Lawyer, judge, congressman, maybe even president. Man, you've taken all the shit those peckawoods can heap on you and still emerged at the top. I'm gonna have Mom buy you a new suit."

Grandma bought a shiny blue ten-dollar gabardine suit for me at Stillman's discount department store and even seemed pleased to do so. Then Dad took me to see Miss Albright, the seamstress who lived around the corner from the rummage sales on Mulberry. Miss Albright, a white woman in her mid-fifties, was especially nice after Dad told her I was going to receive the top academic prize awarded to a Garfield student.

"Greg, I'm so pleased for you," she said. "I remember when your dad brought your first suit for me to alter two years ago. I'm glad things have worked out so well for you." She was too kind to remind me the first suit was from the rummage sale. Miss Albright had the suit ready in two days. Dad then took it to Nick's for pressing. Much to my surprise, Nick did it for free.

Graduation day of 1956 finally arrived. That morning, Miss New-

man marveled at how nice I looked as I sat erect at my desk, fearful of dulling the sharp creases of my gabardine pants. Dad and I
stopped by Aunt Bess's for lunch. We had the usual leftover breakfast biscuits and shared a pot of navy beans. Just as I pushed away
from the table Aunt Bess pulled an apple pie out of the oven—
baked just for me. Still savoring the taste of warm apples and cinnamon, Dad and I walked the six blocks to Garfield for the last time.

We talked about how rough Muncie had been, how I had spent
the first six weeks without books, and how Dad had cut grass in
Louisville for book rent money. We laughed when he said, "They
would've never known you were a spook if the principal hadn't
taken Mike to Aunt Bess after he fell off the fire escape. But I guess
it doesn't matter these days. Schools are changing."

The gymnasium was packed with students and parents when we
marched to our front row seats. We said the Pledge of Allegiance,
then sang "The Star-Spangled Banner." There were speeches by the
principal and the president of the PTA, but I paid little attention to
them. Finally, the time for honors and awards arrived. I leaned forward in my seat. My eyes met Dad's on the far side of the room.
Sober, just like he promised. His face was full of smiles. The basketball coach spoke first. He talked about what a great team we had.
We had just missed being city champs. Brian Settles was named
Most Valuable Player, and the coach said he was sure Brian was
going to make a name for himself in Muncie athletics. I glanced at
Mrs. Settles, sitting behind Dad. I couldn't understand her expression of displeasure. The coach was saying that Brian had a chance
to be a Bearcat basketball star. It was the dream of every Muncie
boy.

Then the principal rose to announce the winner of the Academic
Achievement Prize. "This award and the plaque which comes with
it are sponsored by a group of some of the finest women in Muncie.
No doubt if I read a list of their names you would recognize them
as being from Muncie's most prominent families. They are drawn
together, not only by that honor, but by their focus on American
history and tradition, a tradition that reaches back to the very beginning of the Republic. They value that history and tradition, and
each year ask us to select the one student from our graduating class
who best exemplifies the American standard of achievement. This
year we have a clear winner. A young student who through dili-
gence, hard work, and dedication to learning has shown time and

again the ability to overcome adversity and difficulty, yet grasp an understanding of what learning is all about and what America stands for as a nation."

He announced the winner.

It was not me.

After a deep intake of breath, I glanced at Dad. The smile had vanished, replaced by a cold, knowing mask. Mrs. Settles dropped her head. Searching the crowd for Miss Newman, I saw shock on her face. Dad and Mrs. Settles knew what had happened. She did not. The prize did not go to Negroes. Just like in Louisville, there were things and places for whites only. That was my final lesson at Garfield Elementary School.

# Chapter 11

# Accept the Things I Cannot Change

Shortly after my graduation from Garfield, I noticed Dad was drinking less. One afternoon we sat at Grandma's sharing a two-day-old copy of the *Muncie Press* when he reached for the coffee cup in front of him. Hot liquid sloshed over the edge as he tried to lift it. He set it down, smartly. Again, he tried to pick it up. His hand shook. The cup was halfway to his mouth when it dropped. *Crack!* Steamy black liquid spread in front of us. I grabbed a rag. He sat there ashen-faced, lips quivering.

"Dad, you all right?" I asked, sopping coffee from the table. In silence he moved with difficulty into the next room. "Come here," he said. "I got to talk to you."

He gazed through the window into the alley. I glanced at the grocery sack wallpaper next to the couch where he scribbled notes at night while lying in bed, listening to the radio. He loved to collect what he called "great speech dialogue."

*Welch—to Joe McCarthy: "Sir, have you no decency?"*

*Schools are to be integrated with all deliberate speed.*

An uncomfortable silence filled the room. I settled nervously on the bed. In a soft, almost unrecognizable voice he began, "I'm going away for a little while."

I groaned. "Are the police after you again?"

He frowned. "You act like I'm Public Enemy Number One."

He was going to take "the cure." At first I didn't understand. Finally, I realized he was giving up drinking, again. Grandma walked through the doorway and stood in the kitchen cradling a small brown paper bag. Her nostrils flared when she saw me. "Billy," she screamed, "get off my bed! I told you about messin' it up. You don't give a shit about my things. Buster, tell him to get his butt off my bed."

She pulled a bottle of Thunderbird wine from the bag. I joined Dad on his couch, a few inches from Grandma's bed.

"Buster," she called over her shoulder, "you want a dram?"

"I told you I'm trying to quit. You better too. That rotgut's gonna kill ya."

"Wine ain't gonna kill me, but taking care of you sure is," she said with a huff, and banged the screen door on her way to the yard.

"I thought you was gonna get a job this summer, Dad."

"I'm not in shape to work. I've tried, but I can't control my drinking. I'm having d.t.'s and blackouts. Look."

His hand shook spastically as he tried to steady it in front of him. He leaned forward with a painful look on his face. White, milky pus filled the corners of his eyes. The strong, penetrating scent of Old Spice after-shave reminded me of his last drinking binge. It was a Sunday, just before school ended. Early that morning I rifled through Dad's pants for a church offering while he slept. He had only fifty cents. I pocketed it and congratulated myself on keeping him sober for at least one day. Later that afternoon I returned to Grandma's. Just as I stepped into her kitchen, I saw Dad's head tilted back. He was swallowing something. The shape of the bottle was unfamiliar. As I looked closer, I saw his mouth was wrapped around the aluminum lip of a large Old Spice bottle. In his desperation, Dad was drinking after-shave! The sting of Old Spice was enough to keep me from even splashing it on my face, but never in my wildest dreams could I imagine drinking it. My throat burned in sympathy as I watched him gulp the fiery liquid.

Dad said he would have to sign papers giving the state power to keep him until he was "straight." He could be gone a month, six months, a year. I often wondered why he decided to commit himself that summer. He had tried to quit drinking so many times that I lost count. But a few days without a drink caused the anger and guilt feelings about the loss of his business and family to create a depression of such an intolerable level that he just could not face it. Grandma was always threatened by Dad's struggle for sobriety. It invariably included an attempt to sober her up as well. Although I didn't recognize it then, I believe the d.t.'s and blackouts truly scared him, and like any sane person, he was afraid he was going to die. The men from Alcoholics Anonymous had convinced him that drastic action was required. Dad had sporadically attended AA meetings over the years, but recently AA had begun to play a larger role in our lives. The white men counseled Dad in coffee shops and on street corners. One "sponsor" felt Dad needed a totally different environment. It was hard to be optimistic with a history of so many failed attempts, but self-commitment to the state hospital seemed radical enough to offer new hope. So began the summer of "the cure."

Mike and I joined Dad on the trek to the Delaware County Courthouse. We followed broad stairs to the third-floor courtroom. Sunlight from tall windows filtered onto the polished brown wooden benches. Dad put his finger to his lips and we silently filled rear seats. Ten to fifteen people were scattered throughout the room. A thin white man with his head bowed stood before a black-robed judge sitting behind a raised podium. Leaning forward, I strained to hear the judge.

"You have exactly three days to come up with back support money. If you can't, you'll have some jail time to think about it."

The judge banged his gavel, and a clerk shouted "All rise!" Dad motioned for Mike and me to stand as the judge disappeared through a door behind the podium. Then Dad walked to the front of the room and spoke with a clerk. As Dad rejoined us a strong breeze flowed through the open windows, but he sweated profusely. He drew a handkerchief from his pocket, but his hand shook so much he could barely wipe his brow. Soon a plump deputy sheriff ambled to the wood railing separating spectators from court officials. His belly sagged over the railing as he scanned the room. His gaze landed on Dad.

"Buster, get up here, boy. The judge wants to see you now."

"Yes sir." Dad jumped quickly to his feet. They disappeared through the doors behind the bench. The rest of the spectators drifted out of the courtroom. Mike and I sat alone.

Almost half an hour passed before Dad emerged from the judge's chambers. The fat deputy guided him down the aisle. As they drew near, Mike and I stood uneasily.

"You goin' to jail?" Mike asked anxiously as he stopped in front of us.

"No," he said somberly, "Deputy Andrews is taking me to the state hospital at Logansport. Let 'em lock me up. It's the only way I can get sober."

"Don't worry about him," quipped the deputy. "Logansport's just like a summer camp."

We threw our arms around Dad. I saw tears in his eyes. The deputy pushed him through the large courtroom doors. Mike and I raced into the hall after them. We stepped toward the elevator, but startled again by the sight of Dad in custody, we held back. When the elevator arrived, Dad gave a grim nod good-bye as he left us once more.

A month later we received a five-page letter. At first I was jealous as I read of the three generous meals a day, but my stomach knotted when Dad described the horrors of going "cold turkey." He spoke enthusiastically about a "Twelve Step Program." The letter promised everything would be different when he returned. He'd find a regular job, buy us decent clothes, and, finally, we'd leave for California, where we could begin a new life together.

While Dad spent the summer of 1956 drying out in the alcoholic ward at the Logansport State Hospital, I played at the Madison Street playground. A magnet for Muncie's black community, it had a morning crafts program that kept young children busy finger-painting and making lanyards. Outdoor movies and evening dances lured teenagers. Adults, teenagers, and youngsters alike were all drawn to the late afternoon softball games. Almost every evening as many as one hundred spectators gathered on the ledge alongside the softball diamond to see if pitchers like "Cammie" or "Railhead" could zip the ball past hitters like "Henry B." and "Chubby." If Henry B. didn't hit a home run, he still demonstrated why he was one of the top runners in the state as he rounded the bases. Chubby wasn't as fast as Henry B., but he was Muncie's only bona fide high school All-American football player. When he connected with the ball, it rocketed over the right field fence, the swimming pool, and across Second Street. The sound of shattering glass from the Projects usually accompanied his home runs.

After softball, some of the crowd stayed to watch the evening basketball games. For the past two summers I had lingered at the edge of the playground and watched the older boys. Only in the late evenings after they left did I summon up the courage to sneak onto the court. Now twelve years old and five and a half feet tall, I stood courtside and hoped to be selected when an extra person was needed to fill out the teams. It didn't happen often, and when it did, it was hard to concentrate on the game. During those times, I couldn't believe I was on the court with Muncie Bearcat legends like Carl Miller and Jim Sullivan. By 1956 Muncie Central had secured its place in Indiana basketball history with four state championships. That summer's playground stars were members of the 1954 Muncie Central Basketball team, which lost the final game of the state championship to tiny Milan High School. Jimmy Barnes's lightning-fast hands and George Burks's outside shot were a thrill to watch, but the crowd roared loudest whenever "Big John" Casterlow, a six-foot, six-inch giant, soared high above the rim and snatched the ball almost from the top of the backboard.

One evening I stood courtside as the lively crowd, many fueled by liquor from the nearby Willard Street Tap, watched Big John and his teammates perform. Beer bottles wrapped in brown paper bags were passed through the crowd. After two games, Jimmy and George left, followed later by Big John in his purple-felt and brown-leather Muncie Central letter jacket. I hoped one day to have my own Bearcat jacket. As new teams were selected they were short one member. Chubby, finished with softball for the evening, shouted for me.

I eagerly ran onto the court.

"Who do you want, Earl or Slick?" I sized up Earl, a nineteen-year-old Arkansas native. He had recently moved to Muncie to compete in the Golden Gloves. Though he had lightning-fast hands, he was a basketball novice. Then I stole a glance at Slick. Only on the playground to impress the girls on the sidelines, he trotted onto the court dressed in sharply pressed pants, a starched white shirt, and bright red suspenders. He looked ready for a dance, not basketball. Slick had a reputation for violence. Two weeks earlier, the ball was stolen from him during play, and the quick-handed "thief" headed to the opposite end for an easy basket. Enraged, Slick raced after him. Just as the player made the layup, Slick whipped a straight razor from his pocket and slashed his adversary across the butt. Fortunately, he only ruined a pair of pants. From then on, no one guarded Slick unless there was no other choice.

"I'll take Earl."

Earl and his team were not much of a contest. Twice Earl tried to shoot, and I slapped the ball away, provoking giggles from the girls. As he dribbled the ball up the court a third time, I wondered if he would be stupid enough to give me another chance to make him look like a fool. Sure enough, he made a beeline to the very same spot and jumped to shoot. I leaped to make the block. My timing was perfect and I batted the ball deep into the crowd. Laughter erupted on the sidelines as I glided to the ground in what felt like slow motion. My toes barely touched the blacktop when—*Whap! Whap!*—Earl jabbed me twice in the face. Dazed, I fell backward onto the asphalt and sat there trying to focus. I felt an eyelid beginning to swell. Blood dripped from my nose. Earl towered over me menacingly. Sweat rolled down his dark brown face and saturated his shirt. "Come on, mothafucka, git up and let's see if ya can fight!"

"Man, what did you hit me for? I didn't do nothin'!"

"You skinny mothafucka, you been fouling me all game! Now get up so I can kick your ass!"

His left fist quivered above my head. He leaned toward me.

Warily, I edged backward. He stepped closer. I was desperate. If I took a swing at him, he would kill me. If I took off running, I'd not only lose the respect of the other players, but he would probably kill me anyway. Finally, I eased into a standing position and blurted out, "Man, I'm goin' home to get my daddy's gun! You better not be here when I get back!"

"Everybody knows your juicehead daddy is in the insane asylum. Now fight like a man. I'm gonna knock you crazy too." He took another step toward me. Turning away from him, I forced myself to retreat slowly from the playground. The crowd parted for me as I tried to avoid the girls' eyes.

Miss Dora halted in mid-rock as I walked up the steps. "Billy, what happened? How come your face is all swolled up? Look at that blood!"

"Earl hit me when we was playing basketball."

"Did you fight him back?"

"No ma'am, he's in the Golden Gloves. I came home to get the butcher knife."

"Lordy, I ain't about to let you take no knife up there. Come on in the house," she said, rising from the chair.

Carefully she wiped dried blood from my face. Then she put ice in a rag for me to hold over my eye. She sat beside me.

"Everybody's gonna think I'm scared if I don't go back up there. But I got to take the butcher knife."

"You do hafta go back. If you don't, them boys is gonna think they can run over you whenever they want. But you can't take a knife. You liable to get kilt. When people starts carrying guns and knives, they asking for trouble. You got to go back up there with nothing but your own will. If he starts a fight, just do the best you can."

Shortly before dark I finally gathered enough courage to return to the playground. Several of the players still milled about the court, and I sighed with relief when I saw no sign of Earl. Chubby was there and Big John Casterlow had returned. No one said anything about the earlier fight. Just as I silently offered a prayer of gratitude, I saw Earl walking toward the playground. He and his buddies passed a familiar brown paper sack from the Willard Street Tap among them. Earl took a long swallow of beer, then stalked directly to me. His eyes darted like small fish in a bowl.

"You ready to fight now, you little white nigger?"

My body tensed as I waited for him to take a swing. Just then a huge purple shadow moved between us. Startled, I looked up and saw Big John Casterlow in his Bearcat letter jacket.

"Look here, Mr. Golden Gloves," he said to Earl, "I don't care if you do think you Sugar Ray Robinson. Don't mess with this boy. He don't bother nobody. If you lay a hand on him, I'll whip you myself."

My body deflated like a pierced balloon when I saw Earl drop his fists. Big John stood there like a mountain for almost twenty seconds to reinforce his words. Earl retreated to his group, and snatched the beer bottle out of a buddy's hands. Big John turned toward me and, with a deadpan look on his face, shot me a wink. I wanted to shout Miss Dora's favorite phrase, "Thank you, Jesus!" but we both knew the rules of the playground, and all I could do was nod my head ever so slightly.

After that I only saw Earl a few times. His career as a fighter was soon ended by drugs. He lingered on the edge of the playground, a shell of his former self. Big John left Muncie and I didn't hear much about him until years later, when I was a member of the Bearcat football team. One afternoon following practice a coach told a group of us from the Projects that Big John had been attacked and killed on the streets of Detroit. As we stood in the shadow of the Muncie Fieldhouse, the scene of so many of Big John's public achievements, I didn't care if my teammates saw my tears.

By mid-summer Dad had successfully completed the program at Logansport and was transferred to Nash Rehabilitation Center, fifteen miles south of Muncie, on the northern edge of New Castle. He made rapid progress at Nash, and his recovery from alcoholism was crowned with a job offer as a clerk/typist in the center's business office. A small trailer on the grounds was provided as living quarters. Mike and I began making weekend visits.

The first Saturday morning we rode the ABC Coach bus down State Road 3 to the public golf course where I had caddied for Mr. Poole. Golfers teed up for the long thirteenth hole, which ran alongside a cornfield. Mike laughed as I complained about the hot afternoons spent searching for Mr. Poole's errant golf balls in the tall corn. We crossed the highway and began a four-mile walk along an undulating blacktop road that Dad's letter promised would be "a nice little hike." After thirty minutes, we still trudged beside the steaming pavement, hoping some motorist might take pity on us and offer a ride. Only two cars rushed by, and neither driver gave us more than a passing glance. In the distance, limestone cliffs guarded the Big Blue River, which flowed lazily toward Knightstown. At the crest of a hill, we saw a huge farm. Acres and acres of dark green pastures stretched before us. It was a perfect picture of Indiana farm country. Yet something about the scene was unsettling to me. At first I thought my apprehensiveness was caused by the fact that all the barns, outbuildings, and vehicles were the same dull, institutional color. But that wasn't it. Then I decided it was that all the people were dressed exactly alike—blue caps, blue shirts, blue jackets, and blue denim pants. That wasn't it either. What troubled me most was the aimlessness of the people. At other farms workers scurried about, repairing tractors, loading and unloading pigs, and tilling fields. Here everyone moved slowly and without purpose, as though in a trance. As we walked along the barbed wire separating us from the farm, blank faces turned toward us. At the metal gate, a tattered sign declared INDIANA STATE HOSPITAL FOR EPILEPTICS, NO TRESPASSING, VISITORS REPORT IMMEDIATELY TO INSTITUTION HEADQUARTERS IN COTTAGE D!

We trudged up and down another hill, and I wondered what Nash would be like. Dad wrote it was part of the epileptic hospital complex. Perhaps Earl was right, maybe Dad had drunk himself crazy. Finally, we reached State Road 103 and the entrance to Nash. A small lane snaked up a hill between large, towering trees. As we rounded a bend in the lane, we saw a three-story red brick hospital building high on a ridge. An enormous weeping willow tree shaded the northwest corner of the building. A vast green lawn rolled down the hill to greet us. It was bordered by a flower garden and an elaborate arrangement of painted rocks. A porch with Greek columns and dotted with white and green steel lounge chairs stretched across the front of the building. The chairs were occupied by middle-aged men. Had it not been for the pale gray institutional benches and the gray fire escape cylinders that sloped from the second story of the building, I would have believed Nash Rehabilitation Center was a summer resort. I felt uneasy again, however, as we drew closer and I realized that although these men were not dressed in the institutional blue we saw across the highway, many had the same vacant stares.

We arrived just as the lunch bell rang. Dad rushed us into the dining hall. I covered the roast ham and cinnamon sauce with mashed potatoes until the ham was hardly visible. I stopped chewing only long enough to gulp down milk. Dad didn't even complain as he took the pitcher back to the kitchen for two refills.

The only disappointment was the sharp-smelling yellow bread on the table. Normally I loved all kinds of bread—white, wheat, even pumpernickel and rye—but this bread was terrible. I asked Dad why it was so bad when everything else tasted wonderful. He leaned across the table and put a hand on my shoulder. In a solemn voice he said, "I guess I can tell you now since you're a seventh grader." He paused, and I looked at him expectantly, waiting for a great truth to be revealed.

"Greg," he said in a voice that carried throughout the room, "they put saltpeter in the food. You can only taste it in the bread."

I looked at Dad quizzically.

"So the fellows won't get a hard-on!" he shouted. Laughter rang out as he added, "As much as you've been eating, I bet you don't get a boner till you're in high school." My face turned crimson as he joined the roar of laughter.

That day Mike and I explored the building. We slid down the banister several times, then wandered through the second-floor living quarters. Beds were arranged barracks-style. We were intent on playing in the steel cylindrical fire escapes, but all of a sudden Dad appeared in the doorway with a stern face. "Upstairs are off-limits, boys. Either go outside or play in the lounge."

Mike took off outdoors, and I explored the first-floor lounge. Dark wood wall panels and a large fireplace reminded me of fishing lodges I'd seen in magazines. But instead of a trophy-sized muskie mounted over the fireplace, there was a large plaque in fancy scroll writing:

*Lord grant me the serenity to accept the things I cannot change.*
*The courage to change the things I can.*
*And the wisdom to know the difference.*

I struggled to understand the quote. Dad always said I could change my life, but I was losing hope. We still didn't have adequate food, clothes, or money. It had been three years since Mom left. But maybe now that Dad was sober everything would change. I was still doubtful as I flipped through magazines and strained to overhear the dirty jokes exchanged by four poker players seated at a corner card table. Dad strode into the room with a cup of coffee and a cigarette. He admonished them.

"Charley, you fellows know you're not supposed to be gambling," he said.

"We're not gambling, Jimmy."

"Well, what in the hell are those cigarettes doin' stacked on the table? You know the rules. No gambling here, not even on the weekends when Mr. Wolfe is away."

"Hell, Jimmy, you used to have a sense of humor, even when we was in the drunk tank at Logansport."

Dad took a sip of coffee. "Being sober makes me realize how that bitch I married screwed me. If it wasn't for her, I wouldn't be in the shape I'm in today. Damn, I was bustin' my balls and she's off fuckin' the hired help."

He paused for a puff on his cigarette. A gray-haired player laid his cards on the table and said, "Resentments kill more alcoholics than anything else, Jim."

"Give it a rest, Richard," said Dad. "Two AA meetings a day is enough. I've had it with your armchair philosophy. Why don't you get the hell out of here if you've got it all together?"

Richard shrugged and picked up his cards. "I'm just tellin' you what worked for me. Let it go if you wanna stay sober."

"It must not have worked too well, since you staggered back here in less than six months," spat Dad angrily. "I'll never forgive the bitch who destroyed my business."

"Dad," I interrupted, "you still had the tavern after Mom left."

He glared at me. "Get outside, Mr. Big Mouth. You've been sitting around too long. Go on. It's not every day you've got these surroundings to enjoy."

Mike was tiring of chuking rocks at cans behind the trailer, so we hiked over the state hospital grounds. South of Nash across a grassy meadow we saw children our own age. As we drew closer we noticed many had severe physical impairments, and several even wore old-fashioned Knute Rockne–era football helmets to protect against head injuries. They were under the watchful eye of stern-looking attendants, so we gave them a wide berth and headed to the creek that wound through the grounds. We followed it to a spot where an old tire hung over the stream. A man in blue denim, obviously an inmate of the state hospital, sat on the bank fishing. His red-and-white bobber floated motionless in the middle of the creek. "You catchin' anything?" Mike asked.

His face lit up and he responded, "I snagged a couple of bluegill, but they were too small."

We sat beside him and talked about fishing and the hot weather. Except for the institutional clothes, he looked and acted like anyone on the streets of Muncie. He told us he had been at the epileptic hospital for twenty years—since he was thirteen.

"Yep, some of the guys been here thirty or forty years," he added. "Ain't heard from any relatives. This is all the family they know."

He let Mike toss the bobber into the water a couple of times. Then several cars stopped on the gravel road near the stream's bridge. Our companion quickly lifted his line from the water.

"Well, I better get out of here. You boys better, too, unless you wanta get saved."

Several middle-aged men in suits and women in crisply pressed dresses headed for the creek singing "When the Saints Come Marching In." Mike and I watched a young, hefty man in a suit and tie wade into the water. Ignoring us, he turned to his followers, who congregated along the riverbank. I had seen the baptismal pool in the basement of Christ Temple where those being baptized donned a rubber suit, but this was total commitment.

"Brothers and sisters," he began, "I stand here to offer you a chance to change your lives. This water will purify you of your sins and lead you down the path of righteousness. Come and let me anoint you in the name of the Lord. As His servant, you will have new direction and hope in your lives. You can be saved even in this place of pain and suffering where the diseased, feeble-minded, and weak of spirit live." A wave of his hand indicated he was referring to Mike and me.

The minister continued, "Now I know some of you are afraid of ruining those fancy dresses and new suits. They are only vestments of this world and have no place in the next. You gotta give yourself fully to the Lord. You can't just put your toe in the water to be saved. You gotta believe with all your heart and answer the call. Now is the time if you gonna truly be saved from the clutches of the devil!"

Slowly the converts waded toward the preacher. Placing one hand on their head and another across their chest, he shouted, "Glory, glory, glory! I baptize thee in the name of the Father, Son, and Holy Ghost!"

*Swoosh*, he dunked them one by one into the creek. Water rolled off the suits and dresses as he jerked their bodies to the surface. "Cleansed," the men and women scrambled up the slippery bank, smiling broadly, shouting "Amen! Amen, brothers and sisters!" They stood dripping on the bank, their faces flushed and happy.

Although we passed the daylight hours on our own, evenings were a rare opportunity to see our father sober. As darkness descended over the hospital grounds, the three of us gathered in the cramped sitting room of the small trailer. One night, Dad taught Mike the shell game he'd used to win small bets in Muncie bars. I lay on the couch and watched them at the plywood dining table. He spread three walnut shells in front of Mike. Dad wet a piece of paper with his tongue and wadded it into a ball the size of a pea. Placing the pea on the table, he rapidly moved the shells over and around it. I tried to follow the trail of the pea, but his hands were too fast. "Okay, which one is it under?" he challenged.

"I got it!" Mike shouted, and turned over the middle one.

"Sorry, son," responded Dad with a smile, and turned over the shell on the far right, revealing the pea.

"Do it again, Dad," urged Mike.

Dad repeated the routine five or six times. Mike was still unable to find the pea.

"What's the trick, Dad?" I asked.

"No trick, Greg, just a game of skill and cunning."

"I know what it is!" shouted Mike. "You're hiding the pea!"

Dad turned his palm up. The pea was carefully wedged between two fingers.

Mike tried to mimic Dad, but again and again the pea fell on the table. He was so intent on mastering the trick, he pestered Dad to repeat the sleight of hand for over an hour. The game held little interest for me, and I began reading a tattered novel from the Nash lounge when Dad left the trailer for an eleven p.m. bed check of the dormitory. Mike crawled into the double bed at the rear of the trailer and was soon fast asleep. I continued reading.

Dad returned in half an hour. He leaned back in his chair and began to ramble about his dreams after Nash, getting back on his feet and leaving Muncie. The lone bulb in the ceiling shone directly on his face, and I saw the same zeal and commitment the converts showed on the banks of the stream. Realizing this was more than his usual, drunken rambling, I laid my book on the floor.

"Greg, you gotta work hard in school. What you do today establishes the foundation for tomorrow. I know you like basketball and football, but your number-one goal is to be a lawyer. And you don't want to be just any lawyer. As Dr. Ralph Bunche used to say to us at Howard, 'Don't become a twenty-five-dollar-a-case lawyer. Go into the field of international relations. Make your place in the world scene.'

"These Muncie teachers don't understand you any better than they did me. You can't count on them to recognize your potential. Before I could go to Howard, I had to return to Central High for college prep work since my entire senior year was spent building a goddamn house near Ball State. I didn't learn a thing I needed for college. You've gotta take the most difficult classes you can, even if you have to struggle through them.

"It's a dog-eat-dog world, and you have to be tough. That's why I put you up on the Madison Street playground. You fought every inch of the way. And it will never be any different no matter where you go. You're not some rich white boy who never had to worry about where the next meal was coming from. You've had to beg and plead for odd jobs, carry people's coal, wear raggedy-assed pants and shoes with holes in the bottoms."

I rose to a sitting position on the couch and tried to absorb his message. Such openness and honesty was unfamiliar. I often thought Dad had no idea how hard life in Muncie had been for Mike and me as he reeled from one drunken stupor to another. That night his words revealed he was painfully aware of our struggles.

"Life is going to change, Greg. By the time you graduate from college, I'm going to give you a trip around the world. There is nothing that broadens a man as much as travel, meeting all types of people, and gaining an opportunity for the cross-fertilization of ideas."

He paused and in a lowered voice said, "But who am I to give advice when I have made such blunders? Man, I was once King of the Mountain, but I came tumbling down."

He stopped again, looking into the blackness outside the window for a moment. Then he turned to me.

"All I'm saying, son, is do the very best you can. You have the ability. Your success or failure is up to you."

He reached into his shirt pocket and handed me a small New Testament Bible bound in black, left by the Gideons for the alcoholics at the center. I opened it and read the inscription:

*To my son,*
*Gregory Howard Williams*

*May this Bible provide you some small*
*consolation for all your losses at*
*such an early age.*

*Dad*
*James Anthony Williams*

Mike and I spent every possible weekend with Dad at Nash. When we lacked money for the bus, we hitchhiked. Mike even hitchhiked alone, but that made me nervous. I refused to do it after one driver offered Mike five dollars to let him touch Mike's penis. Despite the difficulties arriving, we almost always had a safe return on Sunday. There was a fraternity among alcoholics' families, and there was never an occasion when a group of Sunday visitors heading anywhere near Muncie refused to give us a ride. Even when the cars were crowded with family members, they always found room for us. Once a Nash visitor made a thirty-mile detour to insure our safe arrival home.

We rarely visited New Castle during the school week, but one Thursday afternoon James, a distant relative from Chicago, arrived in Muncie. He picked up Grandma, Mike, and me to take us to New Castle for a visit with Dad. Once in the car, however, he bypassed New Castle and sped south to Knightstown to visit his wife's family. Mike and I became anxious as he and Grandma began drinking heavily.

To make up for lost time, James roared east on U.S. 40. Less than two miles down the road he scraped a car while attempting to pass it on the divided highway. We began to slide sideways. Fighting for control, James struck the rear of the car in front of us, causing it to jump across the median and collide with an automobile traveling in the opposite direction. We swerved back across the two lanes and headed straight for a tree.

Grandma, in the middle of the front seat next to me, was screaming. Mike was crying out in the back. Though I braced an arm against the dashboard, the tremendous force of the crash hurled me forward. Grandma's head cracked the windshield. Whipped back into my seat, I saw flames leap from under the hood of the car. Pushing the door open with my shoulder, I didn't know how much time I had before the car exploded. Quickly, I dragged Grandma to safety under a nearby tree. Then I returned to the car, wrenched open the rear door, and pulled Mike from the back seat. James staggered away from the car toward the highway. When I turned to look at the car, I realized I must have been hallucinating, because there was no fire.

An ambulance arrived, attendants loaded Grandma and James and then sped off to the Henry County Hospital in New Castle. Even though we were covered with blood, a state trooper placed Mike and me in his car while we waited for the wreckers to arrive. On the way to the hospital he asked us if we were runaways. We denied it.

"Then what are you doing with those colored people?" he asked.

"They're family," I said.

"Don't lie to me. You better tell me the truth before you really get in trouble. Where is your momma and daddy?"

"Our momma don't live with us, and our daddy works in New Castle."

"You're lying. We can keep you in jail until you tell the truth, and not some bullshit about being kin to those niggers."

"We are colored!" I protested. "If you don't believe us, call Nash Rehabilitation Center in New Castle and ask our dad. His name is James A. Williams."

"I'm gonna have the desk sergeant do that, but if you boys are shittin' me, you'll be sorry. I know a place where we can send smart-asses."

With that threat I fell silent. My head throbbed. I was covered with my own blood and the blood of my grandmother.

We finally arrived at the hospital. The doctors stitched a deep gash on my nose and a laceration on the right side of my head. Mike escaped with a few bruises, but Grandma had a broken leg, arm, and collarbone, as well as several other cuts, abrasions, and internal injuries. When I walked out of the treatment room, the officer roughly gestured for me to join him and Mike on a lobby bench.

Soon Dad rushed down the dimly lit hallway. Mike and I ran to meet him. When assured we were all right, he asked about Grandma. The state trooper walked toward us. "Are these your boys?"

Dad immediately responded, "Yes, and that's my mother in the emergency room. Is that a problem, Officer?"

Deflecting the challenge, the officer curtly reported the extent of Grandma's injuries.

Grandma spent six weeks at the New Castle hospital. Upon her release she was still unable to sit upright, and Dad talked Richard Taylor, a local black mortician, into using his hearse to transport her to Muncie. As we pushed Grandma through the hospital door on a gurney, she complained about the hearse, saying, "I ain't dead yet, Buster." She was so glad to be out of the hospital, however, she laughed about it most of the way home. Grandma begged Dad to stop for a bottle of wine. They both finished it as we neared Muncie. The accident left me with two scars for life and a head full of glass fragments that took almost a year to work to the surface. Our relative had a badly sprained ankle and facial abrasions.

I was disgusted with James when he arrived at the house shortly after the accident with a request. We sat on the porch.

"What do you mean be careful about what I say?" I demanded. "You tellin' me to lie?"

"No, Greg, I'm not telling you to lie, but you don't have to tell the insurance adjuster everything you know."

"Why can't I tell him everything I know? What are you telling me not to say?"

"Nothing, Greg. Just forget it."

When he left, Miss Dora sat next to me on the swing.

"Greg, you got to tell white people the truth when they ask you about the accident. You could get in trouble tryin' to lie to them for that old man. You don't have to take care of him. The only time he ever shows up around here is when he's drunk."

When the insurance adjuster arrived to question me about the accident, I recounted everything, including James's afternoon and evening of drinking.

Shortly after the accident, Dad bought a 1949 Hudson for $25 from a hillbilly buddy, Wendell Netherly, who ran N & W Used Cars in New Castle. On Friday nights when he was off duty, Dad would drive to Muncie for us. It was always near midnight when he arrived. He wasn't drunk, but I could tell he had been drinking. After we left Miss Dora's, he would stop at Tisch's Chicken Shack. Then we went to the whorehouse, where Mike and I sat in the car eating chicken while Dad spent money on the girls. We arrived in New Castle around two or three a.m. and crawled into bed. No matter what time of night we made it to the trailer, we were never late for a Nash breakfast.

Saturdays following breakfast Dad drove downtown to Wendell's N & W Used Cars. While Wendell had a few old cars for sale parked beside the garage near the railroad tracks, he was never very busy. Mike played outside on the tracks in the wrecks, but I lingered inside while Dad shared jokes with the mechanics. I hoped that if I kept an eye on him he might decline the beer that seemed to be in constant supply.

It wasn't long before he said, "Greg, you watchin' me like an old mother hen. Why don't you and Mike go downtown and buy some ice cream? Here's a quarter."

Mike and I walked up the Main Street hill, stopping to peer into store windows. We bought ice cream cones at the drugstore near the courthouse square. Then we walked across to the War Memorial and watched the Saturday shopping crowd. Everyone seemed so happy. Around noon we headed back to the garage to urge Dad to make a quick return to Nash so we wouldn't miss lunch. Dad sent us across the street to the Railroadmen's Cafe. As we sat there eating cheeseburgers, I remembered the time Grandpa Cook took me to the same café following a ride from Muncie on the diesel engine. I thought, If he were alive, life wouldn't be so hard for us. After lunch we spent a long afternoon sitting on the railroad tracks. Dinner was served at Nash at five p.m. and Mike and I didn't want to miss it, so around four o'clock we began to nag Dad in earnest. He would finally agree to go after a trip to the drugstore for a package of Clorets so his Nash co-workers wouldn't smell beer on his breath. At Nash, Mike and I raced for the dining room, while Dad stayed behind in the trailer feigning illness.

One night I challenged Dad about the drinking.

"Greg, don't worry about it. I'm only drinking on the weekends. I'm the model of sobriety during the week. I'm just letting my hair down a bit."

"You said if Mr. Wolfe found you drinking, he'd fire you on the spot."

"That's the reason I only drink on the weekends. He goes home.

By Monday morning I'm sober as a judge. You worry about your-self. I can handle it; everything is under control."

One Friday just before midnight, Dad arrived outside Miss Dora's, honking on the horn. Mike and I raced downstairs. As we opened the door I saw the car loaded with Dad's fellow Nash pa-tients passing around a bottle. Sensing disaster, I hesitated.

"Get in, Greg, I'm taking the boys down to the redlight district for a little therapeutic treatment!" he roared.

I knew Dad's time at Nash was coming to an end.

# Chapter 12 Choices

About the time I began junior high school, Grandma Sallie lost her job. The mushrooming fast-food franchises had put the café where she worked out of business. In her sixties, no one would hire her, especially since she could not read. Though she had cooked in Muncie restaurants for over forty years, she had no retirement plan. Dad believed she might be eligible for Social Security benefits. The difficulty was verifying her age. We knew she was born in Bowling Green, Kentucky, around 1890 or so, but no records were available. Dad painstakingly pieced together the limited information known about Grandma's birth by documenting the ages of her sisters and brothers. He then presented it to the Social Security Office. I never saw her smile as broadly as she did the day Dad ripped open the letter confirming her eligibility for benefits and informing her that she would receive a $650 lump-sum back payment. It would take six to eight weeks to process.

In the glow of the moment Grandma cheerfully agreed to share her good fortune. She promised Dad $100 for a new car, as the engine in his old Hudson had thrown a rod. Mike and I were guaranteed $50 apiece for new clothes. Excited by the pledge, I made countless trips downtown, pricing shirts and pants and searching

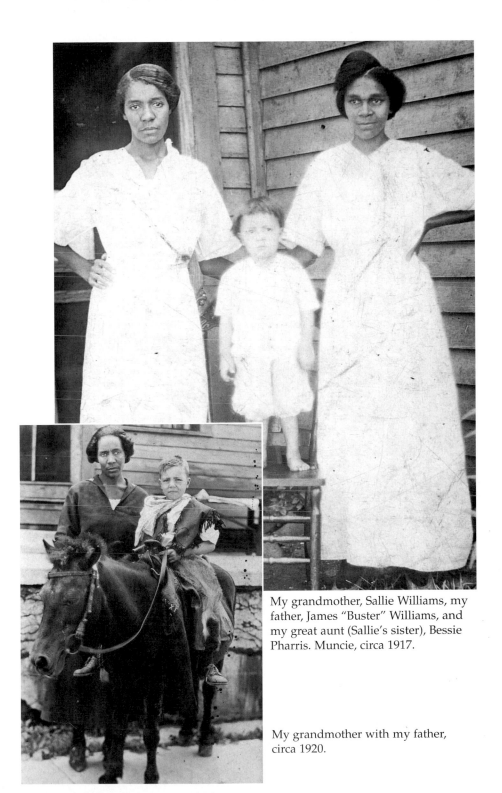

My grandmother, Sallie Williams, my father, James "Buster" Williams, and my great aunt (Sallie's sister), Bessie Pharris. Muncie, circa 1917.

My grandmother with my father, circa 1920.

The Open House Cafe, Gum Springs, Virginia, circa 1947.

My brother Mike and me on Dad's septic tank trunk, Virginia, 1947.

An early snapshot of the family. *Left to right:* my father, my brother, me, and my mother, Mary. Fairfax County, Virginia, circa 1947.

My fourth grade class picture from Garfield Elementary School,
Muncie, 1954.

Mike and me in front of
Sam Wheeler's grocery,
Muncie, 1956.

Mike and Joe Samuel
Thompson (Sam Wheeler's
nephew), Muncie, 1956.

My father at Nash
Rehabilitation Center, circa
1956. He took the "cure" and
was awarded a job as a
clerk-typist.

Wilson Junior High School basketball,
Muncie, 1958.

High school party,
Muncie, 1960. *Left to right:*
Carl Brown, Mayme Barker,
Lorraine Hayes, me.

Relaxing before the Black
Students Senior Prom
party, 1962. *Left to right:*
Michael O'Neil, Marjorie
Hayes, Jean Carol Ivory,
Martha Jo Kelly, me,
Jeanette Blackburn, Carl
Brown, Brian Settles.

Me, my father, and my brother, 1967.

My wedding to Sara Whitney, August 1969. *Left to right:* Sara, me,
Miss Dora, Mike.

Mike and me with our Hayes cousins and their families, Back to Muncie Reunion, August 1992. Our grandmothers, Sallie Williams and Bessie Pharris, were sisters. *Left to right:* Bill Cox, Jewitt Hayes, Virginia (Hayes) Cox, Novella K. (Hayes) Bryant, me, Joy Hayes, Mike Williams, Marjorie (Hayes) Crim, Calvin (Seeing Eye dog).

Miss Dora's home at 623 Kirby Avenue, Muncie, 1990

My family, 1992. *Left to right:* Zach, Anthony, Natalia Dora, Carlos, Sara, me.

for the best bargains. My wish list was scribbled on a sheet of paper I kept with me at all times. I sensed there would be a lot of jostling for Grandma's attention once the money arrived, and I wanted to be ready to rush her downtown.

Two weeks before the money was expected, Dad made one of his irregular safaris through the white hillbilly bars on South Walnut Street. He occasionally frequented those bars in defiance of Muncie's rigid racial lines. Sometimes he was able to cajole a free drink, but more often than not he received a busted lip or black eye from those who challenged his crossing of the color line. Dad's "friends" from these forays rarely lasted longer than a bottle of wine, although some of them continued to wander in and out of our lives. Fred Badders was like a "bad penny." He kept turning up.

In his early forties, Fred had pasty white skin and stood barely five feet tall. Partially bald, he kept the sparse hair he did have matted down with heavy doses of Brylcream. His dandruff flakes were visible almost six feet away. Fred spent most of his time at Grandma's running his dandruff-filled comb through his hair. To me, Fred was the spitting image of a weasel.

It didn't take Fred long to discover we were all waiting for "Grandma's ship to come in," and he began to hover around her night and day. Despite the twenty-five-year age difference, they became lovers. Often I entered her shack in the middle of the afternoon and heard Fred's feet hit the floor as the screen door slammed after me. He burst from behind the bedroom curtain and greeted me with his yellow toothy smile, bad breath, and sweaty face. Standing there in his soiled underwear, Fred was the most repulsive lover that I could imagine. It wasn't that I was squeamish about my grandmother having sex. Joe Turnipseed had often spent nights with her when Mike and I lived in the alley. It just seemed that by choosing Fred she cared so little about herself. While she would never admit it, I believe her interest in him had a great deal to do with the fact that Fred was white. Now I believe her yearning went much deeper than what was evident in the person of Fred Badders. It may have gone all the way back to her rejection by my father's father.

Once Fred was in the picture, the competition for the money became fierce. Mike and I raced to Grandma's every day to see if the check had arrived. One evening the house was deserted. We waited a full hour. Then Dad staggered up the alley, returning from a long afternoon at the tavern. Jolted by the discovery that both

Grandma and Fred had disappeared, he sensed the need for immediate action. We double-timed it to the Kirby Avenue intersection. Within five minutes Dad flagged down a passing friend to take
us to Whitely to see if Grandma was at her favorite bootleg joint.
We found neither her nor Fred. They didn't return that night, or the
next morning. For two weeks we heard absolutely nothing. Were
they dead? Were they in jail? Convinced that Fred was just slimy
enough to take Grandma's money, then dump her somewhere, we
feared for her safety.

Finally, at the beginning of the third week, Grandma returned
alone and broke. We couldn't get much out of her, but Fred followed
two days later. He arrived clad in a garish Hawaiian shirt and urine-
stained white flannel pants. Dad immediately began to curse him.

"Motherfucker, you've got some nerve showing your face around
here, you little sawed-off son of a bitch."

Grandma interceded. "Now, Buster, this is my shack and Fred's
my company. Don't talk to him like that."

"Buster, I don't know what you're talking about. I got Sallie back
to Muncie safe and sound. I just had some business where she
couldn't go."

"Shit, Fred, I should kick your ass," said Dad, rising from the
couch. "You put her on a bus with a goddamn tag tied to her like
she was a dog. Look at this!" He shoved a manila-colored tag with
a wire tie under Fred's nose. It read:

> Sallie Williams
> Destination: Muncie, Indiana
> Can't read or write.
> Please help.

"Now how is that taking care of somebody?"

Grandma interrupted again.

"Don't mind Buster, Fred. He just don't want his old mother to
have any fun. Thinks I'm supposed to sit around here and let it rust
out, while he's sniffing around them old white bitches across the
tracks."

The argument seemed destined to continue forever until Fred
reached into his pocket and handed Dad a peace offering—a half-
pint of wine. Long sips around the room eased the tension, and the
story unfolded. Once the check arrived, Fred didn't even give

Grandma time to pack. He rushed her to the bus station and bought two round-trip tickets to Louisville. Within eight hours they were at Aunt Roxie's, once again a refuge—this time from Dad, Mike, and me.

While Fred snorted with laughter about how they put one over on us, Grandma sat beside him on her bed and giggled like a schoolgirl. Dad soon had half the bottle inside of him and joined the laughter. When Dad stepped to the toilet, Fred gave Mike a sip of the wine. The friendship was sealed when Fred slipped him a pair of loaded dice. Putting his finger to his lips so Dad wouldn't know, Fred gestured for Mike to hide them in his pocket. It was more than I could take when they all began to guffaw at the second telling. I doubt if they even heard me rock the gate back on its hinges as I left. Turning up my collar, I dug into my pocket for the wish list. Raindrops dissolved the ink on the paper as I tore it into small pieces and threw them into the wind.

Although Fred received a chilly reception from me after the Louisville adventure, nothing prevented his regular appearance every month when Grandma's Social Security check arrived. Once it was cashed he and Grandma began a five-day binge of cheap wine and sex. When the money disappeared, so did Fred, until the same time the following month.

Many years later, during a nostalgic walk through the old neighborhood, I saw a short, hunchbacked, elderly white man staggering down First Street. Black teenagers stared disgustedly at him. Something clicked in my mind as I noticed the slicked-back white hair. When he was about five feet away, I recognized the weasellike features and shouted one of Dad's familiar greetings.

"Fred Badders, one time, what's happening?"

Shock registered on his face. In spite of his drunkenness, he knew Buster was dead. He paused and examined me with squinty, bloodshot eyes.

"Greg, is that you?"

I nodded.

"Damn, Greg, it's good to see you. You need anything? What can I give you?"

"Nothing, thanks." Too late I realized my response was too quick and self-assured. The scent of money brought a reflex action.

"Well, Greg, let me hold something. I need a little taste."

I could have resisted, but I had lost the need to hate him any longer for the final wedge he drove between me and my grandmother. Reaching into my pocket, I pulled out a five-dollar bill. He mumbled a quick thank-you and did an immediate about-face, heading toward Dalby's Liquor Store at Kirby and Hackley. There was not a single word about Grandma, Dad, Mike, or the past. For the final time Fred confirmed all my feelings about him.

Shortly after Grandma went on Social Security, Mike and I had our first brush with the law. It all began innocently enough during a baseball game on the railroad tracks with Ken and Sonny, two neighbor boys. We had been playing for half an hour when a loud whistle blew from a freight train barreling down the tracks. We scrambled to the side waiting for it to pass. Mike and I sat on the railroad ties in front of Miss Lucy's gate. Ken and Sonny began hurling rocks at the engine. We watched for a minute or so, then joined the rock-throwing at the freight cars. Soon the train was gone and we were back at our game.

Two days later a Muncie police officer arrived at Miss Dora's with a summons for us to appear in juvenile court. On the day of our "trial," Dad was at Miss Dora's at eight a.m., sober and wearing a suit and tie. We were scrubbed and dressed in white shirts and dress pants from the rummage sales. We walked down the railroad tracks toward town.

"Boys, I hope you liked that special meal Miss Dora fixed last night," Dad said as we crossed the Madison Street underpass. "It may be a long time before you eat that well again."

"Do you think they're going to send us away, Daddy?" asked Mike.

"You boys really messed up this time. What got into you? You know better than throwing rocks. I've told you a thousand times not to do that. If they send you to Plainfield, take care of each other. Some of the worst boys in Indiana are locked up down there. Don't hang around them. They might try to make sissies out of you."

"What do you mean, Dad?" I asked.

"Make you punks, Billy. Fuck you in the butt!"

Though the City Hall courtroom was familiar from the days we spent helping Dad clean and mop it, that morning it was cold and forbidding. More than once during my City Hall "janitor" days I had hopped into the judge's high-backed chair and pretended I was the man in charge. During my fantasies I had sent many men to prison with a smile on my face. That day it was different. Sweat rolled down my underarms as I took a seat on the hard wooden bench.

My eyes fixed on a unknown thin, bald man in the front row. He looked almost sixty years old, and he wore wire-rimmed glasses. His stern demeanor was punctuated by a dark-brown growth protruding from the left side of his forehead. It was as though someone had spit a wad of tobacco at him, and it stuck. When the judge called for the railroad detective, the mystery man stepped briskly to the witness stand. My fear was that he would be incapable of honesty, due to being jaded by years of constant stares at his disfigurement. However, he told the truth, and ended with a plea. "Judge, you gotta do somethin' about this. A witness said these boys been doin' this all the time. It done cost the railroad a bunch of money. We got to scare hell out of these kids."

He returned to his front-row seat and resumed his sphinxlike posture. The judge called for Ken, who at fifteen was the oldest of our group. Clad in denim slacks and a white shirt, Ken moved slowly past his parents into the aisle. Suddenly he dropped his shoulders and swaggered to the front of the room, imitating a "pimp roll" popular among older boys at the Madison Street playground. The judge's face flushed as Ken slouched in front of him and defiantly placed his hands on his hips.

"You have anything to say for yourself?" demanded the judge.

"I didn't do nothing," Ken responded.

"That's not what the detective said. You were sitting back there with a smile on your face. You heard it all. Come on, don't you have at least one little lie to tell me?"

"I said, I didn't do it. It wasn't me."

The judge stared at Ken for almost a minute. "I suppose you 'didn't do nothing' these five other times you've been arrested," he mocked. "Looks like that short stay in jail didn't do you any good."

The judge continued to glare at Ken. Then he almost shouted, "You're going back, big shot, and this time for a whole year!"

One year for throwing rocks! I was in shock. The judge was following the railroad man's recommendation! My hopes for leniency evaporated.

Sonny was next. He had been in trouble before, but mostly for skipping school and fighting white boys at the Wysor Theatre. He had never been to reform school. He, too, nonchalantly strolled before the judge, and he received a month in the county jail. Then it was our turn. With head lowered, I moved slowly forward. My body trembled as I contemplated reform school or jail. Mike swaggered up beside me, jutting out his chin. As I glanced at Mike, I saw a slight sneer on his face. Wild with panic, I wondered why he didn't realize that was exactly what had sent Ken and Sonny to jail. Fortunately, the judge was glancing at papers on his desk. As we stood together in front of the bench, I nudged Mike with my elbow. The judge turned to us.

"I hope you both realize what a dangerous situation you created by throwing rocks at the train," the judge began. "A window in the engine compartment was broken. The engineer almost lost control. Even if neither of you threw rocks at the engine, you were with these two other little thugs, and railroad property was damaged. You are fully responsible for the broken window and everything that might have resulted from that act. We simply cannot tolerate such reckless conduct and I think—"

Captain Guzzi of the Juvenile Division, who up to then had remained silent during the proceedings, suddenly stood.

"Your Honor, if I might interrupt."

"Yes, Captain Guzzi?"

"Your Honor, I would like to say something before you decide what to do with the Williams boys. Frankly, I'm surprised by their involvement. They're good boys. When their father worked at City Hall, they spent all their free time here helping him mop and clean. They've never been in any trouble before, and I'm sure they won't be again. I urge you to give that serious consideration."

The judge was silent for a moment, then turned to us.

"Considering what Captain Guzzi said, I see no purpose in sending you to jail. I'm going to release you, but if you come before me again I won't be so lenient. I want each of you personally to share in restitution for the broken window. Case dismissed."

We left the room in confusion. Though I was overjoyed to be free, the harsh punishment of Ken and Sonny deeply troubled me. Miss Dora said we were lucky Captain Guzzi spoke for us. I agreed and promised myself that would be the last time I would ever be in juvenile or any other court. Mike, on the other hand, was full of defiance.

"They don't send you away the first time you're arrested. I've got at least two or three more chances," he boasted.

From that point Mike became increasingly rebellious. He began smoking around the house, strictly against Miss Dora's rules. When she caught him she issued a stern ultimatum. That stopped the smoking, but Mike began to resent her control. All of a sudden he decided he didn't want to live with us any longer. He began sleeping at Grandma's, but Dad wouldn't share the couch with him and told him to either go home or elsewhere. Mike then moved in with one of Dad's gambling buddies. Sometimes we didn't know where he was for days. Though he made it to school fairly regularly, Miss Dora had no idea where he spent his time, and Dad didn't seem to care. Finally, Miss Dora threatened to have Dad charged with neglect if he didn't get Mike under control. A couple of days later Mike returned home.

Then Dad announced he wanted to spend more time with us. At first I was pleased, but soon realized he meant he wanted us to follow him on his rounds. One day we stopped at Joe's Rib Joint on First Street across from the Projects.

Through the plate glass window I saw a crowd gathered to sample Joe's legendary barbecue. The sweet smell of his famous sauce greeted us as we walked through the door. The crowd was mostly middle-aged men and a few younger women. The jukebox blasted Little Richard's "Tutti Fruitti."

All eyes were on Mattie, a willowy brown-skinned girl, dancing on the shiny linoleum floor. Her body moved in perfect time to the staccato beat of the music. She ground her hips toward the men sitting at the counter, and drew a chorus of "Shake that thang, Momma!" Then she turned her behind toward them. Joe, the "Barbecue King" himself, joined in with a "Good golly, Miss Molly!"

When the music died, Joe shouted at her, "Honey, I got your ribs done, but I don't think you need no hot sauce!"

The room filled with laughter.

As Mattie left the floor, Joe hailed Dad from behind the counter. Joe looked like he sampled almost as much of his barbecue as he sold. His sauce-stained apron barely covered his six-foot, 280-pound frame. He smiled easily, but everyone knew no one caused problems at Joe's place. If his size didn't intimidate troublemakers, the baseball bat he kept under the counter did the trick.

My eyes alternated between Mattie's gorgeous behind and the plate of ribs in front of her. Dad headed to a table near the front. Sitting alone and picking at the remains of barbecue on his plate was "Bear." Despite the cool evening, sweat dripped down the sides of his ink-black face. I noticed an empty bottle of hot sauce in front of him. "What you got to drink, Bear?" Dad asked as he reached the table.

"You know I ain't drinking, Buster. Let me buy you and the boys a Coke."

Bear shouted an order for Cokes, and within a minute Joe lumbered around the corner of the counter clutching three bottles by the neck. As I guzzled the Coke, my eyes remained fixated on Mattie devouring the ribs on her plate. After a few sips, Dad spoke.

"Why don't you boys show Bear your appreciation for the Cokes by reciting the poems you learned last week?"

A poem or a famous speech was always the beginning of our "show." Dad shouted for Joe to unplug the jukebox, and surprisingly, he did so. Then Dad stood. With a flourish of his hat and a bow to the crowd, he began, "Ladies and Gentlemen, tonight I am proud to present my two sons in performance. Greg, my white boy, is going to quote Lincoln's Gettysburg Address, and Mike, the nigger and small-time hustler—just like me—will exhibit the same athletic prowess I did during my Golden Gloves days."

Standing self-consciously, I softly began.

"Four score and seven years ago—"

"Stand straight and speak up, Greg, no one can hear you." He jerked my shoulders, and I gazed into the face of the crowd. Even Mattie turned away from her barbecue to listen. Dad, seated next to Bear, grinned from ear to ear as I continued.

". . . our forefathers brought forth on this earth a new nation conceived in liberty and dedicated to the proposition that all men are created equal. . . ."

When I finished, Mike, only eleven but much stronger than I, did fifty push-ups, the wrestler's bridge, stood on his head, and walked the length of the room on his hands. That always impressed the crowd. They clapped for Mike, but Dad realized he had to do more to hold their attention. He grabbed each of us by the arm, pulled us to our feet, and shouted, "Okay! Boys, now square off! We're gonna see who is the best man. The nigger or the white boy."

Sullenly, I stood, hands at my sides. Mike crouched, fists in front of his face.

"Put up your dukes," said Dad.

I made no move.

"Put up your dukes!" he ordered harshly.

Still, I did nothing. He slapped me across the back of my head. The sound echoed around the room.

"Listen to me, you little peckawood, when I tell you something, do it! Now fight!"

I held up my fists and began circling. Mike hit me on the shoulder and in the chest. I didn't return the punches, hoping Dad would allow us to quit. Then he could crow about how Mike was going to be Muncie's next Golden Gloves champion. As I stalled, Dad slapped me on the side of the face. Full of anger at Dad, I charged Mike and pummeled him. He covered his face, crying. Then he grabbed me and we fell backward, knocking over chairs and tables.

Joe finally shouted, "Sit the boys down, Buster!"

Dad got up from his seat and yanked us apart. He pushed us into chairs at Bear's table. "Mike, you can't fight worth a damn. You're too much of a sissy. Greg kicked your ass."

Mike sat sullenly. Tears came to his eyes as Dad turned his attention to Bear.

"Say, Bear, didn't you enjoy that performance? What about giving the boys something?"

Reluctantly, Bear responded, "Here's a dollar, boys. Buy yourself some barbecue."

Before Bear replaced his wallet, Dad leaned across Bear's plate. "What about lettin' me hold a dollar for a little taste?"

"Shit, Buster, I got sixty-five cents left, that's what wine costs, and don't ask me for another goddamn thing. Man, you always got your hand in my pocket."

Dad jerked back, held up the palms of his hands, and protested, with great indignation. "Wait a minute, Bear, you have witnessed my generosity on many occasions. When I have funds to treat the crowd, my hand is never slow. I've never been a parasite and it's too late to begin now. I'm temporarily insolvent because my ship hasn't come in. When it does, we'll all be ridin' high."

"Buster, the only thing I ever see you ridin' high on is other people's money," said Bear, laughing.

The chair screeched as Dad stood to respond to the insult. "If you feel that way, keep your money." He shoved the sixty-five cents for the wine and the dollar for barbecue back in front of Bear.

Now, I was mad. Dad continued, "I don't have to sacrifice my dignity and manhood for a handout. But this is a bitter pill to swallow after all our years of friendship. You remember when I brought those guns back from the army after World War II. We were expecting race riots and all hell to break loose in Muncie? If that means nothing, take your money back."

He spoke with the fervor of righteous indignation.

Bear, totally exasperated, finally pleaded with Dad, "Please Buster, keep the money. You're a drunk, but you're a good man. There's not a man in Muncie who don't respect your intelligence. If you hadn't been a nigger, I bet you'd been governor of Indiana."

Later, as we were leaving Joe's, I complained to Dad, "Why do you call me white? I'm not white. And Mike's not a nigger. Miss Dora said being a nigger ain't got nothing to do with color. It's a bad, low-down person."

"Billy, you're supposed to be a smart boy, but you haven't learned a damn thing in Muncie. Don't you remember the only time I was somebody was when I was white? In Muncie, I'm just another nigger. You're smart enough to make it out of this hellhole. Your brother's not. He's gonna be a no-'count black bastard just like me, who fucks up everything. Oh hell, he's gonna learn how to hustle and make a buck. I'll teach him that, but he's never gonna climb to the top of the mountain. You need to be a white boy to do that. Mike's already too much of a hustler to change."

Turning, I looked at Mike walking with his head down. I was furious with Dad. Of the two of us, Mike needed the most support. He ached for affection and praise, and constantly suffered from our mother's absence. In the first year after she left there wasn't a single day he didn't mention her name, and he often cried out for her at night. Dad even told Mike his teachers said he had a low IQ. He was in the fifth grade, yet read at the second grade level. His school struggles puzzled me because Dad often taught him long poems, which he memorized with ease. In retrospect, it's clear that he had all the classic symptoms of a learning disability, dyslexia, but in those years little was known about it. Teachers always compared us—me, the sucessful student, and Mike, the failure. Now even Dad did it.

"Mike ain't dumb and I ain't white," I protested.

*Whap!* Dad smacked me on the cheek. "You're a white motherfucker whether you like it or not. Come on back in here and let these niggers tell you both what you really are."

Mike, head down, turned toward Joe's, but I stood anchored to the sidewalk. Dad grabbed my arm and dragged me inside. "Bobby," he said, intruding on a group of ten men and women placing bets with the numbers runner and the repository of wisdom of that night's group. "Greg doesn't think he's a white boy. He says he's just like me and Mike. Tell him he ain't a nigger, even if he wants to be one."

"Buster's right. Him and Mike are gamblers, and hustlers. You okay, Greg, but this ain't you, man. You belong with them smart white folks."

"But I don't want to be white."

"Boy, you got a choice. Take it, and get your ass on outta here!"

I hadn't wanted to be colored, but too much had happened to me in Muncie to be a part of the white world that had rejected me so completely. I believed that most of Dad's problems stemmed from his attempt to "pass for white" in Virginia. The charade created incredible turmoil for him. "Passing" hadn't worked. Why did he want it for me? I also knew being black didn't mean I couldn't be successful. Just the week before, Dad told me about one of the most famous Negroes in America—Walter White. White had been executive director of the NAACP for ten years until he died in 1955. He traveled throughout the country speaking against prejudice and discrimination. Negro communities around the nation greeted him with open arms. Yet he had blue eyes, blond hair, and, most of all, white skin. He was only $5/32$ Negro, but he was "black." If Walter White could choose to remain in the black community and make a difference, so could I. No matter what Bobby, Dad, or anyone else said or thought. I knew who I was and what I wanted to be.

# Chapter 13 Go for It!

Wilson Junior High School was a long walk down South Walnut Street, past the hillbilly bars, past the Park & Shop, even way beyond Ninth Street, which ran east to Garfield School. Brian Settles and I, along with three boys from the Projects, gazed at the unfamiliar Knights of Columbus Hall, Dairy Queen, and Owl Drug Store. After Twelfth Street the area was mostly residential. Tiny frame houses sat close to the sidewalk. Cars full of white men in denim jackets headed to Muncie's south-side factories. All at once, Wilson Junior High School loomed against the morning sky. Three stories of blood-red brick towered over us. It stretched back from the street for almost a block.

Silence fell over the white kids crowding the sidewalk as we sought refuge with other black students gathered at an entryway. From the safety of our small group I surveyed the surroundings. Across the street was a small diner. A gang of white boys stood in front smoking cigarettes. Many sported pegged blue jeans and black leather boots. A few wore silver-studded motorcycle jackets. Some of the boys had long greasy hair with ducktails and sideburns. Just as I smirked at the Elvis imitators, my eyes connected with one short, squat member of the group. His hair was matted with oil except for a lone four-inch strand that sliced down the side of his pimpled face. A pack of cigarettes protruded from the tightly rolled sleeve of his white T-shirt. He stared at me, perhaps wondering why I stood with the black students. His puzzled expression quickly changed to hostility. He held his fist up and flipped his middle finger. His lips curled in a snarl, but I was able to decipher my welcome to Wilson. "Fuck you!"

That was my first encounter with the "Shed Town" boys. Located five blocks southwest of Wilson, Shed Town was an all-white poverty-stricken area of ramshackle housing, unpaved streets, and outdoor privies. There were three places in Muncie where blacks from the Projects and whites from Shed Town met—at Wilson, at Central High School, and in the factories and foundries. By the time blacks and low-income whites toiled together for survival in Muncie's sweatshops, economic realities tempered the hostility, but Wilson was a racial powder keg. Though there was a large group of middle-class white kids at Wilson, they sought mostly to stay out of the crossfire. Between the Shed Town kids and black students, it was all-out war.

The morning classes were a blur as I wondered how I was going to carve a niche for myself in such a tension-filled environment. Descending the basement stairs to the recreation room following lunch, the sounds of Elvis Presley's rendition of "Big Mama" Thornton's song "Ain't Nothing But a Hound Dog" thundered from the jukebox. No black kids would be dancing to Elvis, I thought. Sure enough, the only dancers were white. White students stared at me as I crossed the floor and joined the black students in a far corner.

Elvis's song died, followed by "Rockin' Robin," later remade by the Jackson Five but at that time another "white" tune. Still no black students moved toward the dance floor. We were told the principal refused to allow the Coasters, the Marquees, Bo Diddley, or even Chuck Berry on the jukebox. According to the ninth graders, he said they were "too suggestive." Two black ninth grade boys interrupted us with a more urgent concern. The word was spreading like wildfire that Shed Town kids planned to attack us after school. "Don't nobody leave by themselves. Bring whatever you can find to fight with."

When the final bell rang that afternoon, crowds of students converged on the front door. I gave grim nods to the other black students gathered by the exit as we searched the scraggly bushes in front of the building for sticks, bottles, and rocks. Shed Town boys massed in front of the diner. Racial epithets flew back and forth across the street. The Shed Town boys moved down the grassy knoll toward us. Just then I saw Captain Guzzi, driving the familiar green Juvenile Division police car, turn the corner followed by two other patrol cars. Relieved there would be no fight that afternoon, I followed Brian to the locker room for football tryouts.

Flag football was the game in elementary school. Now was the time for shoulder pads, helmets, and cleats. On the Garfield team I had been the center, but it didn't seem important enough. I wanted to be a leader. After a few warm-up drills, the ninth grade coach, taking over for the day, asked for quarterback volunteers. My arm shot up. He closely scanned the crowd and selected three boys: I dejectedly dropped my arm. Brian addled up beside me and whispered, "Greg, they ain't giving up shit unless you take it." Just then the coach called for more volunteers. Brian nudged me and I raced forward. Five perfect twenty-yard passes, and then I tossed a wobbly ball that fell far short of my intended receiver. Immediately, the coach complained about the bad throw, but he didn't replace me. He kept muttering about the errant pass, and I promised myself I would not make another mistake. I didn't. By the end of practice, I was the seventh grade quarterback.

About the middle of the season, I sat in the locker room tying my cleats when Willie, a neighborhood buddy, approached me. Already dressed, he leaned over and whispered that the coach had asked him to "identify the colored boys" from his list of players. "When I pointed to your name, Greg, the coach acted like I kicked him in the balls."

Willie continued, "I told him your daddy was yellow, and your Grandma was brown, so I was sure you was colored. He ain't happy about having a nigger for quarterback. Watch yourself, Greg."

If I thought I had learned one thing in Muncie, it was that race didn't matter on the playing fields. Everywhere else it did, but in sports the only goal was winning. However, for the first time that very day the coaches began to alternate me with a Shed Town boy. They painstakingly repeated every play with my newly recruited rival. They devoted so much time to the other quarterback, the entire team was puzzled.

For about a week I fumed as the coach pampered his new protégé. One afternoon Brian jogged behind the team huddle and stood beside me. Dirt and sweat covered his face, hidden under the helmet. He said, "Don't let that motherfucka take your job. It belongs to you!"

That was easy for him to say. Although we were the same height, Brian outweighed me by twenty-five pounds, and he liked to hit people. I didn't. Standing there I realized I didn't even like football. Maybe I should quit, I thought, and turned to look at Brian once more. He must have read my thoughts, and shook his head. I realized he was right. I would fight.

I approached practice with new purpose. When the coaches taught my rival techniques never showed me, I scrutinized every move, every nuance. Then I practiced them myself. I became more of a student of the game than I had ever been. My eyes were constantly on my rival—watching—waiting—looking for weaknesses. I volunteered to play defense, something I had never done before. Though outweighed by the linemen, I fought my way through them to the Shed Town boy, dishing out as much punishment as possible. Soon he began to flinch when he saw me coming. Pain vibrated from my shoulder pads when I hit him, but I was consoled by the knowledge that it was nothing compared to what I inflicted upon him. When it was my turn to quarterback, I stood behind the offensive line taking the full brunt of the onrushing tacklers to gain extra time to complete my passes. The afternoon the coaches stopped play to order me out of the way of tacklers as soon as I released the ball, I knew I had won. They didn't want the first-string quarterback injured. After that, the only time my quarterback job was in jeopardy was when another event occurred far away from the football field.

The night before one late-season game, I played basketball at the Madison Street playground. Toward the end of the evening, an argument with a younger boy turned into a shoving match. He was much smaller, and I had no desire to fight him, nor did he appear to want to fight me. So after an exchange of obligatory threats and curses, I turned to leave. As I walked off the basketball court, he hit me in the back of the head with an empty beer can. The blow didn't hurt, so I gave only a halfhearted chase, more to please the onlookers than to try to catch him. When he dashed across Madison Street and disappeared into the white Projects, I decided he'd have enough trouble over there, and I left for home. On the way I stopped by Grandma's. As I leaned under her kitchen faucet for a drink, she walked into the room and screamed.

"Billy, what happened?"

Reaching back, the wound felt wet and sticky. My hand was covered with blood. Grandma washed the wound with a damp rag.

At school the next morning my head began throbbing, and I went to the nurse. She immediately summoned the football coach. "Why didn't you go to a doctor to get it stitched up?" he demanded.

"We don't have any money."

"What the hell do you mean you don't have any money? What kind of crap is that?"

"Coach, my dad ain't working."

"We have an important game this afternoon. Come on, let's get it fixed."

He drove me across town to Dr. Botkin's office. The doctor decided it was too late to stitch the cut, so he placed a special bandage over the three-inch gash. I would have a permanent scar behind my ear as a reminder of the beer can episode. "Doc" Botkin explained that a hard blow to the head might reopen the wound, but if I put a thick sponge over the cut and taped it on my head, I might be able to play. That afternoon the coach gathered sponges and bandages from everywhere in the school, and we were in the dressing room an hour before the game cutting and taping them to my head. I could barely squeeze on my helmet when he finished.

The Madison Heights Pirates roared onto the field. They were some of the biggest junior high boys I had ever seen. Several must have been over two hundred pounds. Their bulk and the ominous skulls and crossbones painted on their black helmets made my stomach churn. They kicked off to us, and raced down the field growling and shouting. I picked up the ball on the thirty-yard line, hurtling straight up the field. Three linemen, each outweighing me by at least forty pounds, converged toward me, on a collision course. I gritted my teeth and pointed my head to the biggest guy's stomach. *Boom!* My helmet flew off on impact, and I ended up on the bottom of a five-hundred-pound-plus heap of flesh and pads. Wobbling from the pile, I struggled to force on the helmet. The opposing players fell silent. My heavily bandaged head made it look like I belonged in the intensive care ward of the hospital rather than on the football field. We beat the Pirates by forty points. I was learning a lesson from athletics that was to carry over in so many other aspects of my life and times in Muncie. Something was starting to grow inside of me that would absolutely never let me give up or quit. In later years I sometimes wondered if that trait was a blessing or a curse.

Wilson's racial tension was fueled by older white dropouts, who hovered around the school eager for an opportunity to prove their manhood. They stood ready to enforce the cardinal rule: "Black boys do not talk to, flirt with, or date white girls." The girls perched on the concrete steps in front of the "greasy spoon" diner were an identical version of the boys: pale and pimply-faced, with cigarettes hanging limply from their mouths. It was no sacrifice to never talk to any of them. In fact, I wasn't interested in any girls, black or white. I had taken to heart Dad's admonition that I must be single-minded to reach my goals.

That fall, Brian began to pester me about a party at the Boys' Club, a youth center on South Madison Street. The party didn't appeal to me, and it was only after Brian accused me of not liking girls that I realized I had to take action. Less than a week remained before the event. As I waited to play basketball at the Madison Street "Y" one afternoon after school, I wondered how I would find a date. Three junior high school girls were talking courtside. Jane was a tall, chocolate-brown-skinned girl with short hair and a round cheerful face. She wore white hiphuggers that revealed the attractive contours of her body and a yellow halter top covering her full breasts. As I studied her I began to understand why she distracted so many of the basketball players. Mayme, my classmate from Garfield days, was slightly taller than I, and solidly built. Though always friendly to me, she could be tough and aggressive. In the short time we had been at Wilson, I saw Mayme stand toe to toe against some of the white boys I avoided. I was often glad to join her on walks home from Wilson. Lucy, the third girl, had attracted my attention earlier in the summer during Friday night playground dances. There wasn't a dance step she didn't know. She spun, twisted, and boogied across the floor. Guys literally lined up for the slow dances. Lucky partners were molded against her body and they moved together as if connected at the hip. Those slow dances never failed to produce beads of sweat on her partner's face. As I thought of her, I remembered one summer evening I overheard her embarrass one shabbily dressed boy who had the nerve to ask her for a dance. Sobered by that recollection, I decided to avoid the risk of being the object of her cruel humor.

When Mayme and Lucy were distracted by a friend, I approached Jane. We stood side by side, our eyes on the basketball court. Fearful of facing her, I blurted out my plea for a date. Her head snapped toward me. I stared hopefully at her for an agonizing few seconds. She zinged back a loud and clear "No." Hunching my shoulders, I slunk to the other end of the basketball court nursing my rejection.

The next afternoon the three girls were again on the playground talking animatedly. As I passed, they fell silent. Trying to appear nonchalant, but certain they were ridiculing my ineptitude, I focused on the game. Later I saw Mayme alone, and sauntered to the edge of the court beside her. This time I tried small talk first, but I wasn't very successful. Finally, I just blurted out my request. The slightest breeze could have knocked me over when she whispered, "Okay."

Later that evening Mayme's mother called. "Were you serious?" she asked. "You weren't playing with Mayme, were you?" She wanted to know if I really intended to escort Mayme to the Boys' Club party.

I tried to figure out the reason for the call. Mayme's mom knew my dad. She knew who I was. The only explanation that made sense to me was that this was Mayme's first date, just like mine.

"I just wanted to check." she said. "Mayme's looking forward to it. Bye."

Now that I had a date, I realized I needed to buy some decent clothes to wear. I thought Aunt Bess would be my best prospect for a loan. Uncle Osco rocked in his favorite porch chair while keeping an eye on the playground softball game. He let fly a long stream of dark-brown tobacco juice into the can beside the rocker as I opened the gate. "Bessie ain't home," he said. I looked carefully at him. Dad said he was so tight he could "squeeze a buffalo off a nickel."

"Uncle Osco, can you loan me ten dollars? I need some clothes. I'm looking for a second job. I'll pay you back a dollar a week when I find one."

"That's a lot of money, boy," he said, paused for a moment, then bent over, pulled on his tattered slippers and walked into the house. He passed the window in his bedroom and headed toward the old wardrobe. Although the location of his money was supposed to be a well-guarded secret, Mike and I knew he kept it hidden in an old Stetson hatbox on top of the wardrobe. Leaning toward the window, I listened intently for clues. Soon I heard him groan and knew he must be reaching for the box.

"You're different than Buster and Mike," he said when he handed me the money. "Them rascals never pay you back. Man, I loaned 'em money like a fool. But all you have to do is tell me what'cha need. Greg, I know you won't let me down."

The fresh smell of denim filled the air in the jeans section of the J. C. Penney store. I searched through six piles of jeans before I found anything close to my size. In exasperation I bought a pair with a twenty-six-inch waist and thirty-inch length. The length was close, but they hung off my waist. The tag indicated there would be some shrinkage. I then spotted a shiny orange long-sleeved shirt with black quarter-inch stitching on the collar. When I realized it could be worn outside the trousers to conceal the loose waistband of the jeans, I knew I was set. At home I carefully hid the clothes so Mike wouldn't wear them before the big day.

At last, the evening of the party arrived. After dressing I even went by Dad's for a dab of after-shave. Then it was off to the Projects. Mayme answered the door. She wore a crisply pressed blouse with a full skirt. Every curl of her short black hair looked as if it had been given personal attention. I even noticed a trace of lipstick and darkened eyebrows.

We walked south along busy Madison Street. Mayme spoke quietly, and I began to see a new dimension to her personality. She revealed a softness I had not seen before. She spoke wistfully of the summer tea parties our neighbor Mrs. Poole gave for her daughter, our classmate Anne. Mrs. Poole arranged outdoor tables and chairs in her backyard with freshly cut flowers, delicate glassware, and even china. Once, following a day of caddying for Mr. Poole, I was invited to the tea party. The lemon meringue pie was unforgettable.

Any time a fight at Wilson appeared imminent, Mayme raced to Anne's side to shield her during confrontations with the white kids. I teased her about protecting Anne just so she would be invited to the tea parties.

As we laughed, I began to notice cars slowing down and drivers gawking at us from the heavily traveled street. Were we laughing too loud? Then I realized—they were shocked to see a "white" boy on South Madison Street with a black girl. Though neither of us said a word, Mayme too sensed the surrounding hostility. The hardness returned to her face, and we began to walk faster and speak in monosyllables. A teenager leaned out a car window and shrieked, "Nigger lover!" Other drivers honked their horns.

By the time we reached the Boys' Club, I felt like we had run a gauntlet. Couples gathered in front of the building waiting for the doors to open. I recognized several white classmates from my Garfield days and, eager for a friendly greeting, waved to one, but he stared past me. As we drew closer I nodded to another, but still received no response.

Inside the building, bright red-and-white streamers hung from the ceiling. Over a dozen cardboard carnival booths were scattered around the area. Leaving the animosity of Madison Street behind us, Mayme and I were soon swept up in the amusement of the evening. We laughed at each other's clumsy efforts at bobbing for apples and tossing the rings for small prizes. With Mayme, I began to feel I could make mistakes and enjoy the games without being called childish. We were giggling so much that I doubled over. Yet, I began to notice that, even among our classmates, unfriendly faces followed our every move. Soon their antagonism engulfed us, but we struggled to maintain our smiles as we doggedly went from game to game. It was hard to keep up the facade, and I was relieved when it was time to leave.

After saying good night to Mayme, I walked to the playground. Alone, I sat on a bench overlooking Madison Street, watching the cars race by. No heads turned toward me. Now I was an anonymous speck of salt under the dim streetlight. I wrestled with the fact that Muncie would not permit me to date white girls, and apparently couldn't tolerate seeing me with black girls either. Muncie's white community would only be satisfied with an inconspicuous and unobtrusive eunuch. My very existence made people uncomfortable and shattered too many racial taboos. Dating for me was going to be like swimming in shark-infested waters. I would have to give it up. Just as I was ready to yield, I remembered one afternoon earlier in the summer when I accompanied Miss Dora on a visit to Sister Johnson.

It was a long walk to a section of town called "Industry," where a few blacks lived. When we arrived, Sister Johnson offered us blackberry pie and lemonade. I quickly became bored listening to the two women talk guardedly about backsliding church members. When Sister Johnson's daughter, Hattie, returned from a trip to the grocery store, the women whisked us outside to the backyard. As we walked out the door, Sister Johnson leaned toward Miss Dora and began church gossip in earnest. With her reputation for long-windedness, I knew we would be lucky to be home before nightfall.

Hattie was a lovely, honey-skinned girl with sparkling green eyes. In church she was shy and quiet, and her folks *never* let her come to the playground. They had the reputation of being the strictest parents in the church. The backyard was large and grassy except for a spot near the alley where there was a swing and a wooden shed. Hattie hopped on it.

"Push me, Greg," she ordered.

Grabbing the rope, I tugged, then pushed hard on the wooden seat. She swung forward and floated back. Again, I reached out to her. This time my hands slipped off the wood and slid across her backside.

Giggling, she said, "Careful, Greg." Encouraged, I touched her again when she swung back to me. I began to slow the swing and slide my hands around her thighs. The swing was almost at a standstill when she hopped off and skipped toward the shed with an inviting smile. I cast a nervous glance toward the house and followed her.

The smell of sawdust was in the air, and quarter-inch spaces between the wall slats filled the room with ribbons of sunlight. Fresh-cut firewood and kindling was stacked neatly against one wall. No sooner had I closed the door than Hattie threw her arms around me. She planted a kiss on my lips, and I buzzed from the pleasant, moist sensation. She held me to her body till I felt her warmth. "Open your mouth," she commanded. I complied, and she pushed her tongue inside. I was tingling in places I didn't even know tingled. She whispered, "Wanta see my titties?"

Breathless, I managed a nod. She unbuttoned her blouse and revealed two small firm breasts. A nipple swelled with my touch. She grabbed me again for another open-mouth kiss. I drew her closer and began to slide her dress up her thighs. My hands reached soft nylon panties. As my knees began to shake, I clutched her for support. Her hand slithered down my pants. Just when she touched me a distant noise pierced the fog that enveloped us.

"Hattie! Hattie! Sister Dora's got to go! You all come on back to the house."

She jerked away, buttoned her blouse, and was out of the shed in a flash. Trembling violently, I tucked in my shirt, and stood in the shed for almost a minute adjusting my pants.

That night as I sat alone in the park, enticing thoughts of Hattie and Mayme filled me with determination not to give up girls—no matter how angry it made anyone.

Shortly after the first of December, Dad lay on the couch at Grandma's during one of our regular visits there. Suddenly, he said to Mike and me, "Boys, there's one thing I want to tell you. I've decided not to buy you any Christmas presents this year."

We both looked at him in silence. Christmas in Muncie had been disappointing enough, but were we to forgo even Dad's famous rummage sale "treasures"?

"Don't look so disappointed. I've figured out a way for you to have presents. But you're going to have to rely on your own ingenuity instead of my generosity."

Mike and I gave each other knowing looks. We recognized the pitch. Dad had a job for us.

"Yesterday I hitchhiked to Indianapolis and bought some Christmas cards wholesale. I'm willing to let you sell them and you can earn enough to buy your own presents."

Rising to leave, I told him selling Christmas cards didn't appeal to me, and he could forget about giving me any presents. However, once Dad had a moneymaking scheme, there was no escape.

"Sit down," he ordered. "I'm going to teach you the principles of self-motivation and good salesmanship whether you want to learn them or not. It's time you started paying your own way around here and not relying on Miss Dora or me to look after your every need and desire.

"Early tomorrow morning I want you to go downtown along West Jackson Street. Those white folks have some money, but they are not wealthy enough to be offended by two raggedy-assed boys coming to their doors. If you're not successful there, go on across the bridge toward the university. Those folks have more money, but probably won't be as receptive to your hustle."

That Christmas, my dream was a pair of Hood basketball shoes just like those worn by many of the boys on the seventh grade team.

Though similar to the popular Converse All-Stars, the Hoods had a neat raised leather pad over the toe of the shoe and a sharp quarter-inch cut just before the tongue. My teammates claimed the shoes not only looked classier than Converse, they helped you jump higher as well.

Early Saturday morning Mike and I traipsed up and down the West Jackson Street neighborhood knocking on door after door. Mike had those appealing brown eyes and a special knack for selling. He was sold out by lunchtime. My pitch wasn't quite as effective, but after every sale I counted my money to see if I had enough for the shoes. Mike agreed to help me, and soon I had reached my goal.

"You know we're supposed to take the money to Dad first."

"I'm not gonna do it," I said, tossing him the canvas bag, still half filled with cards.

"I'm gonna tell Daddy on you right now," he said. "I bet you get a whippin'."

"I don't care if I do," I lied.

As I headed downtown, Mike raced home. The clerk handed me a pair of size-nine Hoods, pure white except for a blue line around the top of the rubber soles. The leather toe pad gleamed in the fluorescent light of the store. I could hardly contain myself as the clerk laboriously laced the shoes. I slipped my foot inside and it felt like I was stepping into a velvet cloud.

Carefully, I gave them back to the clerk. He placed them in the box and I handed him eight dollars and fifty cents, all in coins. It was a happy walk through town, but as I turned down the railroad tracks toward home, I was overcome by guilt, and I decided to stop at Grandma's and face Dad.

"What in the hell do you think you're doing spending my money?" Dad boomed. "I should whip your ass. Did you think I was giving you the cards free? I want the money I spent, not to mention a return on my investment for my time and labor going to Indianapolis."

Walking toward him at the table, I said, "I'm sorry. Do you want my shoes?" I placed them in front of him.

"No, I don't want your shoes, goddammit!" he said, knocking the package to the floor. I kneeled to pick them up and looked toward him.

"Do you want me to take them back, then?"

"No, I don't want you to take them back. The more sacrifices I make for you boys, the less you appreciate them. You're just like your momma. You don't appreciate a goddamn thing I do for you. I should have left both of you long ago. But no, I stick around here to help you out and what do I get in return? Absolutely nothing. You boys don't do a thing for me, and think of all the opportunities I've forsaken for you. I'll leave Muncie and let you two see how well you get along on your own."

Mike moved toward Dad. Tears streamed down his face.

"Daddy, don't leave," he cried.

Dad roughly shoved him back. "Get away from me with that shit. This is the final straw. I'm tired of having the responsibility of two ungrateful little peckawoods."

Too proud to beg, I stood motionless, but Mike, who had done nothing wrong, continued to plead.

"Please, Daddy, don't leave us. We promise to be good. What can we do? I'll sell all the cards myself."

"Neither one of you can make me change my mind. I'm so mad that I could bite a ten-penny nail in two. I invested my last five dollars in those cards, and now I don't have shit but what Mike brought home." I had rarely seen Dad so angry. Mike, Grandma, and I stood there quietly waiting to see what would happen. Finally, Dad faced us. "You boys are going to church to ask forgiveness," he said. He stopped pacing and turned to look out the window of the shack.

"This is Saturday night. No churches are open," I said hopefully.

"What about Reverend Reese's across the street from Miss Dora's?"

"I guess it's open," I admitted.

"Well, get up there and pray to God for guidance. Ask him how you are going to survive Muncie without me to support you. How you gonna be somebody without me? Now get out of my face. I might have pulled myself together again if you two hadn't been such a burden."

As Reverend Reese delivered his sermon that night to the ten people scattered about the room, my mind was elsewhere. I wondered why I had been so driven to buy the shoes. As selfish as Dad could be, I couldn't bear the thought of him abandoning us. Although he gave us little support, his presence made the uncharted waters of Muncie easier to navigate. I regretted that I had allowed myself to be controlled by my compulsion to get what I wanted.

The next morning we walked to Grandma's after Sunday school, dragging our feet. Was Dad gone already? Walking through the door, we sensed a different mood. Wine bottles littered the floor. Mike's money was gone. Dad was trying to sober up. Now it was his turn to feel guilty. Mike was the one without a Christmas present that year.

# Chapter 14

# Big Shoulders

As my ninth grade year began at Wilson, I had one goal above all else—to excel in school regardless of the obstacles. Dad said education was the key to success, and I believed him. It was the only way I knew to escape the harshness of Muncie. Long, long hours passed as I hunched over the card table in my room reading history, drafting English compositions, and struggling to understand science.

One day after school while I worked feverishly to finish an algebra assignment so I could study for a biology quiz, I received an urgent call.

"Get over here," Brian insisted. "Paula ain't gonna wait all day to give you some. You gonna be third."

"I don't wanta be third."

"Lester is already here. You got to be third."

"I'm not gonna be third."

"For someone who ain't ever got any you sure are particular. Just get your butt over here before Momma and Vicki get home."

The phone buzzed in my ear as I stared out the living room window toward Brian's house, trying to decide what to do. A flood of emotions overcame me. Fantasies of Paula's lovely brown-skinned body filled my mind. Sharing her with two other boys however, troubled me. But my adolescent hormones prevailed and I pulled on my jacket and stepped onto the porch. As the chill of the damp afternoon penetrated my body, from deep in my subconscious Dad's warning surged to my brain. "Don't get any girls pregnant. Don't get any girls pregnant." His nasal intonation of "prag-nant" made it sound so distasteful. Every time Dad was sober, I heard the story about how the pregnancy of a girlfriend from Whitely, my half brother Jimmy's mother, ended his college career. According to Dad, her brother came after him with a "shotgun marriage" in mind. Dad hopped the next freight out of Muncie and stayed with friends in Milwaukee for almost a year. When he returned to Muncie, it was to wheel hot glass from factory furnaces. His college days were over.

That afternoon as I lingered on the steps trying to decide whether to join my buddies or not, I couldn't shake Dad's mournful description of college plans gone awry. As I closed the door and dropped on the couch, the phone buzzed again—ten rings. I ignored it.

Mike was always far more worldly. One Saturday afternoon as we attended the twenty-five-cent matinee at the Wysor Theatre I realized how different we really were. Mike, Brian, and I arrived just as the newsreel clips lit up the room. Brian spied, across the balcony, a Shed Town girl who had spurned him earlier in the year. Mike claimed the girl was interested in him. "No way, man. She don't like your ugly ass," protested Brian.

Rising to the challenge, Mike strolled across the theater. From the reflected light of the movie screen we could see her smile as he sat next to her. We could hardly keep our eyes on the Buck Rogers serial flashing in front of us as Mike slipped his arm around the girl, and was soon kissing her. During intermission, he followed her from the balcony. Mike caressed her behind and winked to us as he passed.

Every time the door opened during the second feature I snapped around to look for Mike. He didn't return. After the movie we found him standing under the marquee puffing a cigarette and grinning triumphantly.

"You didn't get any. You lying your ass off," contested Brian.

"Yeah I did, right back there in the alley," responded Mike, pointing to the narrow passageway that ran alongside the theater. "And when she got on the bus to Shed Town, I said, 'You just been fucked by a nigger.' "

Mike passed it all off as a joke, but I feared the girl might claim she was raped. Miss Dora and Grandma often recounted how during their youth in the South, young white women frequently lodged false claims of rape. Mike had heard the same stories, but they did not faze him.

All that next week Mike's boldness was the topic of conversation at school. One afternoon as we walked home, Brian, who seemed to be on a constant crusade to help me lose my virginity, lamented, "Why can't you be more like Mike? What's wrong with you, man?" Another friend added, "Even your old man still gets a lot of pussy."

That day we took a different route home from school, north on Walnut to Second Street into the "colored red-light" district. It wasn't much more than a poolroom, Bob's Tavern, and a corner frequented by prostitutes, but fights and stabbings occurred regularly. Less than a year earlier a drinking buddy of Dad's went berserk in the area. Holed up in an abandoned building, he shot and killed a white passerby and held the police at bay for almost an entire day. In the early afternoon, police shouted over the bullhorn that school kids would soon be passing through the area, and they were giving him one last chance to surrender. Apparently, he didn't want to endanger the children, so he put his mouth over the rifle barrel and blew his head off.

We had just turned the corner onto Second Street when the front door of Bob's Tavern flew open. Charlie Leachman, the bartender, had one hand on the back of a man's neck, the other on the seat of his pants. Two steps outside the door, Charlie heaved the drunk into the air. Wincing, I turned aside as the man's face bounced across the cobblestone surface in front of the tavern like a rock skipping across water. How could anyone endure punishment like that? I wondered. The drunk lay on the ground writhing in pain. As we crossed the Mulberry Street intersection, he rolled toward us. It was Dad!

My buddies fell silent. We stepped on the curb. I was amazed to see there was no blood.

Brian glanced toward me. "Need any help, Greg?"

Too embarrassed to respond, I waved them on, wishing that I too could sneak past. Yet at the mention of my name Dad raised his head from the cobblestones and gave me a glassy-eyed stare.

"Greg, come 'mere and help me up," he slurred.

Leaning over, I asked what happened in the bar.

"Charlie got mad 'cause I was beatin' the fellas with the shell game."

One eye was swelling shut. His rummage sale blue serge suit was ripped at the collar and on the sleeve.

"I'm all right," he said, trying to raise himself up on his elbows. He slipped back to the cobblestones and lay there for ten seconds. "You gonna have to carry me home."

I stood in silence.

"Carry me home, goddammit! You think I can walk? Use the fireman's carry. Come on now, Big Shoulders, I got to see Momma before Fred gets her money."

Dad rarely called me "Big Shoulders" unless he wanted something. Most of the time he called Mike and Brian "Big Shoulders," since both of them were much more solidly built and muscular than I. Dad said they could stand toe to toe with anyone—black or white—in Muncie. I always felt I too had "big shoulders," but he just hadn't noticed. I knew I could lift him. I was now nearly six feet tall. I knew the fireman's carry too. During football practice I lugged Brian's 185-pound frame the length of the field. My concern was the embarrassment of carrying Dad past people I knew, but he lay there semiconscious, spittle drooling down his chin.

Angrily, I yanked him to his feet. "Ow!" he squealed, then nearly fell to the sidewalk once more. Leaning underneath him, I pointed my shoulder toward his crotch, took his right ankle, and let him drop across my back. For the first half block he didn't seem much heavier than my football shoulder pads. Some of his wine-drinking buddies stared out John Knight's barbershop window as I passed in full stride. By the time we reached the pool hall, his weight became oppressive. Soon the Projects loomed in the distance. Certain my friends would see me, I dreaded that part of the journey. At Elm Street, I decided that carrying Dad past my buddies' was more than I could endure, and turned north toward the railroad tracks, adding three blocks to our journey. By now Dad felt like a sack of bricks, and I needed a rest. He was semiconscious when I laid him on the rail bed in front of Dague's Coal Yard. I sat beside him to catch my breath. As I looked at him I didn't know whom to feel sorrier for, my father or myself.

Only two more blocks, I thought, and picked him up once again. Near the Madison Street underpass, I saw two friends throwing rocks at bottles perched on the rails. Then I felt a dampness on my shoulder. A few more steps, and I became wetter. Stretching my neck skyward, I looked for clouds. There were none. Then I realized the dampness was only on one shoulder—the one under Dad's crotch. Standing in the middle of the underpass, I wanted to toss him two stories below into Madison Street traffic and be done with him forever. For a brief second I seriously considered it. Instead, I pulled his legs in front of me to hide the stain. That made him much heavier. When I jostled him he began to grumble about being uncomfortable. Soon I carried him almost like a baby, with feet in front of me and head over my shoulder. My friends stared as we approached. They said nothing, and I was thankful. Although I was embarrassed, it was rare for children from the neighborhood to "play the dozens," or ridicule another's family. Passing them with a brief nod, I recalled that an older neighborhood friend once told me the best way to survive Muncie was to find some humor in my misfortune. At age fifteen, I tried mightily but I saw no humor in carrying my drunken father home. Pushing open Miss Lucy's gate with my knee, I dumped Dad in Grandma's dirt yard. He opened his eyes.

"Carry me in the house, dammit!" he yelled as he struggled to all fours like a dog.

"Forget it!" I yelled back. "Get in there yourself."

"You need some pussy to clear up those pimples!" he yelled at me. "Try to be more like your brother and me."

I barged out Grandma's gate into the alley and ripped off my foul-smelling shirt. Bare-chested, I raced home.

With all the locker room talk of sex it was hard not to think about it constantly, and one Saturday afternoon when Hattie and Sister Johnson came to visit, I couldn't think of anything else. Though it had been almost two years since Hattie and I were alone in the woodshed, I often fantasized about her. Her family continued to be very strict and wouldn't permit her to date, not even boys from the church. However, that didn't stop Hattie from flirting with many of us. And with the passage of two years she had ripened into a perfectly sculptured honey-skinned beauty.

That afternoon, she sat alone in our front room while Sister Johnson, Miss Dora, and Grandma gossiped in the kitchen. After greeting the ladies, I felt a deep inner tug to the living room. A rich combination of sensations filled me as I nervously settled on the couch across the room from Hattie. She stood over the furnace register. The warm air blowing into the room lifted her dress ever so slightly, and I could see the beginnings of her thighs. She beckoned me with a subtle tilt of her head and a mischievous smile. I lost all willpower. Slipping off my shoes, I tiptoed across the stiff linoleum floor. A tingle of excitement shot through me as the warm furnace air enveloped us. We embraced in a long kiss over the register.

I stroked her hips as she gave me a teasing look. Another long kiss, and she whispered, "What you got in your pocket, rocks or sticks?"

Perspiration covered us as we stepped away from the heat vent. She settled into the chair. I leaned across the arm, holding on to another kiss. My back ached from the awkward angle, but I refused to let her go. Every nerve in my body seemed to be pulsating frenetically. She looked at my pants as we separated, and giggled. "I see what it is now," she said. I moved in front of her on my knees and put my hands on her thighs.

"Wanta see something?" she whispered. A hoarse response was all I could manage as I remembered a similar question two years earlier. After casting a brief look toward the kitchen, she slowly slid her dress up smooth muscular thighs. After another glance to the kitchen, she drew it to her waist. She wore no panties.

As she leaned forward to kiss me, I slid my hands around her firm bottom. Gently, I pulled her toward me. Her tongue probed deep in my mouth. I began to caress her inner thigh. She opened her legs wider and moved to the edge of the chair. My hand went up the inside of her thigh. She moved closer, head back. As she gyrated trancelike, I probed deeper and deeper with my fingers. She moved with pleasure. She then opened her eyes and tugged the shirt from my pants. Her hands touched my bare skin. She reached deep down for me. Just as she touched me the words "Prag-nant, prag-nant" circled over my head like two vultures. Short of breath, I didn't know what to do. She grasped me tightly and shot me a sultry challenge. It was the longest second of my life. I withdrew her hand gently.

She gave me a puzzled look as I stood. "I'm coming *right* back," I whispered urgently.

I raced to the attic and shoved my bed back to the corner. "Cut down that racket, Greg," I heard Miss Dora shout from the kitchen. Searching frantically, I rolled the linoleum back to the middle of the room, but the three condoms I kept hidden there were nowhere to be found. I rolled more linoleum back, sliding the bed to the other corner. Still, nothing. I rummaged through my dresser, under my clothes, trying to remember if I'd hidden them somewhere else. Then I realized Mike must have taken them. In desperation, I reached into my book bag. After a few seconds of frantic fumbling I tiptoed back down the stairs.

Hattie broke into a grin. "What's that?" she asked, suppressing a giggle and looking directly at me.

It was my plastic pencil bag, held on by two rubber bands.

"I'm not gonna let you put that inside me," she whispered as I knelt in front of the chair.

"Come on," I pleaded as my hand went under her dress once more, and I drew her to the edge of the chair. She began to laugh, but I covered her mouth with a kiss. My hand slipped around her hips. I was so focused on Hattie, I barely heard the loud "Ahem!"

Grandma stood in the dining room looking directly at us. She remained frozen for a long second, and then abruptly turned to the kitchen. Hattie's eyes flew open as I roughly pulled away from her.

"Grandma," I murmured, jumping to my feet, as Hattie jerked her dress over her knees and began to smooth it.

I was halfway up the attic steps in one hop. I heard Miss Dora's voice as she entered the dining room.

From the attic window, I watched the women say good-bye at the gate, and heaved a sigh of relief as Grandma quickly departed. My body shook with fear as I wondered if Miss Dora or Sister Johnson knew anything was amiss. Later that evening, Dad, with Mike as his messenger, ordered me to the alley.

"Damn, I don't understand it," he said. "I spend all my time planning your future, and all you wanta to is stick your dick in every girl that walks. I don't want you to ever forget that getting a girl 'prag-nant' can ruin your life. You gotta start thinking with your head instead of your dick. You must be crazy trying to screw that girl right under Dora's nose."

"You told me to do it, Dad."

"That's wine talking, boy. You gotta be careful. I bet you didn't even wear a rubber."

"Yeah, I did," I replied without describing my makeshift substitute.

Dad was right, I was crazy.

I renewed my vow to focus all my energy and attention on schoolwork and basketball. By January I even made the starting five and continued to kindle my dream of becoming a Muncie Central Bearcat. I made A's and B+'s in most of my classes. One February evening I sat with Miss Dora at the kitchen table, showing her an A I had received on a book report. The phone rang. It was Brian. He got right to the point.

"Rachel says Janie is still waiting for you to call, Greg. What's happening? You gonna do it or not? Man, if you play your cards right you could finally get lucky."

I never told Brian about my misadventure with Hattie, fearful he would ridicule my feeble efforts. All the girls adored Brian; the black girls who dated him openly, and the white girls whom he met clandestinely. Not only was he a star in football, basketball, and track, by the ninth grade he was six feet tall and strong as an ox. He once carried six would-be tacklers twenty yards across the football field before they were able to bring him down. During basketball games I remember the squeals of joy from the girls as his muscular body floated in the air after snatching a rebound. One female classmate even fainted when Brian autographed her basketball program following a twenty-five-point-game performance. I never quite understood how he could be so blessed. He was a tremendously successful athlete, incredibly handsome, a good student, and he still had time to pursue every girl who gave him the slightest glimmer of interest.

Mrs. Settles tolerated Brian's rambunctiousness as long as he made decent grades. The only time she put her foot down was on the subject of white girls. Mrs. Settles talked about evil white women and how black men had been lynched for talking to them. I guess that was the primary interest Brian, or any of us, had in white girls—they were forbidden.

I protested softly into the phone.

"Janie's white, and I don't want to get into trouble."

The sounds of water running from the kitchen faucet enabled me to speak freely. "Your momma warned us. You know she's worried about you gettin' beat up or lynched."

"Ain't been no lynching in Indiana since the 1930s, Greg. Momma just gets excited," he said in exasperation. "Anyway, we're talking about you, not me, and the teachers don't care what you do. You're almost white. They ain't gonna bother you. If you don't talk to the woman, you're lettin' the brothers down. We're going to think you ain't into shit. She digs you, and you got to go for her."

"But what if I don't like her, Brian?"

"I ain't heard of nobody that don't like gettin' some, Greg."

Two days later on the way to the locker room to dress for a basketball game, Brian stopped me outside the door. "Janie's upstairs at the balcony entrance. I told her you'd get tickets for her and her little brother."

Reluctantly, I headed toward the balcony. Janie and a young boy stood near the entrance. After a bit of small talk our hands touched when I gave her the tickets. We faced each other in silence. She was not too bad, I thought, as I tried to overlook the dullness of her hair and rather unattractive glasses. I realized the Shed Town boys would go crazy if they even saw us standing this close together. Those boys scared me two years before, but after several fights and a mild feeling of invincibility, I no longer feared them. Balancing on Muncie's racial tightrope added to her appeal. Brian was right, I thought. I could do what I wanted.

I asked Janie to meet me after the game.

It was all so easy. No police rushed into the hall to arrest me. It was like I asked her to loan me a pencil.

That night it was hard to keep my mind on the game, but it didn't make much difference. The coach kept me on the bench most of the evening because of a fight earlier in the week with a white teammate from Shed Town. While I managed to score two baskets, I was called for four fouls. As Brian led us to victory, I stared across the gym floor and up into the stands at Janie.

The final buzzer had hardly died before I streaked across the floor to the showers. Upon leaving the locker room, I scanned the hallway for teachers. Seeing none, I darted upstairs. Janie stood outside the balcony door, alone.

We floated down the broad hallway, turned a corner, and huddled in a secluded alcove of lockers. I leaned against one and Janie stood less than a foot away. We stared at one another, uncertain about what to do next. After an awkward silence she whispered, "You know, Greg, I like you a lot."

Moving closer, I put my arms around her. She snuggled up to me. Leaning down, I gave her a soft kiss on the lips. Then a second, longer kiss. My hands caressed her back and fell to her waist. I pulled her tighter. Then my hands dropped even lower across her hips. Our kisses lasted longer. Feeling her breasts against my chest, I reached for the top button of her blouse.

The staccato beat of leather heels on the concrete hallway jolted me back to reality. We broke away from each other and moved out of the alcove toward the gymnasium. We were less than two steps from the lockers when Mr. Bennett, my English teacher, rounded the corner. When he saw us, his jaw jutted forward. We struggled to appear nonchalant.

"What are you two doing up here?" he barked. "Everyone's supposed to be out of the building! Get on downstairs!"

Quickly, we descended the steps and exited the building. Janie hailed her brother, and I joined Brian, who stood near the bicycle rack. There were no good-byes. Brian shook his head with exasperation, but managed a sympathetic smile.

"Well, tell me the sad story. I know you didn't get into anything. You weren't in there long enough. What happened?"

"Bennett caught us."

Brian's smile vanished. "Oh, shit, you're in trouble. Bennett definitely don't like the brothers messin' with white girls."

The next morning Mr. Bennett's discovery was common knowledge among the black students. All of us were tense when he walked through the door. The usual "first joke" of the day was omitted as he tersely announced a massive homework assignment to be started in class and handed in the next morning. Just as I breathed a sigh of relief and opened my book, Bennett sent me for water to clean the blackboard. When I returned, he intercepted me in the hallway just a few steps from the classroom door.

"I'll take that," he said, snatching the can from my hand and spilling water on the floor. "You stay here."

I stood there wondering what he would say. I had little time to consider the possibilities. He set the water can on the floor inside the room and slammed the door. His owlish face and thick bifocals bore down on me. His breath smelled of stale cigarettes.

"You know," he said, our noses almost touching, "I saw you with Janie yesterday."

I couldn't deny it, so I said nothing.

"What do you think you're doing? You're not supposed to be fooling around with her. That's not allowed at Wilson.

"You better get it out of your mind that you're ever going to date any white girls. That kind of thing is just not done in our society. It's not going to be acceptable in my lifetime or yours, and it will never, ever happen here in Muncie!

"You have some potential. You could be a credit to your race. Maybe you can be a teacher like me, but if you start messing with white girls, you're going to have more trouble than you can handle."

I was nervous, but I felt Mr. Bennett was proving Dad's assertion that most of Muncie's teachers were stupid. I focused my attention past him down the hall to the statue of Woodrow Wilson, the name-sake of the school. Just a week earlier our history teacher told us Wilson was the leading proponent of the League of Nations after World War I. Wilson sought to bring peace to the world. I was gaining an understanding of why he failed.

Bennett shouted, "Pay attention when I talk to you! You think you're something special just because you're a ballplayer. Well, the rules apply to you just like everyone else!"

Mr. Rea, the math teacher, stuck his head out his classroom door to investigate the hall commotion, then ducked back inside.

"Playing basketball doesn't make you any different from the other colored boys."

He paused for a moment, then as if struck with an insight, said, "I bet this wasn't your idea. I know who put you up to this, and if he doesn't straighten up, he's going to find himself in hot water as well. Mr. Brian Settles is going to learn a very hard lesson if I ever catch him stepping out of line.

"I thought you had more sense than to be coaxed into this. I don't ever want to see you talking to any white girls again. Do you understand that?"

He waited for an answer. His tirade left him breathing heavily, and his pale skin had turned purple. He looked like he might ex-plode at any moment.

"Yes, sir," I said. His final command was, "Go see Miss White. She wants to talk with you too."

Sadly, I travelled the long corridor to Miss White's room. It was my first private visit with her despite the fact that she was a guidance counselor and was supposed to provide individual academic and career counseling to all students. Miss White was a tall, gray-haired, anemic-looking woman in her mid-fifties.

"Sit down, Gregory," she said sharply. Judging from the way Miss White grimly pursed her thin bloodless lips, one would have thought I was Jack the Ripper.

"Mr. Bennett says that you have been dating white girls?"

"I haven't been dating any girls," I said defiantly. "I only talked to one girl. What's wrong with that?"

She drew her chair closer to the table and clasped her bony hands firmly in front of her. "Don't use that tone of voice with me, young man. We know everything that goes on around here, and a lot more about you than you might think."

She paused to let me chew on that for a moment.

"I've been wanting to talk to you ever since I found out you were colored," she said. "You're a special case. Everyone at Wilson knows about you and your problem. But next year you'll be at Central. When school starts I want you to speak to each and every one of your teachers and tell them you are colored. They will know what to do. I'll write them a note too.

"Now about this business with Janie. It is simply not acceptable for you or any other Negro boys to socialize with white girls. If you continue this, you are going to create a lot of problems for yourself. I don't want to have to talk to you again. You've been a pretty good boy and not a bad student. You could be a credit to your race." They both seemed to like that phrase. "But if you persist in violating Wilson rules you will be suspended."

Forty long minutes passed as Miss White lectured me in her office. The halls were deserted when I finally made my way back to class. Actually, I was relieved to have an excuse not to call Janie, a reason my buddies would accept. I didn't want the problems I would face from teachers—and the Shed Town boys—if I pursued her, especially when I felt no particular attraction to her. Though I had tried to project indignation and courage, the encounters with the two authority figures left me badly shaken, confused, and hurt.

What infuriated me most was that in spite of my good grades, both teachers saw a limited future for me. I prayed they were wrong.

When I think back to the brief interlude with Janie and all the "guidance" I received on "dating," it's hard not to be angry. I really did need counseling—but on how to deal with my father. It was about that time he started spinning totally out of control. One afternoon in late April 1959, while on my way home from an afternoon of reading at Maring Branch Library, I saw him stagger down the middle of Madison Street. The shiny blue gabardine suit caught my attention first but I thought my eyes were playing tricks on me as I spied two army surplus ammunition belts crisscrossed on his chest, Pancho Villa style. He had discarded his brown "stingy brim" fedora for a green steel army helmet. A canteen and first aid kit jangled on the webbed belt around his waist as he held up his hand to stop traffic. Cars whizzed past with drivers angrily blaring horns. Seeing me standing in front of Haag Drug Store, he snapped to attention and saluted. Over the din of the horns he shouted, "I'm going to Cuba to join Castro! *Viva la Revolución!*"

Fidel Castro was important news in America. Even the conservative *Muncie Star* contained detailed accounts of how Castro's army forced the corrupt Batista government out of power. Castro himself had just completed a triumphant visit to the United Nations in the middle of April. He stayed at Hotel Teresa in Harlem during the visit, killing and frying chickens in his room. Dad called him a "friend of the Negro." I didn't bother to return Dad's salute that afternoon. I took off running.

Apparently, Dad was unable to find a ride to Cuba. The following Saturday night he arrived at Miss Dora's way past midnight—drunk. She had kept her word through the years and generally never let him in the house when he was drinking. I was thankful she was so firm. Her house was a true refuge. That particular Saturday night, he pounded on the door for twenty minutes. Miss Dora finally let him inside for what he promised was a brief visit. I was still half asleep when he shook me.

"Wake up! I got something for you."

As I sat up in bed, he pushed five smelly one-dollar bills under my nose. "Here, you said you needed money to buy school pictures."

"Thanks, Dad," I said, tucking the bills safely under the mattress.

"But I needed it five months ago. It's too late to order them now."
I lay back on the pillow. He hovered over me, his brown fedora
almost touching the low ceiling.

"I just ran into your Uncle Dick down on South Walnut," he
continued, ignoring my sarcasm. Uncle Dick was Mom's ex-brother-
in-law and an alcoholic. Dad and Dick often crossed paths in Muncie's hillbilly bars. "He said your mother was in Muncie this past
summer. Did you see her and not tell me?"

"You know me and Mike ain't seen her in over five years."

"Don't lie to me," he said as he leaned closer. His wine breath
made me blanch. I could see the grizzled gray stubble on his unshaven face. He continued accusingly. "I bet you seen that bitch and
didn't tell me about it. You always were like her."

"I swear, Dad," I said, raising my voice. "We haven't seen her
since we arrived in Muncie. We've never talked over the phone, and
haven't even gotten a card or letter from her."

Miss Dora's voice rang out from the bottom of the stairs. "Buster,
come on down and go home! Leave those boys alone."

"Shut up, Dora, this don't concern you!" shouted Dad.

"Anything in my house concerns me. Now come on down from
there."

"Go on back to sleep, old woman. You just mad I won't marry
you. I don't need an old woman. I'm gonna get me some young
white pussy."

Alarmed, I jumped out of bed and pulled on my blue jeans. I
clamped my hand across his mouth. "Dad, what's wrong with
you?" I whispered. "Why are you talking to Miss Dora like that?"

He shoved me against the sharp corner of the chimney and pain
shot through my back. Grabbing his arm, I tried to hold him. He
wrenched free and staggered across the faded linoleum floor. I followed him to the top of the steps and looked down. Miss Dora had
left the doorway, but in a few seconds she reappeared at the bottom
of the steps with a butcher knife.

"Buster, don't nobody talk to me that way in my house! I'm
gonna cut you sure as my name is Dora Terry!" She started up the
steps toward him. After the first step I knew she meant business. In
the five years we lived with her I could count on one hand the
number of times she had been upstairs. Reaching out, I yanked Dad
behind me and stood at the top of the steps.

"Don't cut Daddy," I pleaded. "He didn't mean what he said.

You know how he is when that wine gets a hold of him. You know it ain't worth going to jail over."

She paused on the third step. Then she lowered the knife to her side.

Dad began again. "That's right, you better stop. I'm a Golden Gloves fighter, and you know better than to come up these stairs."

I looked down the dark stairs. By the moonlight I saw a foreign expression on Miss Dora's face. I knew she was going to stab him if he didn't stop.

Mike, now wide awake, raced out of his room and grabbed Dad by the arms. Yet Dad wouldn't shut up.

"That's right, bring your old fat self on up these steps."

She was two more steps closer to us. I put my hand over his mouth again. He jerked his head back and tried to bite me, but I held my hand flat against his face like I was feeding sugar to a horse.

"Miss Dora," I pleaded once more, "let me and Mike take him home. He's drunk and crazy. If you kill him, you won't kill much, but you and him are all we have."

We all stood there in silence less than five steps from one another.

"Miss Dora," I continued, "Mike and me don't want anything to happen to either of you. Please let us take him to Grandma's."

She stood silently for what seemed like an eternity. Our fate was in her hands, as it had been for the past five years.

"Please, Miss Dora," I begged again.

Finally, she said, "Greg, you and Mike get him out of my house. If he ever talks like that to me again, I swear I'll slice him up like an old rooster." She backed down the steps and moved toward the kitchen. We waited till we heard her chair scrape across the floor, then Mike and I dragged Dad down the stairs. Only when my feet hit the cold sidewalk did I realize I had forgotten my shoes. I felt no pain as we raced Dad to Grandma's.

The final event of the ninth grade year was the "graduation" ceremony. Parents and families assembled in the gymnasium to hear music and speeches marking the transition to high school. The ceremony began with a procession of couples into the gym. Boys without a female companion marched at the rear of the line. For over a month I procrastinated in selecting a partner. I dreaded arousing the curiosity of white parents when I marched in front of them with a black companion. Still, my buddies pressured me.

"Man, you gonna be the only brother that's walking alone at the back of the line. You gonna be there with all those pimply-faced crackers."

Finally, I asked Danita, one of my classmates, to walk with me and she accepted. When I told Dad I would be making the graduation walk with Danita, he exploded. "Why in the hell would you pick her? She's black as coal!"

I was too shocked by his words to respond. He continued angrily, "I've planned your future carefully. I'm not going to stand by and see you wreck—"

I interrupted him quickly, fearful of what he might say next. "I'm going to the graduation with her whether you like it or not." I really liked Danita, and I had felt lucky when she accepted the invitation. To have Dad say such mean things made me furious. He carried on for the thousandth time that he wanted me to have the future he never had.

"A rich white girl is what I see in your future. You might have to live in the ghetto, but you don't have to subsist on its food. Life is going to be easier if you have a white wife."

"You're the one who wants to be white, Dad, not me. What about Mike?" I demanded. "You never try to run his life like you do mine."

"The ghetto's already got him, but you can get out, son. I'm just interested in what's best for you."

"We're not getting married, Dad," I added sarcastically. "But if we were you wouldn't have a damn thing to say about it." I slammed Grandma's screen door behind me.

On graduation day, we formed lines outside the gymnasium. I steeled myself for the inevitable stares and whispers I knew awaited us. The line moved slowly. I said little to Danita and began to perspire heavily. At the front of the line stood Miss White and my favorite shop teacher, Mr. Murphy, ushering students into the room. His familiar chuckle and hearty "Congratulations!" rang out down the line of graduates as we moved closer and closer to the entryway. Though I never really liked shop, Mr. Murphy was such a pleasant teacher that I enjoyed being around him. Miss White smiled gracefully at everyone. She had given us two final lessons in her guidance class, dining place settings, and cordiality in introductions. As we inched closer I anticipated at least a warm send-off from Mr. Murphy, and maybe even a friendly acknowledgment from Miss White.

After all, I was following her instructions. I saw the packed gymnasium through the open doorway. Danita and I stepped in front of Mr. Murphy and I waited for a pat on the back before we faced the hostile stares of the crowd. I smiled broadly. Miss White's face was cold as ice. She said nothing. Mr. Murphy's mouth dropped wide open. Unable to muster even a single syllable, he stood there and gawked. Finally, he was able to recover enough to wave us into the gymnasium.

Until that very last moment, I had hoped for support from somewhere. It didn't come. In a way I was relieved. If they had been supportive, I would have had to care about them. With hands intertwined, Danita and I faced the crowd alone. I expected hostility, and was no longer surprised when it came. As Danita and I strode into the gymnasium I saw the same angry eyes I had seen three years earlier on my first trip to Wilson. Only this time among the sea of frowning faces was one belonging to my father. As we strode past his row, Brian Settles smiled and whispered, "Way to go, Big Shoulders."

# Chapter 15

# Persistence

In September of 1959, Muncie papers reported that Central High School had its largest enrollment ever, 2,546 students in grades ten through twelve. The old brick building, crowded with less than a thousand students when Dad was a sophomore in 1929, was literally bursting at its seams. Early that first morning, I felt the electricity in the air as I navigated the wide marble steps jammed with students. Though Wilson had ended badly, I was optimistic about my new environment and hopeful about the different people. As I started up steps to the third-floor classrooms, a solid mass of humanity moved down toward me. An upperclassman smirked and pointed to a One Way down arrow stenciled in big block letters on the wall. Frantic that I would be late for my very first class, I rushed down the hallway, through another crowd, and ascended the "up" steps. The sound of the bell echoed as I settled into my seat.

I felt a surge of excitement as my new English teacher shared his plans for that first semester. We would read speeches, plays, and novels, starting with Charles Dickens' *Great Expectations*. Even Spanish and geometry class generated the same high interest. The only concern that nagged at me as I hurried from class to class was whether Miss White had followed through on her threat to apprise

all my teachers of "my problem." The science teacher began by calling the roll. I was last. After "Gregory Williams," he paused and
asked, "Are you Gene Williams's son?" I had never met Williams,
the white Delaware County prosecutor, not even during the City
Hall days when Dad introduced us to almost every Muncie politician. But I had read about him in the paper. He was a tough crime
fighter, and a well-known member of Muncie's elite. I smiled with
relief as I shook my head no. The simple question kindled the hope
that my new teachers would be unbiased and more supportive of
my desire to excel academically. I felt that I would have a greater
chance of succeeding if I could avoid the racism which had infected
the junior high school.

At lunch I entered the cafeteria and saw Ben Cook, a white
cousin. In the joy of a new beginning, I gave him a friendly smile.
His eyes widened in panic, and he quickly avoided my gaze. I realized he was going to be the same as at Wilson—no contact or
recognition. I simultaneously felt rejected and relieved. He, with his
slovenly attire and Shed Town buddies, was not someone with
whom I cared to be connected in any way.

There were two cafeteria serving lines, the "à la carte" line, with
a wide selection, and the cheap "A" lunch line. Ben made a dash
for the "à la carte" side. I stood in the small "A" lunch line, thankful
I had the necessary thirty-five cents. A pang of jealously overcame
me as I watched Ben pile his tray high with sandwiches, chips, and
desserts. I realized I did not have four extra pennies for a second
carton of milk. But Mrs. Reese, our neighbor, worked in the cafeteria. As she served the food, she winked, and she gave me very
generous portions.

After lunch, some students gathered on the sidewalk in front of
the building. Peeking out the glass doors, I saw many of the same
white boys who had loafed at the diner across from Wilson Junior
High School. Now they perched on the hoods of souped-up Chevys
and Fords, smoking and flirting with many of the same girls. I
climbed the marble steps to the auditorium. The smell of musty
wood filled the air as I scanned the cavernous room. It rose almost
three stories high and spanned over a hundred seats wide, starkly
divided into three distinct sections, north, south, and a broad vacant
middle. Black students huddled together on the south side. Whites
filled the north. The middle section flowed between them like a deep
unnavigable river. This was worse than Wilson, I thought. At least

there I could hide in our corner of the recreation room. How could I maintain the anonymity I desperately wanted? Goose bumps popped out on my arms as I realized that, on the very first day, I had to make a fateful choice. If I sat with the white students on the north side of the auditorium, the blacks would believe I didn't want to associate with them. Yet, if I joined the black students, I would be an all-too-conspicuous "white" face in a sea of the multiple hues of brown.

I stood glued to the floor, turning my dilemma over and over in my mind. Finally, aware I had no real decision to make, I slowly moved down the aisle to join the black students. Another cousin, one of Aunt Bess's grandchildren, whom we playfully called "Jemima," sat in the middle of a chattering group of boys and girls. She was a beautiful, angular-faced, brown-skinned teenager, with long black braids. She hailed me immediately. Her mother, Aunt Elizabeth, had fed Mike and me on countless Sundays when we trekked to her house in Whitely for chicken and dumplings and fresh-baked rolls. Giving her a relieved wave, I plodded down the aisle, unsure of exactly where to sit. There were so many new faces among the black students. I had an aching fear that even though I had made my choice, they might not accept me. Finally, I spied a vacant seat on the aisle. I took it, making my commitment, but remaining on the edge.

As I sat there self-consciously, feeling the burning stares of white students from far across the room, Jemima rose from her seat. Every muscle in my body relaxed as she sat beside me. Drawn by her bubbling presence, a group of students soon surrounded us. Some of the fellows were Bearcat football and basketball stars I had watched during summers at the Madison Street "Y." I reveled in the stamp of approval Jemima provided, but the lunchtime conversation took a turn that made me uncomfortable.

It all began when one boy speculated about what he might do if he had skin like mine. He claimed he would leave Muncie, pass for white, and get a good job. Another boy, who reckoned that lighter skin would bring him easy access to white girls, was quickly silenced with a chorus of hissing. Though I tried to feign disinterest, a third boy asked me point-blank why I didn't sit with the white students. I could only muster a weak "I don't want to." A senior basketball star, perhaps understanding my choice better than I did, spoke up.

"Greg is making his life less complicated. If he sat over there the white kids would find him out in a minute, and he'd be an outcast. He's over here with us, telling them, 'Here I am, deal with me!' Don't bother Greg. He's where he belongs."

Once the lunch period ended, I bolted from the auditorium and eagerly climbed the stairs to Miss Bartlett's history class. She was a slightly built, white-haired woman. I bristled when a classmate referred to her as a "skinny old broad." I liked her from the very beginning and it seems that I made a favorable impression on her as well. One afternoon about the fourth week of school, her eyes swept the class and came to rest on a plain-faced girl with a big smile. "Cheryl," she said, "what was the most important city in ancient Sumer?"

Cheryl said nothing. After a few seconds, her smile began to wither. I was sure she knew the answer. She was probably the smartest student in the class. However, that day Cheryl began to furrow her brow as Miss Bartlett waited. Finally, Cheryl admitted, "I don't know."

Then Miss Bartlett asked her seatmate. She didn't know either. One after another she moved around the semicircle of chairs seeking the answer. One after another the students shook their heads and mumbled.

"I don't know."

Holding my breath, I prayed that the question would make it all the way around the room to me. I would be the last person to respond. Finally, I breathed a sigh of relief when it was my turn.

"Gregory, will you give the class the correct answer?" Miss Bartlett said with great confidence in her voice.

"Ur," I almost shouted.

"Excellent!" she added. "Class, Gregory was not clearing his throat. The correct answer is Ur. I wish the rest of you were as diligent as Gregory in their homework. He reminds me of a young man I had as a student a few years ago, Tom Raisor. Many of you will remember him as a basketball star, but to me his most important quality was his commitment to education. Now he is a successful Muncie lawyer. Like Gregory, he didn't always have his hand waving in the air, but I knew if I wanted the correct answer, I could turn to him."

Although her praise did little to endear me to my classmates, I didn't care. At last, I had discovered a teacher who not only recognized my ability but compared me with a successful lawyer. From then on I spent every spare moment studying history, including almost every second during lunch hour. Receiving the highest marks in class fueled my motivation. Even some of my white classmates sought my help on difficult assignments.

Midway through the semester the results of our IQ tests arrived. We read at our desks while Miss Bartlett conferred with us, one by one, in the hallway. School rules did not permit her to divulge the exact score, only an approximation, and a ranking of below average, average, above average, or outstanding.

The freshly buffed wooden floor squeaked as I strode from the door. Towering over Miss Bartlett, I waited to be anointed as outstanding. She scrutinized the paper in her hand. Her angular face took on an unusual sharpness. She looked toward me, then at the paper again. In a monotone she said, "Gregory, your IQ is above average."

I leaned closer, wondering if I misunderstood.

"What does 'above average' mean?" I asked hesitantly.

"It means your IQ is somewhere between 105 and 115."

My shoulders fell. I turned away to mask my disappointment. As I stumbled back into the classroom, my eyes connected with my rival, Cheryl, across the room. Feeling somehow unworthy, I averted my gaze and stared at the floor. For the rest of the period, I was lost in a fog as I mentally tried to reconcile my high grades with the "low" IQ test. As the class filed out of the room, Miss Bartlett beckoned to me.

"Gregory, I know you're disappointed by the IQ results. And I'm at a loss to explain why there is such a disparity between your performance and that score. I've never seen anyone work as hard. To be honest, I've had a lot of so-called geniuses in my classes over the years, and rarely did they live up to their billing. I'd much prefer to have someone like you. Instead of taking the test results in a negative way, you need to try to see them in a positive light. To achieve the high goals you have set for yourself you will have to work a lot harder than some students, but the important point is that you know you can compete with the very best. You've proven your ability. Students with much higher IQs for one reason or another often have failed to equal your performance."

Her words of encouragement helped alleviate my pain, and I resolved to take her advice. Almost every day after class, I lingered at her desk with a final question. One afternoon she asked, "Gregory, is Ben Cook your cousin?"

Ben Cook! Most of his class time was spent perfecting his "smart-aleck" image. He rarely gave a correct answer on the oral quizzes, and never seemed to have any interest in his homework. Miss Bartlett constantly admonished him in front of the entire class to stop talking and pay attention. The semester was almost over and this was the first week he had spoken to me. "Yes," I admitted reluctantly.

"He mentioned it last week. With his grades, I couldn't believe he was from the same family."

Now I understood why Ben shocked me by striking up a conversation that Monday. I responded coolly, until he mentioned my mother. The exchange ended when the bell rang. Now I realized he only hoped to gain some approval from Miss Bartlett by revealing our family ties.

The rest of the week I concealed my anger and hoped for snippets of information about my family. During the few brief minutes before the class bell rang, I heard the first news of my mother in six years. She had remarried, lived outside of Washington, D.C., and my younger brother and sister had grown so much I would never recognize them. A pain shot through my chest as he casually revealed the astonishing news that my mother had visited Muncie several times over the past years! At that moment I felt complete and utter devastation. I struggled to hide my feelings, but my grasping question—"What's she like, Ben?"—revealed my longing. He leaned back in his seat and paused as he realized he possessed one thing I desperately wanted. He doled it out, tidbit by tidbit, expecting me to chuckle at his jokes, marvel at his insights, and politely wait as he paused to leer at passing girls. Freezing a smile on my face, I swallowed all my pride and sat there attentively. I hated my mother for giving this boy power over me, and I hated myself for begging Ben for a tattered and yellowed dime store photo of her. That night in the solitude of the attic, I placed the photo on the card table in front of me while I did my homework. I asked her a thousand questions, but wanted the answer to only one. Why had she abandoned us? Finally, I had to turn over the small snapshot.

Toward the end of the year, Miss Bartlett asked us to write about some aspect of World War II or its aftermath. Although Fort Belvoir was a distant memory, I was still fascinated with military lore and wanted to write about the army. I moped around the house most of the weekend unable to choose a topic. Miss Dora asked me what was wrong. Because she had only an eighth grade education, and I was in the tenth grade, I was certain she couldn't help. "Nothing" was my sharp response. Though I rebuffed her several times, she continued to prod gently, and finally in exasperation I admitted I had to write something about World War II.

"What about how they treated colored soldiers?" she asked.

Though I remembered my conversation with Uncle Jim about the mistreatment of black soldiers in World War I, I thought it was different by World War II. That afternoon Miss Dora described a U.S. Army of which I was totally unaware. Both her brothers served in World War II, and she recounted their experiences in a rigidly segregated military, living in different barracks, eating in different mess halls, and even fighting in separate units. It wasn't until long after the war, in 1948, that President Truman issued an executive order banning segregation in the armed services.

The next day I searched through the Muncie Central Library for books and articles to confirm what Miss Dora had told me. I found nothing. Even Miss Bartlett was unable to recommend specific books or magazines, so I turned to my two best sources, Mrs. Settles and Dad. Mrs. Settles wrote to Indiana University and was able to collect news articles for me. She even located President Truman's Executive Order 9981, issued July 26, 1948, which stated: "It is hereby declared to be the policy of the President that there shall be equality of treatment and opportunity without regard to race, color, religion or national origin."

Dad confirmed Miss Dora's description of the army, and had a few of his own personal experiences to add, such as being required to assemble with both black and white troops when soldiers were accused of off-base misdeeds. When we talked about President Truman, Dad astonished me by announcing that he had met him when Truman was a U.S. Senator from Missouri.

To help finance his year at Howard University, Dad took a part-time job as a switchboard operator at the exclusive Gunston Hall Girls School. Senator Truman's daughter was in residence while he worked there. Truman often visited in the evenings after a day at the Capitol, but if he arrived during the evening meal he had to wait, as there were strict rules against disturbing dinner, when the students spoke only in French. While waiting, Senator Truman traded stories and off-color jokes with Dad. Truman told one joke that Dad never forgot.

"It was the light-skinned colored boy's first day of school. The teacher asked, 'What's your name, young man?'

" 'Dopey,' he answered.

" 'Dopey, that can't be right.'

" 'Yes ma'am, that's it.'

" 'Come on, tell me your real name. Don't you at least have a last name?'

" 'Yes ma'am. Jones, Dopey Jones.'

" 'Surely your first name is not really Dopey, is it?'

"The boy bowed his head and said, 'Well, no ma'am. It's Opium.'

" 'Opium. That can't be. That's the seeds of a white poppy.'

" 'Yes ma'am, that's it. I got a white poppy.' "

Nonetheless, Truman ordered the armed services to desegregate, and he received praise in my report on the army. I received an A+. Although I had learned to appreciate Miss Dora's common sense and faith, I had not realized how much wisdom my second mother possessed. She seemed to enjoy my newfound curiosity, and shared amazing stories about her family and life as a young girl in Arkansas. Her stories of brutality against black inmates at a prison camp near her home in Grady, Arkansas, were confirmed years later in a newspaper exposé and movie.

For the first time I read the famous "Middletown" studies, written by Robert S. and Helen Lynd. Muncie had been selected by these prominent sociologists for the first in-depth study of a "typical American town." My goal was to learn more about Muncie's black community, and I was disappointed to read that the Lynds had selected Muncie in 1924 because it had "few black and foreign-born citizens." They sought to study "a homogenous native-born population." Nonetheless, Muncie's racial climate was analyzed and the city was found to be a "hotbed of Ku Klux Klan activity." I was astounded to discover that the Lynds did not cite a single interview with a member of Muncie's "negro community," though blacks constituted roughly six percent of Muncie's population. In spite of their highly acclaimed work the Lynds were clearly prisoners of the prevailing attitudes of their time.

Digging through the library, and eye-opening talks with Dad,

Miss Dora, and Mrs. Settles, kindled a desire to study history and become a history teacher. My father discouraged it.

"It's too hard to get involved in politics if you're a teacher. Teachers can't take the time off. You want to make history, not read about it."

"I don't want a life in politics."

"Maybe you don't, but you want to have the option to say 'That's not for me.' Teachers don't have that option. Not only do they lack the time, they don't have the money or training."

"But I love history."

"Knowledge of history is important and you should study it by all means. It just doesn't lead anywhere you want to go. Plus, there's a lot of prejudice in teaching you can avoid as a lawyer."

What Dad said made sense. In all my years in Muncie, I never had a black principal, teacher, or coach. Yet the more Dad talked about my future, the more I wondered if it was his dream or mine. That year Dad was managing longer periods of sobriety, and had made amends with Miss Dora. She even permitted him visits in the evening to make sure I did my homework. One night he was upstairs in my room sitting on my bed while I sat cross-legged on the floor with my geometry book in my lap.

"Howard University is 'the capstone of Negro education,'" he lectured. "When Arnold Robbins and I hitchhiked there in 1936, it was the breeding ground of the finest Negro scholars in America. For my politics class I had Ralph Bunche, who later became Undersecretary of the United Nations. For philosophy I had Dr. Alain Leroy Locke, the first black Rhodes Scholar and author of *The New Negro*, the most important book on the Harlem Renaissance of the 1920s. I chose Mike's middle name, Alain, in reverence to Dr. Locke."

I asked Dad about his grades.

He paused and shifted uncomfortably on the bed. Looking out the window at the activity in front of Roach's Cafe, he admitted, "I'm not proud of my grades. I made a D in Bunche's class, and barely a C in Locke's. I spent too much time with the women and I always had to hustle for a dollar. I've made a lot of mistakes, but not getting my education was the biggest. Life would be different for all of us now if I had clung to my dreams. But you are going to be different. You have established your goals and you will not deviate from them.

"Goals can be achieved. Bunche and Locke are proof of that. With perseverance, self-discipline, and motivation you can make the dream a reality. Never forget that the harder you work, the higher you'll go. I'm convinced you can do it, and I won't let you settle for anything less."

As my sophomore year ended, I began the usual search for a summer job. I went from store to store: Woolworth's, Steck's, Men's Town, Bazley's Meat Market, Ball Stores, and even Nick's Shoe Shine Parlor, receiving rejection after rejection. Since I still had one part-time job, cleaning Turner's Tire and Wheel Alignment late every evening, I decided to develop my basketball skills for Bearcat tryouts in the late fall. I had made the J.V. basketball team my sophomore year, but of the fifteen boys, I probably ranked tenth. The varsity coach was unlikely to take more than five juniors for the team next year. I vowed to spend every spare minute that summer on the basketball court. When I revealed my plan to Dad, he objected. He said that if I didn't have a full-time job, I had to go to summer school.

Burris High School on the west side of Muncie was the laboratory school for Ball State Teachers College. A high percentage of the Burris students were from Muncie's more prominent families. As I walked the two miles to campus, I fantasized about meeting a rich girl who would fall madly in love with me and her parents would want to support me all the way through school. The bloom faded when the first students I saw were two Shed Town girls who had dropped out of Wilson because of teenage pregnancies. Summer school, I quickly learned, was not for advancement but for make-up. When school was dismissed at noon, I jogged home. Often I beat the crosstown bus, using its snail-like speed as an excuse for not riding it. The truth was that I rarely had the ten-cent fare.

Mr. Buley, the Madison Street YMCA playground director, always smiled and waved as I trotted onto the hot asphalt basketball court. The heat kept most others off the court until around three o'clock. By four there were enough players to begin the afternoon games. Games usually lasted until seven or eight in the evening.

One August afternoon four fellows from the all-black Indianapolis Crispus Attucks team arrived on the playground. Black athletes from Richmond, Anderson, Marion, and Kokomo often traveled to Muncie, but it was a real treat when the Crispus Attucks fellows appeared. They were some of the best athletes in the state. The Indiana High School Athletic Association had barred Crispus Attucks High School from the state basketball association for years because Indiana high school athletic officials feared white schools wouldn't want to play the black athletes from Crispus Attucks. Once in the system, however, Crispus Attucks teams captured three state championships and produced superstars like Oscar Robertson. That day I stood on the sidelines, pouting over not being selected to play with two members of the previous year's Bearcat squad. Angrily, I called for the next game, and asked the Attucks guys to play with me.

The combination of the snub and the desire to impress my Indianapolis teammates energized me. Even the two Bearcats who rejected me for the earlier game shook their heads in disbelief as I won the first game with a left-handed jump shot from deep in the corner. When one of my teammates from Indianapolis said in a deep bass voice, "You're lookin' good, Slim," I knew I had a chance for the Bearcats. We played for over two hours without losing. During a break I noticed Dad standing at the edge of the playground. He motioned for me. I walked toward him, wondering if he was drunk. As I drew near, I noticed his rummage sale suit still held its press, but his eyes were glassy. He wasn't drunk, but I could tell he had been drinking.

As I stood on the ledge and looked down at him, he lifted a familiar rectangular cardboard box to me. For about a year Dad and Grandma had been able to receive welfare food commodities from the Township Trustees office. Once a month we were given "surplus" food, which included a brick of cheddar cheese, a sack each of beans and rice, a tin of powdered eggs, and a box of powdered milk.

"Take these up to Miss Dora's. I've got an appointment."

Quietly, I argued that I didn't have time—basketball practice was more important. Then I leaned over and in a whisper added, "Plus, I don't want people to see me carrying welfare food through the Projects."

"You won't mind having this when your belly starts growling. Now get it on home! You've got to realize there are more important things in life than basketball."

Dad turned and headed in the direction of the tavern. I waved to my buddies from Indianapolis and picked up the box to carry it home.

For five years Miss Dora's home had been a haven compared to life at Grandma's, but that spring A. D. Smith, a devout member of Christ Temple Church and the widower of one of Miss Dora's best friends, spent more and more time around the house. A.D. was a short, heavyset, dark-brown-skinned man. His stark silver-framed glasses matched his rigid personality. I cannot recall a conversation of more than two or three sentences with him, although he was always cordial. Every Sunday, without fail, he took Miss Dora to church, and to dinner following services. On Wednesday nights he escorted her to Bible study class, and on Fridays to choir practice. Most evenings they sat on the front porch talking until after dark. One evening when I arrived home and saw them holding hands on the front porch I became very nervous. Sensing marriage might be imminent, I worried about the implications for Mike and me.

Miss Dora's financial picture was bleak. Postal had not raised her twenty-five-dollar salary in five years, and never paid one cent in Social Security for her. His health deteriorated daily. His pale white skin now seemed almost transparent as it stretched across sharp bones and blue veins. He lost so much weight he literally looked like a walking skeleton, except he could barely walk. Every morning Miss Dora lifted him from his bed like a baby and carried him to his favorite porch chair to gaze out the window over the intersection of Charles and Madison streets. When I passed on the way to school, and saw his feeble wave of the hand, I realized his days were numbered.

Both Mike and I had part-time jobs, but that hardly covered school clothes and other necessities. Miss Dora, at age fifty-eight, would have a hard time finding another job as a cook and a maid. Even if she could find work, she was no longer strong and healthy. A.D. had retired on a pension, which provided a steady source of income. If they married, Miss Dora would continue to receive his pension after his death. That was a strong financial incentive to marry him. It was clear he wanted to marry her.

I was eavesdropping when I heard another issue resolved.

"Dora, there's one thing I want to talk about," said A.D. as he sat at the kitchen table. He paused and then continued hesitantly. "It's the boys."

"What about the boys?" she asked guardedly.

"Well, me and some of the other church members just don't understand why you keep 'em. You don't get anything for it. You have to use your own little bit of money to take care of 'em. And they got people here in Muncie who should be worrying about 'em. Especially they daddy, who could get a job if he had a mind to. He don't even want to work. He just goes around drunk all the time with gamblers and hustlers."

Miss Dora responded, "Maybe Buster could get a job if he wanted one, but that don't have nothin' to do with my boys. I know I ain't they real momma 'cause I didn' birth 'em, but I been takin' care of them for years, and they never give me no trouble, neither one of 'em."

"I ain't saying they bad boys," countered A.D. "I'm just saying they ain't your responsibility."

"A.D., one thing I want to get clear 'fore we get married. Them boys was here when you got here, and gonna be here when you gone. And if you don't like that, I don' see no reason for us to get married."

The final words were barely out of her mouth before A.D. gushed an apology.

"Now, Dora, don't get yourself upset. I'm sorry. I just wanted to tell you how I felt about the boys being here. This is your house, and if you want them to stay, that's up to you. I'll never say nothing about it again."

They were married in a private Justice of the Peace ceremony in a matter of days. I can still recall Miss Dora beaming like a schoolgirl, flushed with happiness, as she walked through the front door. She wore her finest Sunday dress. She had curled her hair and even wore a tinge of rouge. In the magic of the moment I kissed her and congratulated A.D. That evening as I lay in bed I realized that she had been willing to sacrifice her joy and even economic security for us.

There were some adjustments to having A.D. in the household. To avoid his complaint that we were a financial drain on him, we were forbidden to eat any of his food. There was a separate shelf for us in the refrigerator, and generally Mike and I left his treats alone. One night, however, I was starving after a basketball game, and his barbecue rib dinner from Roach's was too tempting. I gobbled it down without thinking. A.D. was good enough to pronounce me forgiven after a sincere apology.

There was more excitement in the house, as A.D. brought a radio and television to the marriage. They absolutely loved the Lawrence

Welk show, but were always in bed by nine p.m. Mike and I had free rein with late-night TV, as long as we turned off the living room lights and kept the volume really low.

Things seemed to go well, until that summer evening when Dad asked me to carry the welfare food home. I had just turned the corner onto Kirby Avenue when I noticed an unusual flurry of activity in front of our house. Five cars were parked there. Older women walked toward the gate carrying bundles. As I drew closer, I recognized the women in the plain, long black dresses carrying food into our house. They were members of Christ Temple Church. Then the director of the Mortuary stepped outside the front door. Overcome with panic, I raced down the street. Miss Dora hadn't been feeling well, and she had high blood pressure. I barged through the front door. The church sisters scowled when they saw me dressed in shorts, which were not permitted in the church. I paid no attention to them. Just then Brother Webb, the Christ Temple assistant pastor, walked out of Miss Dora and A.D.'s bedroom. His curly hair was slicked back with pomade oil. He looked straight at me.

"Gregory, I've got some bad news for you." I prayed Brother Webb wasn't going to tell me what I feared in the bottom of my heart. Just then Miss Dora stepped around the door and with tears in her eyes said, "A.D.'s dead."

I bounded forward to put my arms around her as I sobbed uncontrollably. Dad was right. Some things were more important than basketball.

# Chapter 16

## Teammates

My summer basketball routine ended on August 15, the day Indiana high schools officially began football practice. Though fearful that the lack of constant drill on the playground might destroy my chances to make the Bearcat basketball squad, I looked forward to varsity football. The previous year, I was the sophomore team's starting quarterback. It had been hard to secure that spot, competing against three star quarterbacks from Muncie's other junior high schools. Most of them could run faster or had better skills than me. From the very first day the coach seared two facts in our minds. We were some of the very best athletes ever to be assembled at Muncie Central High School, but we wouldn't "be worth a damn" if we didn't "sacrifice all for the team." Then he added—to our group, which was almost equally mixed with black and white players—"I don't care if you're from Shed Town or Whitely, Industry or the fancy West Side, we ain't gonna be shit unless you come together as one." For the skeptics, our coach quickly proved he was more than a philosopher. When teammates slacked off blocking assignments, he lined up across from them and on the snap of the ball whacked them across the helmet with a massive forearm. Few of my teammates risked earning his displeasure more than once. His message was loud and clear: either be part of the team or quit. We lost several boys, including my major rival. When the coach told me I was his number one quarterback, he added that if I slacked off "your ass will be drawing splinters on the bench." During that practice he drew all the players together and said I was to be protected at all costs. At six feet and 150 pounds, I needed all the help I could get. Once the coach made his unequivocal choice, even my white teammates readily accepted me as the leader. Tim Freeman, the mammoth-size son of the head football coach at Ball State, anchored the line at center. He approached me after practice and pledged never to let anyone get to me, and that if we ever needed an extra yard he expected me to put my cleats on his back and vault over him. Charlie Brady, normally a quiet and shy 240 pounds, made a similar vow. We won nine games and lost one that sophomore season, playing against major conference powerhouses. What was most important to me was that all the players, black and white, developed incredible respect and friendship for one another both on and off the field. I had never witnessed that before in Muncie.

By the time the fall of my junior year arrived we were even bigger and stronger. As we began the varsity season, Brian Settles was six feet, two inches tall, 190 pounds, and still growing. He had the potential to be an All-State defensive end. The press and coaches touted Ronnie Hudson, over six feet tall and 225 pounds, as an All-Conference lineman. Charlie Brady and Tim Freeman were also aching to show their incredible skills.

The varsity season began disastrously. We lost the first four games, each by an increasing margin. Our new coaches experimented with different people at every position—except quarterback. I wasn't given a chance to play at all the first half of the season. On September 30, the fifth game of the year, we faced Indianapolis Technical High School. "Tech" was rated as one of the strongest teams of our North Central Conference. Size-wise we should have overpowered them, but we were unable to move the ball. Pacing the sideline behind our coaches, I hoped for action. But the game dragged on and on with me as a spectator. Finally, the lighted end zone scoreboard showed less than three minutes remaining in the game. Even though another defeat was imminent, the starting quarterback remained on the field. I gave up hope of playing and my thoughts turned to a hot shower and a warm bus ride back to Muncie.

Just then I felt a slap on my shoulder pads. "Come on, Gregor!" One of the assistant coaches, George Punzelt, was in front of me with his freckled face and bright red hair. "Wake up! It's time to do your stuff!"

Looking over his shoulder, I saw our starting quarterback hobble off the field with a player supporting him on each side. His face contorted with pain as he held his right foot off the ground. George continued. "He may have broken his ankle. Just get in there and play ball control. We want to run out the clock. Go talk to Coach first."

Buckling my chin strap, I trotted down the sidelines. The head coach was a big man, almost six feet, six inches tall. In his heyday, he was an All-American football player. Around Muncie he was a coaching legend, leading Central High School to frequent conference championships. In the last few years, however, Central usually ended up in the league cellar. Ex-members of the team said the coach hadn't introduced a new play into his offense in the last ten years. Every conference coach knew exactly what to expect.

"Williams," he said gruffly, "get in there and hold it together. Run out the clock. Do you think you can do that?" he asked sarcastically.

"Yes, sir," I said, ignoring his tone, and raced onto the field.

My hands, still cold from the fall night air, stung as Tim Freeman slapped the ball into them, but I managed to hold on to it and hand it off to our halfback for short yardage. There was time for one more play, and as I stood behind our huddle I looked to the sidelines and caught George's eye. I raised my right hand to the side of my face and made a slight throwing motion. My plan was to throw a deep pass to our star halfback, Jim Boyce. There was no doubt he was fast enough to get under a thirty-five-yard pass, and during the pregame warm-up I had thrown three deep ones to him. Again I gestured to George, but the decision from the sideline was unmistakable. Both coaches pointed to the ground. I took the final snap and fell on it.

As I reached the sidelines the head coach solemnly looked at me and said, "Well, Williams, it's on your shoulders now." He took a long stride to catch the other coaches and was gone. Just then Ronnie Hudson sidled up to me. In spite of the chill of the evening, his face was covered with sweat and dirt. He looked back over his shoulder to see if anyone was within earshot, then leaned closer to me.

"Just like those white mothafuckers. He's only let you play two minutes all season, and now expects you to save his ass by becoming a star."

I nodded in response. If I succeeded, the coach would take all the credit for molding me into a key player. If I failed, his decision not to play me earlier would be vindicated, and the search for another quarterback would begin.

Monday was an upbeat day. The coach surprised almost everyone when he walked onto the practice field with a new clipboard of freshly diagrammed plays to counter Richmond's All-State 250-pound tackle. When he said, "Okay, Williams, it's time for you to be a man," I didn't take offense, but determined to show him I had been a man for a long time, he just hadn't been looking.

As we prepared for our Richmond game, the 1960 presidential campaign was in its final stages. John F. Kennedy was on a whirlwind tour through the Republican Midwest trying to wrest it from Richard Nixon. Morning classes were dismissed at eleven, and students spilled out of Central High School to hear Kennedy at a noon courthouse rally. Only a few classmates drifted away as the crowd streamed north toward the courthouse to see one of the few presidential candidates who considered Muncie worth visiting. Hundreds of people packed the Courthouse Square. Strangers, jammed together, talked animatedly with one another. Others jostled for a better vantage point to see the action. Bedecked in red, white, and blue banners, the platform faced the Republican headquarters on the east side of the square. I threaded my way by Judge Carson's law office, where Dad and I had painted, mopped, and cleaned for so many hours. At the Wysor Office Building the dense crowd stalled my progress. I leaned back against the cool stone wall and turned my attention to the stage.

Almost every important Indiana Democratic politician was there: senators, congressmen, mayors, and party leaders. I recognized many of them from newspaper pictures and television. I recalled a few from the days when Dad worked as a janitor at City Hall. Finally, Kennedy appeared at the rear of the platform. Shaking hands and slapping backs, he squeezed his way through the throng to the lectern. Just as he reached the microphones, and stood there giving his hair that trademark flip, some "big shot" politician rose from the front row of chairs behind him. The "pol" leaned across the podium and kissed Kennedy on the cheek. Even from a distance I could see shock register on Kennedy's face. I had seen male politicians give a friendly embrace to female supporters, but I had never seen one male politician kiss another. When the crowd roared its approval, Kennedy ignited them again by throwing a kiss to the crowd. The response was deafening.

Who was the mystery man? Dad had taught me to analyze events through "the process of elimination." First, since the man was in the front row, I decided he must be an important Indiana politician. Second, no "small time" pol would have had the nerve to jump the political hierarchy like the brazen "kisser." That only left a senator or congressman. Since Indiana had only one Democratic U.S. senator, I wondered if it was him or one of the few Democratic congressmen. Whoever he was, he would not sit down. He continued to wave to the crowd. The mystery politician twirled his hat in the air. Standing and straining to see above the crowd, I tried to catch a glimpse of him as he turned toward the south side. I couldn't believe my eyes. It was Dad!

My heels sank to the sidewalk and I hunched my shoulders. I raised my eyes toward the stage once more to make sure I wasn't mistaken. Sure enough, Dad stood with both arms in the air like *he* was the presidential candidate. Finally, I saw an arm reach from behind him and tug on his sleeve. Thank God, Dad got the message and took his seat. Through the cheering and screaming, I continued to wonder how in the world Dad had managed to get on stage. Although I could barely concentrate on Kennedy's words, his crowd-pleasing humor and charisma were so apparent I sensed I was listening to the next president of the United States.

That afternoon following football practice I stopped by Grandma's, but Dad wasn't there. After Wednesday's practice, I stopped again. As I walked in the door, Grandma sat in the kitchen with one foot soaking in the washtub and the other across her knee. She carefully worked a double-edged razor blade around her corns. Finally, she held the blade at her side and turned toward me. I asked about Dad.

"Drunk, in jail. It's s'posed to be in the paper," she huffed, turning back to her feet.

I raced to the grocery store for a paper and stood outside feverishly thumbing through the pages. It was in the City Court column. "James A. Williams, 601½ Railroad Street, guilty of public intoxication, fine $25 and costs." I read it again to make sure, but knew there was only one James A. Williams at 601½ Railroad Street. Fred Badders had mentioned once that fines were served at five dollars a day. Depending on "costs," Dad would remain in jail at least a week, because he was broke and jobless.

Mike discovered that the sheriff permitted visitors on Thursday nights, so the next day we pooled our money for a carton of cigarettes and made our way to the Delaware County Jail. We crowded into the waiting area with about thirty other families for half an hour before a turnkey motioned for us to enter a hot steel cubicle. Inside were two small eight-by-ten-inch plate glass windows. There were tiny holes drilled in the wall to allow voices to travel from one side of the cubicle to the other. We saw Dad's face through our window. He appeared to be speaking but we had to lean close to hear him.

"Kennedy's the man of the hour," he said with pride. "And I was right there with him. When he's elected, I can cheap-note for days for being the only person in Muncie who kissed him."

"Yeah," interjected Mike. "The fellows at Bob's been talking about you all week. Bear said he gonna buy you a chicken dinner when you get out."

"Why did you get arrested if you're such good friends with Kennedy?" I asked.

"After the speech . . ." he began, and I put my ear closer to the holes to hear him over the din, "I spied a police car driving through the alley. I recognized the officers and raised my hand to stop them. I said, 'Gentlemen, take me home. I just kissed the next president of the United States!' They said, 'Buster, we got a home for you. Get in the car.' "

"Well, you got what you deserved." I chuckled. "You shouldn't have been up on the stage drunk anyway."

"Hell, I just had a little taste. I was looking to the future, son. It was good publicity. I might even run for city judge. I couldn't pass up that opportunity. Anyway, it's not that bad in here. I have a decent place to sleep, plenty to eat, and don't have to listen to Mom's harangue."

"What about my game?" I asked. "You said you would come to Richmond. This is the most important game of my life."

"I'm sorry. I'd like to be on the sidelines. It'd be worth the trip to see you show the coach how stupid he was for keeping you on the bench all season. Anyway, I told the sheriff all about you and he said he would let 'me and the boys' listen to the game on the radio."

That's great, I thought. My biggest cheering section is going to be "A" block in the Delaware County Jail.

On the bus ride to Richmond I sat alone to psych myself up for the game. For the first half hour, I wondered how life could have been worse. I'd had virtually no playing time during the season, and the coach clearly did not want me to lead the team. Richmond even had the home field advantage.

Shame dominated my feelings when I thought of Dad in jail. I had such mixed feelings for my father. I wondered how I could love and hate him so much at the same time. I allowed myself to dwell with sadness on all that might have been. As we passed through New Castle and the halfway point to Richmond, I realized negative thinking would not help me do my best. "Stop feeling sorry for yourself," I said. "Some of this is funny as hell. Kissing the next president?" I chuckled softly when I decided that Dad's being in jail was a blessing in disguise. He was safe, sober, and far away. I wouldn't have to worry about him standing at the stadium railing, shouting drunken instructions to me.

The October air was crisp as we ran onto the field. Our sophomore team had beaten Richmond on this very site the previous season, but there had been only a few spectators. Now it seemed over five thousand people filled the stands. The noise was deafening, as the crowd cheered for Richmond. We lost the coin toss, and I paced the sidelines waiting for our turn on offense. Looking onto the field I watched the Richmond quarterback, Sonny Sage, the Red Devils' All-State candidate. He had been a rival of mine since the ninth grade. Everyone who saw him talked about how talented he was and believed he was a sure bet to play big-time college football. Sweat rolled down my back as I stood beside George Punzelt and watched one of our defensive men knock down a Sage pass. Richmond had to punt.

Punzelt turned to me and said, "Okay, Gregor, let's show these boys how to play football!"

Sage trotted off the field as I raced toward my huddle. As his number disappeared into the crowd, I said to myself, "Sonny Sage, you've never beaten me, and I'm not about to let it happen tonight."

We decided to take it right to their All-State lineman to see how good he was. Our redesigned offense called for two blockers on him. I shoved the ball into Jim Boyce's gut, and he ran right behind Ronnie Hudson as he blew the All-State tackle off the line. Jim gained fifteen yards, and a first down, on what should have been a five-yard play. We were moving, but we still didn't know whether our first run against their All-Star tackle had been a fluke.

I decided to try a quarterback sneak. Hunching over Tim Freeman, I barked out the signals. My eyes were straight ahead as I moved the team in cadence. Tim slapped my hands with the ball, and I ran laterally down the right side of the line, looking for the opening but tensing my 165-pound frame for a collision with a 250-pound wall. Right in front of me Ronnie slammed his shoulder pads into the tackle's stomach. Surprised to still be on my feet, I quickly turned up the speed for a ten-yard gain before a defensive back hauled me down. Even as I tumbled to the ground, I felt no pain. I knew we could win.

The game became a battle of attrition. We moved twenty yards and had to kick. They moved twenty yards and had to kick back to us. Finally, we reached scoring territory, but a pesky Richmond safety intercepted one of my passes. Richmond couldn't capitalize on the turnover, and soon we threatened to score again, but we couldn't penetrate the end zone.

The fourth quarter arrived with the score deadlocked in a 0–0 tie. As the clock ran down to the final minute, we ripped off a long gain, and after another run found ourselves on the Richmond one-yard line, poised to score and win the game. My teammates bent over with their hands on their knees. Their purple jerseys were covered with dirt and grass. A cloud of steam rose from our huddle. I looked through it at the Richmond defense, searching for a way to beat them. I felt I had the answer. "Okay, I'm going to take the ball off tackle again. Ronnie, I'm going to be right behind you. Knock that big mothafucker on his ass." Just then I felt a slap on my shoulder. It was a runner from the sidelines. "Coach wants Nick to take it off tackle."

Damn. I groaned to myself, wondering if the fact that Nick was white influenced the decision. "Okay." We jogged to the ball for the final time. The clock ticked off the last seconds. If we were going to win, it had to happen on the final play. For the last time that night, I leaned over Tim Freeman and barked out the signals. He slapped the ball in my hand and I spun to my right. One long step, and I stuffed the ball into Nick's stomach. Two steps into the line he fumbled. Richmond recovered. The gun rang out.

The game ended with a 0–0 tie. It wasn't what we wanted, but we were glad to take it back to Muncie. We arrived near midnight and walked through the deserted downtown. As we passed the jail I saw the cell block was dark, and I wondered if Dad had heard the game. It was almost one a.m. when we reached the Madison Street YMCA. Teenagers were streaming out the door at the end of the regular Saturday night dance.

Two former Muncie Central football stars stood on the steps outside the building. As soon as they saw me one said, "Damn, Greg, you should have heard the radio broadcast. Man, they were talking about you all night. They said, 'This Williams is a player. We're going to hear a lot about him from now on. He came off the bench and led the Bearcats to tie one of the best teams in the state.' They didn't criticize Coach, but he sure looked bad for not playing you before."

By my junior year I was less self-conscious about where I sat in the auditorium. I still spent most of my lunch break studying history. Dad was ecstatic when I took my grades home for the first six-week period. My grade in U.S. History was A++ with an appended note: "Greg has scored more points than were technically possible!" As soon as he saw the note, Dad snatched it from my hand and headed for the tavern to brag about my accomplishments and look for free drinks.

Actually, the major reason I worked so hard in history that fall was to impress a classmate. Maxine had flawless, creamy, light-brown skin and a warm, friendly face. Short, reddish brown curls framed her ever-present smile. She often wore a yellow dress that clung to the curves of her body. It was easy to talk with her, and she surprised me by appearing interested in what I had to say. From the very first day of school I longed to ask her for a date, but she was seeing a fellow in his early twenties. Certain she had no romantic interest in me, I held back. One afternoon following class Maxine casually asked me if I would be at the postgame dance. Immediately, I knew I would be there.

The best dancer in school was my football teammate Jim Boyce. As we stood in the showers after practice that day, I told him I wanted to go to the dance on Friday but didn't know how to dance. My instruction soon became a neighborhood project. Several teammates, Jim's girlfriend, Alma, and two of her neighbors crowded into his small living room on East Jackson Street to coach me. Finally, Friday night arrived. On the football field we soundly defeated our opponent. As soon as the gun sounded I raced to the locker room. I was in and out of the shower before Jim had the tape removed from his ankles. Ronnie and Brian still sat on the bench in front of their lockers, blaming each other for missing the tackle on our opponents' only touchdown. I fidgeted at the door waiting for them, and considered going on ahead to the dance, but that meant I'd have to walk through town by myself. The previous week some Shed Town boys attacked a black couple walking home after the game. Finally, the six of us left the stadium and walked downtown, past Woolworth's and Sears. I paused at Morton Standt's Jewelers' clear glass window to check my face for game bruises. The fellows were halfway down Jackson Street past Lem's Mandarin Inn when I caught up with them. Jim was singing, "Let's do the hitchhike baby." They were in line behind him keeping step. In front of the Rivoli Theatre Jim ordered, "Okay, Greg, I want you to practice that spin I taught you last night."

"How I'm gonna do that? Ain't no girl to dance with."

"Grab a hold of Ronnie."

I looked at Ronnie Hudson, who seemed almost as big out of uniform as he did in it.

"I ain't no broad," protested Ronnie.

"We know that, man. Just stand still while Greg practices his spin," said Jim.

Ronnie stood scowling under the Rivoli marquee lights. "Come on, Greg," challenged Jim, and I took Ronnie's hand for two quick spins.

"Shit, Greg, that ain't it," said Jim as he grabbed Ronnie's hand and did a double spin and dip under his outstretched arm.

I tried it again, but my feet got all tangled up.

"Well come on, Greg. Let's see your slow dance style."

"Wait a minute," shouted Ronnie. "I ain't gonna let Greg be

grinding with me here in front of the theater." Ronnie backed into the darkness away from the marquee lights.

We headed for the dance, held in Muncie's version of Harlem's Birdland Cafe, at 714 East Seymour Street. The Birdland was a one-story, concrete block building next to the railroad tracks. A large crowd congregated on the paved area just outside the door. The Birdland didn't serve alcohol, but the smell of beer, wine, and marijuana was in the air. Older fellows trying to pick up high school girls often arrived drunk and shared their bottles and drugs. I thought we would never get through the crowd, especially when friends began congratulating us. It was almost eleven p.m., and I was worried about missing Maxine. Finally, Jim noticed I was nervous and shouted for Ronnie to forge a path through the crowd and lead us inside. It took almost a minute for my eyes to adjust to the darkness as I frantically scanned the room for Maxine. Jim spotted her. Her gold hoop earrings gleamed in the light as her smile filled the room.

"Don't be waitin', brother," Jim said. "No tellin' who's gonna be comin' through that door."

Reluctantly, I sauntered over to her.

"Say, Maxine, how ya doin'?" I asked meekly.

Her low, husky voice melted whatever confidence being the star quarterback of the night had given me.

"You guys played a pretty good game."

"Yeah, but I got hit hard a couple of times. You should see the cleat marks on my legs."

As the words tumbled out of my mouth I wished I could have pulled them back. At that moment the jukebox began to wail with "For Your Precious Love." I asked her to dance.

"You sure you're not hurt too bad?" she challenged with a broad smile. Self-consciously, I took her hand and we slowly moved to the dance floor. Finally, face to face with her, I drew her body tightly to me. Leaning over, I brushed her neck with my lips. I fell deeper and deeper into her embrace, drawing in the sweet fragrances of her body.

"Greg, the record's over," Maxine said, pulling me back to reality.

We were the last couple on the dance floor. As Maxine rejoined her girlfriends, I caught her boyfriend Ray eyeing me from the doorway. He was a handsome guy, but so arrogant, I couldn't understand what Maxine saw in him.

I walked back to Jim, who was standing with my cousin "Ducky."

"Give me some skin, bro, you lookin' good!" said Jim. "You were in there so tight with the woman I started sweatin' from watchin' you."

Ducky added, "You're lookin' good, cuz. I dug your crouch, man." Then turning to the other fellows, he said, "Soon as Williams goes out on the floor, he falls into a crouch and gets as close to the woman as he can. Man, you couldn't see no daylight between Greg and Maxine. He goes right for the money."

Ducky continued. "You shoulda seen the look on Ray's face when he walked in and saw Greg grindin' with his woman. Man, I thought he was gonna jump out on the floor and try to put some knots on my cousin's head. Then we'd have to turn the whole place out!"

Across the crowded dance floor Ray was shaking his finger in Maxine's face. I couldn't understand why she took that kind of treatment from him. She could have had any guy she wanted.

"You're in luck, cousin. Ray's headin' out the door. You better get over there and talk to the woman."

I had several more dances with Maxine and was flying high when they played "Save the Last Dance for Me." Not wanting the night to end, I summoned up all my courage and asked to walk her home. She stopped two blocks from her house at Kirby and Macedonia.

"This is close enough," she said, drawing close to me.

"Can't I go all the way home with you?"

"No, I've gotta do the rest alone. Daddy doesn't like to see me with boys."

Uncertain if I would be rejected or not, I leaned down to kiss her good night. She didn't resist my first kiss, and I slipped my arms around her. Our lips touched and she opened her mouth to let my tongue meet hers. We stood locked together for almost ten minutes. Even the chill of the late fall night could not pull us apart.

After another long embrace, she said, "If I don't get home soon, Daddy's liable to come after me and see us standing here on the corner."

I knew it was time for her to go. Her father had a reputation as a "wild man" where his daughters were concerned. I watched her disappear down the street.

Now that I was an official Bearcat football hero, more girls seemed attracted to me, especially white girls. Some of them even began to call me at home. At first I really wasn't interested. I recalled the firestorm my short interlude with Janie had caused at Wilson. But Maxine's boyfriend monopolized her time, and she made it clear he was the guy she wanted. The white girls kept calling. Every time Miss Dora answered the phone she handed it to me with an anxious look on her face. There was one particularly persistent girl who phoned every day. Although she refused to give her name, her phone voice was so enticing I continued to talk with her. She obviously knew a great deal about my activity around the school. She even described Miss Dora's house perfectly. When she offered to meet me anywhere I chose, my interest soared. Some of the other black athletes on the team talked about calls and offers of secret dates, even though the same girls rarely acknowledged us during the school day. I was almost ready to arrange a meeting with my mystery caller when a sixth sense cautioned me. I told her I was unable to plan anything until the weekend.

The next day we finished practice early, and I was less than a block from my house when I noticed a light blue Chevy moving slowly down Kirby Avenue. Two white girls were in the car. It slowed almost to a stop in front of my house. I slipped behind the tree in front of Roach's. The car picked up speed, but I recognized them. The driver was my mystery caller. It was Candy Gardner. We had spent an entire semester together in history class, and she never spoke to me.

Certain Candy would continue to call, I needed to find a way to deflect her interest. I called one of my buddies on the football team who was crazy about white girls. I told him that Candy was available and interested. As I walked to my first period class Monday morning he grabbed me in the hall, and swore they'd had sex all Saturday night. "I owe ya, man," he said. A week later he gloomily confided he had "the clap."

Football continued to take up most of my time. When we played Kokomo we weren't able to surprise them the same way we had Richmond. They gave us a 41–0 beating and a lot of punishment. Late in the game, after making a handoff to Jim Boyce, I raced to the opposite side of the line attempting to fake the defense. As I turned my head downfield to see if Jim had made any progress, shoulder pads slammed into my stomach. My back hit the grass like a shot. The hit was so hard that my socks, taped to my legs to keep them up, dropped on impact. Opening my eyes, I saw six-foot, eight-inch, 225-pound Jim Ligon getting off me. Most Indiana sports enthusiasts said Ligon's real athletic prowess was basketball, but after that night he had my vote for All-American defensive end.

Dad, sick again from drinking, listened to the game from his couch at Grandma's. He wrote the words of the local sportscaster on her grocery sack wallpaper. "When Ligon hit Williams that time, his molars must have shook."

Dejected over the loss, I was almost the last player dressing after the game. Just as I waved for my buddies to go home without me, a coach walked through the locker room.

"Greg, would you drop by the office before you leave?"

The room could hardly pass for an office. The desk was flush against the wall, and there was only space for three chairs bunched together. He motioned me to a seat beside the desk. I wondered if he was going to criticize my game performance.

"I've wanted to talk with you for some time, but never got around to it. I was wondering how things were going. I like to know my players so if problems arise, I might be able to help them. I try to look out for you guys."

I wanted to believe he was sincere. However, experience had taught me there was a "Mr. Bennett" around every corner whose principal concern was to discover if I was dating white girls. Quickly sensing that this discussion might be heading in that direction, I looked past him, locking my eyes on the green concrete wall.

"I understand you and your brother don't live with your mother or father. How do you take care of yourself?"

Momentarily disarmed by the unexpected approach, I thought maybe he really did want to help me. I explained our dependence on Miss Dora. He, like so many others, didn't seem to believe she wasn't related to us. I thought of the numerous women in our neighborhood who struggled to care for others' children in need without assistance or acknowledgment. Yet I dared not show any anger or accuse him of racial insensitivity. Once he had spent almost half an hour of practice time talking about the deep understanding and friendship he had developed with one of his former "colored" players. The following day, he thoroughly embarrassed the only black senior starter on the team by accusing him of being a poor role model and failing to provide leadership. The tongue-lashing he gave the athlete made the rest of us cringe. Now he claimed he wanted to look out for me.

I considered telling him how hard it was. Maybe he could help. I needed more weight and often felt faint from hunger at practice. He seemed to express a genuine interest in my welfare, but so many "concerned" people had let me down in the past. I decided to trust him a little, but not too much. He might think I needed another job instead of playing football. He might even try to convince me to quit the team.

"Yes," I admitted, "it's hard, but I have a part-time job and make enough to get by."

He asked me how much I made.

"Three dollars a week for cleaning a law office."

"But that's barely enough for lunch."

I forced a halfhearted smile to convince him that everything was okay.

"I think I can get you a job around the school sweeping the cafeteria for free lunches," he said. My spirits soared. He paused. Then, looking toward the open door, he continued in a low monotone.

"Oh, yes, there's another thing I want to discuss with you."

The wooden chair became harder. I fidgeted and averted my eyes. I felt caged. I wanted to run from the room. My body tensed as I braced for the next question. I knew what it was going to be. I waited while he tried to sound nonchalant.

"What about dating?"

"What about dating?" I questioned, feigning ignorance. I realized we now had arrived at the true purpose of the session. He leaned closer, his yellow-stained teeth bared in a half smile.

"Well, who do you date, Greg?"

"Nobody in particular. . . . Sports and studying take a lot of time."

"You must have some girls that you see from time to time."

Finally, I stopped fencing with him and said, "Yes. There's one girl I mess around with." I was thinking of Maxine. He no longer disguised his interrogation as casual.

"Is she white or colored?" he asked bluntly.

"Colored."

His forehead wrinkled with suspicion. "Do you see any white girls?"

Even if I dated every white girl in the school, there was only one acceptable answer to that question.

"No."

He stared at me for a moment, then he relaxed.

"Tell me about the girl you are seeing. Are you going steady?"

I thought when I told him I wasn't dating white girls the conversation would end. It was obvious he wanted to know more, but as he probed, I made him repeat each question. As I lied about Maxine he continued to press for more details. Both of us became uncomfortable, and I leaned away from him toward the door. Finally, weary of our cat-and-mouse game, he dismissed me.

As I walked along the corridor into the locker room, I saw a black teammate who had overheard the conversation while dressing in the locker room. I put my finger over his lips so he wouldn't acknowledge me. Once we were safely outside the building, I nodded in agreement as he said, "I don't think you should have told Coach all those things. It ain't none of his business. You never know how white people will use that information. Even if they say they want to help you, that doesn't mean shit. Any way it goes, they've got you over a barrel."

I was grateful the coach had not totally disarmed me by expressing interest in my family situation. The truth was, I was without a job. The lawyer had fired me for losing his office key during an overnight football trip. I desperately hoped the coach would remember I needed a job to pay for lunches, but he never mentioned it again.

Perhaps the coach's concern about my dating white girls made them more appealing. The next morning as I stood in the hallway near my classroom, I noticed an attractive brunette struggling to open her locker while balancing an armload of books. I walked over and helped her open the locker. She gave me a friendly "Thanks" and left for class. Several times that week when I saw her at the locker, I began casual conversation about school and the upcoming game. At first she was friendly, but after a few days she became cold and distant. Later that week I decided to go to Concannon's Bakery for a cream-filled cupcake for lunch. As I made my way out the Charles Street exit, I found my path blocked by a white football teammate. I didn't know him very well. He was a short and stocky senior lineman. I tried to sidestep him, but he moved in front of me. Thinking he was playing a practical joke, I laughed. However, there was no friendly response. "What the fuck are you doing talking to my sister?" he snarled.

"I don't know what you mean."

"Don't lie to me. You been hanging around her locker all week."

Then it dawned on me. I had never asked the brunette her last name. Although he outweighed me by over sixty pounds, I had no fear of him. My only thought was how lucky his sister was to be so pretty, when he was so ugly. However, I wasn't crazy enough to say that out loud. Tensing my shoulders and arms, I waited for him to swing at me. I edged away so he would be unable to grab me in a wrestling hold.

"Man, I don't know what you're talking about," I said, trying to figure out how I would fight him. "Her locker is right across from mine. I can talk to anyone I want."

"I tell you what, nigger, if you say one more word to her I'm gonna kick your black ass."

The threat shocked me more than it frightened me. I didn't expect it from him, my own teammate. He had protected me from the onslaught of opposing teams. I stood there dumbfounded while he walked away. Once I recovered my senses, I decided not to let him intimidate me. Later that afternoon, when I saw his sister at her locker, I walked over to her, leaned against the wall, and began a conversation. She grabbed her books and fled down the hall.

That night after midnight I awoke to the sound of glass breaking and tires squealing. Racing downstairs, I found Miss Dora standing in the living room with a brick in her hands. Broken glass from the front window covered the floor and Miss Dora's sitting chair.

She held the brick up to my face and said, "White girls mean trouble!"

Our next game was the perennial state champion, Reitz High School, in Evansville, on the southwest tip of Indiana. It was almost a five-hour trip. About fifty miles north of Evansville we stopped in a small town for gas. At that time across America's South efforts were under way to desegregate public transportation. Demonstrators traveled in racially mixed buses. As we milled about the gas station, one local white adult, perhaps noticing the mixture of white and black boys, approached me as I stood alone at the soft drink machine. "Are you all Freedom Riders?" I was aware of Freedom Riders from newspaper pictures of whites beating them as they arrived in Mississippi and Alabama towns. I recalled the segregated bus terminal in Louisville, but that was across the Ohio River. I was certain Indiana wasn't as hostile as Mississippi. Yet from the tone of the man's voice, Freedom Riders obviously were not welcome in southwest Indiana.

The game went badly. We were down thirty-three points by the end of the first half. On every play an opponent was in our backfield almost before I received the ball. Someone was missing his blocking assignment. I soon confirmed my suspicion that it was the teammate who had threatened me. In the huddle, I complained, "Damn . . . your man is getting in the backfield before I do. Block that SOB!" The angry lineman still made a halfhearted effort. At halftime I pulled aside the coach who had expressed so much interest in me and told him what was happening.

"What's wrong, Williams? Afraid of getting knocked on your butt?"

The game ended with a 66–0 drubbing. As we walked toward the locker room, the fans threw rotten vegetables, popcorn boxes, and empty Coke cups at us. Then one group near the exit began chanting.

"Niggers!"

"Niggers!"

Outside the stadium as we waited for the bus, a small crowd of boys shouted.

"Niggers go home!"

"Niggers go home!"

The coach was silent.

# Chapter 17

# "Born in the Wilderness and Suckled by a Boar"

The air in the cavernous Muncie Fieldhouse was heavy with anxiety as football players tried out for the basketball team. Stardom in elementary school, junior high school, and on the junior varsity meant nothing. Following a long grueling scrimmage, the coach ordered us courtside. The old wooden bleachers creaked and groaned as thirty athletes scrambled for a place. All eyes were fixed on Coach Prendergast.

"It's tough deciding who's gonna play and who isn't. The problem is, Muncie Central has enough talent for at least five excellent teams. Most of you could play on virtually any other team in the state. This is especially hard for me because I remember what it's like to be cut.

"The skill level we have here today makes it tough to choose. I may make a mistake, and I have made them before, but if I do it's my mistake. There are many factors that I consider. I want players who will give me one hundred percent. I also have to look to the future. If I have two boys of equal skill level, and one is a junior, and the other a senior, unless that senior is going to play a lot for me during the year, I think it's better to keep the junior."

I silently prayed that was the case for me.

"I want to thank each of you for your time and effort, and now if I read your name, take your place on the foul line."

He called the first team as expected: Brian Settles, Bill Dinwiddie, Melvin Jolly, Richie Williams, Curt Ervin. Then he named the next five. He was going to take only two more boys. He named the first: Bob Campbell. The anxiety almost suffocated me. Had my basketball career ended? Finally he said, ". . . and Greg Williams."

I took my place on the foul line. Five years of total commitment to basketball was rewarded. I was a Muncie Central Bearcat.

As the basketball season began in earnest, my teammates and I became one-dimensional. Our sole objective was to be the best basketball team in the state of Indiana. Practices were often more grueling than games. Every Wednesday we had a nonstop two-hour practice, which helped the coach decide who was going to play in the upcoming games. My skills were improving, but I was not a serious threat to replace any of the stars. In fact, I was lucky to play most games. One of my old adversaries from the Projects teased me in front of the lunchtime auditorium crowd.

"Greg is so far down the totem pole, the other night when the team was ahead thirty points the coach said, 'Greg, get up so we can send in the bench!' "

By the middle of the season Indiana sportswriters placed Brian Settles on the list of the top twenty-five basketball players in the state. Although I was slightly taller, he outweighed me by over twenty-five pounds. Since most of our play was fighting around and under the basket, weight was critical. The Wednesday scrimmage after Thanksgiving began casually enough, but we had only run up and down the floor twice before Brian elbowed me in the face. A bloody nose sharpened my intensity, and soon we were fighting like two alleycats, pushing and shoving for the same square foot of space. A shot bounced off the glass backboard. Brian hovered beside me for a rebound. Just as the ball hit the rim, I stepped in front of him and threw my left elbow into his stomach. He doubled over and flew butt-first to the foul line. I grabbed the rebound and raced down the court. Brian pushed himself off the floor and bolted after me like a raging bull. When he was about halfway down the court, the coach yelled, "Hey, you guys, cut the rough stuff! Sit down and cool off."

That Friday we played upstate rival South Bend Central. Though they had a good team, we quickly took control of the game. As I sat alone at the end of the bench, I hoped for a chance to play at least in the fourth quarter. But then, shortly after the second quarter began, I heard my name. I peered into the nearby bleachers to see if Dad was there, drunk, trying to impress a friend. I didn't see him, but I kept hearing it.

"Greg. Greg."

I turned and faced the coach. Red-faced, he leaned over from the other end of the bench, beckoning me.

"Greg, dammit, pay attention. I want you to get in there for Brian."

Elated, I raced to the scorer's table. I scored several baskets, but another substitute took my place as the quarter ended. The coach motioned for me to sit next to him.

"Don't be so glum, Greg. You're gonna play a lot more. The way you've been hustling in practice makes me think I've found the strong sixth man I've been looking for all season."

It was absolutely clear that my formula for success was to assault Brian on the court. Every day at practice I went after him like a mortal enemy, yet away from the fieldhouse we were inseparable. Our team developed into one of the best in Indiana that year. In fact, we were the only team to beat the eventual state champions, Kokomo, during the regular season.

One Saturday night just before Christmas we dominated a very mediocre team from Fort Wayne Southside. Brian looked like an All-American athlete when he intercepted a pass and dribbled the length of the court for an easy layup. As he crossed the foul line, he slipped on a paper cup thrown by a spectator.

X rays revealed a torn ligament in his knee. Rather than operate, the doctors decided to let it heal itself. I was sorry that Brian's season had ended, but immediately hoped I would see more action.

The next week, Coach Prendergast called me into his office. He got right to the point. "Greg, since Brian is out for the rest of the year, I have to make some adjustments."

He leaned toward me, almost touching noses. "I've decided to bring Dennis up from the B team."

Dennis, a white boy, was the starting B team center. Although unformed as a player, he was six-foot-six, almost four inches taller than me. Though I was a better shooter, and could even outjump him on occasion, the four inches made a big difference over the course of a game. The coach wanted more height.

He continued. "You're the logical one to drop to the B team. Start practicing with them and dress for their games. You don't need to dress for the varsity any longer."

There was no discussion, no diplomacy, no effort to make the demotion less painful. I was devastated. Now I knew what the coach meant when he said he could pick and choose whomever he wanted. Under pressure to maintain Muncie's winning tradition he would not gamble on a "promise" or "maybe."

Just before the season began he told us, "The old sportswriter, Grantland Rice, said 'It's not whether you win or lose, but how you play the game.' At Muncie Central it's whether you win or lose."

After my first B team practice, it was obvious I didn't fit into that coach's plans and would receive little playing time. My motivation soon evaporated.

Basketball season ended with an awards banquet. Woody Hayes, the Ohio State University football coach, traveled from Columbus to speak at the ceremony. He likened human potential to a bar of gold that each of us could choose to shape. By using our talent, we could create different treasures, gaining recognition in different ways. He said we could each choose to make baskets, lamps, or finely tuned watches with our bar of gold. I felt I had spent years trying to be the best basketball player I could be. Satisfied that I had worked hard all season, I was anxious for recognition and a varsity jacket for my contribution to Muncie Central basketball.

My award was a small emblem given to B team members. I was embarrassed and ashamed to stand in front of my varsity teammates to accept the same award I had received one year earlier. I dropped it in the trash on the way home.

During the summer I was able to find only a couple of part-time jobs. I returned to the basketball court with renewed dedication to redeem myself as a Bearcat basketball star. I did continue to improve. Almost all the courtside spectators assured me that glory awaited me my senior year. I even began to relax a bit that summer, and took up fishing with my basketball buddies: Brian, Carl Brown, and Melvin Jolly. The White River, which snaked through Muncie, was pretty pathetic, but it was all we had. We plumbed its rocky five-foot bed for carp and catfish, always hoping that some bass or other sportfish might mysteriously find its way into the slow-running waters.

One night we fished at the High Street dam near the fieldhouse until almost ten p.m. In four hours of fishing no one had caught anything—except Brian, who snared an eight-inch carp. His line became tangled as he tried to lug it across the rocks. To save the fish, I stepped on the rocks to loosen the line, slipped on moss, and fell into the river up to my waist. Brian finally managed to reel in the "prize" carp, and we decided it was time to call it a night. We climbed the muddy embankment to High Street and walked south past a popular drive-in for white teenagers. Carl wanted a Coke, but we knew blacks were barred from the drive-in like every downtown restaurant. Even the cafeteria, where athletic teams ate postgame meals, was off-limits at all other times. As we passed the drive-in we heard shouting.

"Hello, colored boys! Hello, niggers!"

"Hello, colored boys! Hello, niggers!"

We tightened our grips on our fishing poles. Looking into the parking lot, I recognized the faces of Central and Wilson classmates. A crowd formed as students spilled out of the restaurant. They raced to the edge of the parking lot, but stopped as if there were an invisible fence. We walked by silently, trying to ignore them. "Let's get the niggers," someone shouted from behind us. I looked over my shoulder. A white boy in ducktails stepped into the street. He was followed by another, then another. Soon a mob filled the street, shadowing us for an entire block, chanting.

"Niggers!"

"Niggers!"

"Niggers!"

Finally, at the Main Street intersection, right under the streetlight, without a word passing among the four of us, we turned to face them. For a brief second, a hush fell over the crowd. If there was any mistake before, there could be none now. They could see we were four well-known Muncie Central athletes. These same students cheered wildly when we mastered conference rivals. From somewhere in the darkness, I heard, "Get the black bastards." The mass of bodies started moving once again. Still, we held our ground. I glanced at Carl, Brian, and Melvin. They stood firm.

The crowd halted ten yards from us, taken aback by our unyielding stance. Two Shed Town boys from Wilson pushed through the group carrying baseball bats. An empty beer can fell at my feet. A stone hit me in the shoulder. I heard an "Oof!" and turned to see a large rock glance off Carl's ankle.

A shower of rocks and bottles fell over us. We glanced at each other, then sped off at a dead run past the courthouse and down Walnut Street. Even loaded with fish and fishing gear, we easily outran our pursuers and finally reached Brian's house. We sat in his living room most of the night, trying to comprehend the attack. Brian, the star of the basketball team who was receiving scholarship offers from all over the country, said, "Don't matter what you achieve or how big you get, you'll always be a nigger in Muncie."

We avoided the High Street fishing hole near Orv's the rest of the summer. By fall, I was so focused on atoning for the way my basketball season had ended the year before that I could hardly concentrate on football. Night after night I jolted awake in bed covered with sweat, convinced that if I didn't make the basketball team it would be the end of the world. Fear of failure constantly plagued me.

Again, football players had only a brief chance to show our basketball skills. Coach Prendergast delivered almost the same speech of the previous year about difficult decisions and how he knew what it was like to be cut. He announced the team one by one. "Settles, Dinwiddie, Brown, Johnson, Hill . . ." I counted eleven and didn't hear my name. I prayed twelve would be my lucky number again. This time it was not to be. My athletic career at Muncie Central was over.

That final year of high school, Dad landed his first regular job since being fired from Nash Rehabilitation Center five years earlier. He was a janitor at a fast-food restaurant. Like most of the menial jobs he found in Muncie, this one ultimately bored him as well. He was never able to adjust to the drudgery of cleaning and mopping, and finally began to drink on the job. He probably managed to hold on to the job because he worked from eleven p.m. to seven a.m., alone. Late one Friday night shortly after being dropped from the basketball team, I heard the phone ringing. I rolled over and looked at my clock, three a.m. Miss Dora called upstairs to say Dad was on the phone.

Furious about having to leave the warmth of my bed, I stomped downstairs in my bare feet.

"What took you so long to get to the phone? You been playing with yourself?"

"I'm trying to sleep like most normal people at three a.m. What do you want?"

"What do you mean, what do I want? You better be careful. I'm still master of your fate, and can kick your butt. I want you and Mike down here on the double to help me clean up the place. If you want any lunch money this week, get your ass out on the porch. I got two policemen coming by to pick you up in their patrol car. I just fixed them sandwiches, and they owe me a favor. Wake Mike. Hurry up!"

I was so angry I wanted to slam down the phone, but I didn't want to disturb Miss Dora. I considered defying Dad, but remembered that the next day was his payday. The squad car arrived as promised.

After issuing orders for us to sweep, mop, clean, and carry out the trash, Dad headed downstairs to the basement banquet room and stretched out on a long, foam-covered bench. He was asleep within seconds. Mike and I made an expert mop crew due to our "training" at City Hall. We raced through the job. To make it interesting we plunked quarters in the jukebox and turned it to full volume. Ray Charles, James Brown, and B. B. King blasted through the restaurant. We danced around the tables, spinning mops and brooms like they were girls. Early morning pedestrians gazed through the plate glass windows at us as if we were mad. Once the work was finished we raided the freezer. Soon we were grilling hamburgers and deep frying mountains of french fries. Then we started on the deserts. First we ate pie and sweet rolls, then doughnuts. We topped it all off with ice cream sundaes. At six-thirty we woke Dad so he could swallow several cups of black coffee and greet the day-shift workers who arrived at seven a.m.

The adventure wore off in about three weeks when Dad lost his entire paycheck gambling before he arrived home. My resentment was still smoldering when he called the following Saturday morning. I refused his order.

"What the hell you mean you're not coming?" he shouted over the telephone. "If you don't come down here, I'm not giving you a nickel when I get paid today!"

"As I recall," I hissed back at him, "I didn't get any money last week."

"If you don't get down here, I'm gonna kick your ass as soon as I get off work. All I do for you, and you don't appreciate shit."

Softly but firmly I said, "I'm not coming. I'm going back to bed, and if you want to see me when you get off work, I'll be here."

"You think you're a big shot, don't you? If you hadn't been so goddamn smart you wouldn't got cut from the team, Mr. Bearcat Failure. If it weren't for me, you'd still be a little snot-nosed sissy gettin' his ass kicked by all the boys on the playground. Man, you don't know who you're messing with. I was born in the wilderness, suckled by a boar, got four rows of jaw teeth and always room for more."

"Good night Dad."

"You can stay home if you want to, and I'll take care of you in the morning. Now get Mike up, and tell him to get on down here."

"He doesn't want to come down either."

"Get him on the telephone, motherfucker, before I get a gun and come after your ass right now!"

I climbed the stairs and woke Mike. We talked while he waited for a ride. Mike begged me to come with him, but I stood firm.

The squad car arrived and transported Mike to the restaurant. He worked alone while Dad slept. I was up and dressed at seven-thirty, sitting on the porch waiting for the showdown. Mike arrived about ten o'clock, and told me Dad was at Bob's Tavern, drunk already, and telling everyone how he was going home to kick a Bearcat's ass. I realized it would be a long wait, so I left to visit Brian.

Back home around four, I was in the bathroom when I heard the front door slam and heavy footsteps trudge through the living room. The bathroom door swung inward.

Dad looked as though he had crawled through the sewers. I suspected he had been thrown out of Bob's Tavern again, or he had gotten in a fight. His rummage sale homburg sat back on his forehead. He tried to give me an evil stare, but his eyes were too glassy to focus. "I'm here to take care of you," he said.

"Do you mind, Dad? I'm trying to use the toilet."

"You've been trying to hide from me. I've been looking for you all day."

"You couldn't have looked too hard. I've been here."

"Oh, you still trying to be a smart boy, are you? I see you're gettin' too big for your britches. I'm gonna have to teach you a lesson. Get up!"

He slapped me on the back of the head. I glared at him, and he jumped into his fighter's stance. I stood to fasten my pants. He was about two feet away, standing directly in front of the bathtub.

"You'll never get too big for me to handle you."

He slapped the side of my face with his open hand. I tried to remain calm. Fortified by my inaction, he hit me again in the face, this time with his full fist. The sting of the punch brought tears to my eyes. Although underweight, I was very strong from playing football and basketball. Many of my friends joked that, pound for pound, I was the strongest man in the high school. I didn't think Dad could beat me in a fight, but I really didn't want to fight him. Yet when I saw a third punch coming, I knew I had no choice. I blocked it with my left hand and punched him in the chest with my right as hard as I could.

Dad tumbled backward into the bathtub. I don't know who was more surprised—Dad, that I had hit him, or me, that I'd finally had enough. The punch focused his eyes. Looking at me, he saw a boy. The chest pain told him he had been hit by a man. Pulling himself out of the bathtub with as much grace as he could muster, he carefully avoided touching me. When standing, he edged out of the bathroom and said, "I should get a gun and kill you, motherfucker! I brought you into this world, and I can take you out. I tell you one thing, if you ever hit me again, you'll be a sorry son of a bitch!"

Dad stormed out of the house. He never hit me again, nor did he ever mention the incident. Although my eye was swelling shut, and the pain was excruciating, I felt an exhilarating sense of freedom on the day of my eighteenth birthday.

That winter I joined a basketball team sponsored by the black Madison Street YMCA. We traveled to Anderson, Richmond, Kokomo, Fort Wayne, and even Dayton and Springfield, Ohio, to play other black teams. In spite of the travel, good-sized crowds, and spirited play, it was a poor substitute for a spot on the premiere basketball team in the state of Indiana. Although I was no longer a Bearcat, Brian kept me up-to-date on news that didn't make the papers. He made a good recovery from the knee injury. The press touted the team for a top-four finish in the state tournament.

Late one evening around eleven o'clock I sat on the floor in my room studying when I heard a pebble hit my window. Brian rarely visited my room, saying the attic was either zero degrees and dropping in the winter or one hundred degrees and rising in the summer. But when something important came up he would signal for me to let him in. I led him upstairs silently to avoid waking Miss Dora. I sat on my bed, and he pulled up a chair. Brian had an unfamiliar nervous look in his eyes.

"There's gonna be a lot of shit in the paper tomorrow," he began. "I want to tell you before you read it.

"Me and three other brothers are off the team and in a lot of trouble."

There was nothing Brian could have said that would have shocked me more. I was hoping I would soon be seeing him wearing a gold state championship ring.

"What in the hell happened?"

"Initiation."

Part of the Muncie Central athletic ritual was upperclass hazing of sophomores. We called it "initiation." It usually consisted of pouring a dose of hot liniment in a jockstrap, throwing a fully clad sophomore into the showers, or taping legs and ripping off the tape. When I was a sophomore, four of us managed to foil an initiation attempt during an overnight trip to South Bend by locking and barricading our motel door. Some of our teammates weren't so lucky. The upperclassmen doused them with beer and soda and roughed them up with punches.

"You guys weren't on an overnight trip, Brian," I said.

"It was on the bus coming back from Indianapolis."

"On the bus? Weren't the coaches on the bus?"

"Yeah, but they were up front."

"What happened?"

Brian hesitated, and then with an embarrassed look he slowly said, "We scared 'em, and . . . and . . . made 'em play with themselves."

"Touch their dicks?"

"Yeah," he answered, looking at the floor. "We were high. Some fans gave us some beer after the game."

"You mean the coaches didn't do anything at all?"

"They said they didn't know what was going on."

"How could they not know what was going on? Didn't the sophomores holler?"

"Yeah, but we told 'em to shut up or we'd kick their butts."

Brian explained that a parent of one of the sophomores threatened to file charges if the coach didn't kick the participants off the team.

I sat on the bed looking at Brian. I thought about the letters he collected daily from colleges offering basketball scholarships. That was all destroyed, unless the coach was behind him.

"The coach will have to go to bat for you to get a scholarship now," I said hopefully.

"Well, you can forget that. He sat us down in the room and said, 'You rotten, low down sons of bitches how could you do this a week before our most important game. I'll never forgive any of you.'"

Brian shared his grief and heartache, then urged me to talk with the coach about a spot on the now decimated team. I felt, however, that the coach was not a man who admitted mistakes. He had dropped me once and I was finished.

Both of us stared at the floor. Brian's name was going to be splattered all over the newspapers, and his incredible basketball career would end in shame.

The expulsion of four top black athletes was the scandal of the year. For weeks there were news items and letters in newspapers all over the state. Racist jokes and cartoons made the rounds, and there were rumors that the incident was of a "homosexual" nature. The event divided the community sharply along racial lines. Outrage that black athletes had embarrassed Muncie and lost a state basketball championship flared through the white community. Black folks expressed the view that it was just one more example of dual standards. What were considered harmless pranks by white players were severely punished when done by blacks.

# Chapter 18

## State of Indiana v. Gregory H. Williams

One advantage of Dad's janitorial job was that he was able to buy an eight-year-old '54 Ford convertible for two hundred dollars. He claimed it was my "senior year present." At least he put it in my name. Early one November afternoon, I stopped at Grandma's on the way home from school to borrow "my" car to take Miss Dora to the supermarket. Dad was talking with an old gambling buddy, Buck, who rested on the couch. I asked for the car keys.

"You have five dollars for gas?" Dad challenged.

"The bus only costs fifteen cents."

"Then you better take the bus," he said with a laugh. He rose from the bed and walked to the old Philco next to the window.

"Why do I have to pay five dollars to use my car?"

A shrill blast of radio static filled the room.

He snapped off the switch and turned to face me. "I gotta have gas to go to Indianapolis tomorrow."

It turned out that he wanted to visit a wholesale house where he bought watches for five dollars each and sold them in Muncie for twenty-five dollars. The "scam" was to take the watches into local bars and surreptitiously show the case, which had a tag that said "As Advertised in Life Magazine, $75.00." Bar patrons who had a bit of larceny in their hearts would assume immediately that the watches were stolen. He and Buck especially liked to work this "con" on the young hustlers in the neighborhood who apparently had more money than sense.

Buck rolled with laughter when he told of "one smart-assed dude" who refused to pay more than fifteen dollars for the watch. Buck said Dad gave an "Academy Award–winning role" with tears in his eyes, claiming he was giving the watch away, when he took the "young blood's" money.

When I learned they planned to leave for Indianapolis early in the morning, I was nervous. A night of heavy drinking was already well under way, and I was certain danger lurked on the road. Though I did fear for their safety, my real concern was that something might happen to the car and end that convenience. I spent a half hour arguing against the trip without success. Reluctantly, I agreed to skip school and drive them to Indianapolis even though it would be my first day's absence in two and a half years.

That evening at dinner when I told Miss Dora of the trip, Mike decided to join us. He had already missed about as much school as he could and still expect to receive credit for the semester, so I argued against his joining us. But Mike was developing a strong will of his own and resented my efforts to control him.

Miss Dora felt neither one of us should gamble on a trip with Dad and Buck. She even dredged up the memories of our nightmare with James Fields when he crashed into the tree near Knightstown and almost killed Grandma, Mike, and me. I dismissed her fears and proclaimed nothing could go wrong because I would be in charge.

Frost was still in the air when Mike and I arrived at Grandma's at seven-thirty the next morning. Buck and Dad sat at the kitchen table, their hands wrapped around cups of black coffee while Grandma stoked the fire in the potbellied stove. As the four of us headed to the car, Mike raced to the driver's side and opened the door.

"No, Mike!" I said sharply, and pointed to the passenger's side.

"Aw, Greg. I want to drive." Turning to Dad, he said, "Daddy, can't I drive? Greg gets to drive all the time."

Mike had only recently passed his driver's test, and I had little confidence in his driving ability, but I realized arguing would be futile. We followed State Road 67 out of Muncie, and to my surprise,

Mike drove well. He didn't keep both hands on the wheel like I suggested, and he sat almost sideways, but he kept the car at a steady even speed. Mike looked sharp. He had raided my sparse closet, and was wearing my only sport coat. Glancing in the back seat, I also had to admit Dad's sharply pressed gray pinstripe rummage sale suit gave him the look of a prosperous businessman. Even Buck was a changed man. The stubble on his face was gone and his hair glistened.

As we passed Mounds Park and State Road 67 turned south, I heard Dad say, "Wanna taste, Buck?" My head snapped to the rear to see Dad pull a bottle of Thunderbird wine from his inside jacket pocket. He took a long swallow before passing it to Buck. I had a sinking feeling in my stomach, but all I could do was look ahead. Mile after mile of barren farmland quickly passed, and soon I spied the Indiana State Reformatory at Pendleton. The thick, gray, thirty-foot walls loomed over the flat Indiana landscape. Two older basketball teammates from the Madison Street YMCA were there, one for armed robbery, the other for a murder committed during a burglary. As the reformatory faded behind us, I briefly wondered about life behind the walls.

Just outside the town of Ingalls, we began to race through sleepy little villages dotted with old, abandoned gas stations. Two miles down the road from Fortville, Buck shouted from the back seat, "Pull over, Mike, I gotta piss!"

Mike glanced at me for approval. I nodded, and gravel clattered against the undercarriage as he pulled off the highway. He braked to a stop about fifty feet from a farmhouse. Buck crawled out of the car and stepped behind a large oak tree. Dad leaned out the open door and tossed his now-empty wine bottle into the farm yard.

"Damn, Dad," I said, turning to the back seat, "don't you know we can get fined fifty dollars for littering?"

"Hell, don't worry. That farmer can break the bottle up for glass and make a few cents off it."

"You'd probably want a cut from it too." I chuckled.

"You know," he said, "you're getting too big for your britches." He punctuated his remark with a long sour wine belch.

Five minutes passed. I yelled for Buck. Then I saw him step toward the farmhouse. Halfway across the yard he began to walk in circles, laughing and singing.

"I got my Mojo working! I got my Mojo working!"

Puzzled, I called out, "Buck!"

When he faced me, I saw what he thought was so funny. His pants were unzipped and his penis hung outside his trousers. Just then I noticed an elderly white woman peeking from behind a curtain in the farmhouse. Sensing disaster, I dashed for Buck and tried to draw him to the car. He resisted, still singing.

"I got my Mojo working! I got my Mojo working!"

Mike jumped from the car. Together we pulled Buck's two hundred and forty pounds across the yard. As we pushed him inside, Dad said, "Hell, Buck, I didn't know you were a singer." They both convulsed in laughter. Gravel flew across the road as Mike jammed the accelerator for a quick getaway. Five minutes down the road, as I began to relax, Mike noticed a state police car in the rearview mirror.

"It's coming fast, Greg."

Just then the loud wail of a siren filled the air. I prayed he would whip around us and roar down the highway. The siren pierced the air again, and the trooper sharply gestured for Mike to pull to the roadside. Desperately trying to stay calm, I asked Mike if he had his license. He reached for his wallet with one hand and gave it to me. There was no license.

"Oh, yeah, I forgot. I loaned it to Rudy. Do you think they'll arrest me?"

The trooper gave another long blast of the siren. "Damn, Mike, stop the car," I said.

While he pulled to the side of the road, I handed my license to him. Less than thirty seconds later the officer stood beside Mike. I took the registration from the glove compartment while Mike handed him my license. He asked, "What's your date of birth, Gregory?"

Mike paused and then said, "November first."

I was born November 12.

"What's the year of your birth?"

"Nineteen forty-four."

I was born in 1943.

"Is this your license, young man?"

Mike lifted his face to the officer. Just then another state police car with red light flashing and siren wailing approached in the northbound lane. It slowed and pulled to the side of the highway.

The officer sat observing the state trooper who now glared into our car.

"Well, is this your license, young man?"

"No," Mike said slowly.

"Then whose is it?"

Stretching across the front seat, I looked up to the trooper. "It's mine, Officer. My brother didn't have his license with him so I let him use mine."

"Don't you know that's against the law? Hell, a license is not a bus pass. You can't let anyone use it. Don't you know that?"

"Yes sir, I'm sorry," I said, and hung my head.

"That's not the reason I stopped you. We got a call about a colored guy exposing himself back down the road. Do you know anything about it?"

Just then Dad piped up from the backseat.

"I'm sorry for the misunderstanding, Officer. My friend Buck and I are on the way to Indianapolis on a business matter and he felt the call of nature. We looked for appropriate consolation quarters, but were unable to find any gas station where he could satisfy his urinary desires."

I tried to silence Dad's blathering with a scowl. He dismissed me with a wave of the hand and continued.

"I remember when I was in charge of the toilets at the Muncie Fairground last year. We always made sure one was never at a loss to find public facilities. I stood at the door and told all my customers as they walked through, 'Come right in and shake hands with "Old Jock" your best friend. Shake him high and shake him dry, and don't forget little Sammy Dean from Bowling Green when you pass by.' "

"Who in the hell are you?" asked the officer as he peered into the back seat.

"I'm James A. Williams. I was candidate for the Indiana State legislature in 1938, and more recently in law enforcement myself in Washington, D.C. I was a member of the General Services Administration Police assigned to the Pentagon, and authorized to enter all federal buildings in the Washington, D.C., metropolitan area.

"These are my sons and if there has been any infraction of the law, I am fully and solely responsible for their activities. These boys live alone with me, and I've raised them to respect and obey the law. Any shortcoming on their part is a mere temporary transgression and—"

Buck, now alert, if not sobered, by the solemn stare of the state trooper, broke into Dad's monologue.

"Shut up, Buster!"

The officer turned to me and said, "Gregory, come back to the car."

Forlornly, I made my way along the gravel shoulder to the police car, and hunched over in the front passenger side.

"It looks like you're the only one that knows what the hell they're doing. I should arrest both of them for public intoxication, and your brother for driving without a license. I don't want to, but I've got a problem. An old woman just called the station, scared shitless."

I looked in the trooper's craggy face for a clue. He continued. "She was jabbering about some colored guy doing a war dance in her yard with his pecker stickin' straight out."

"But, Officer," I interjected, "he was just taking a leak. We didn't think there would be any more filling stations before Indianapolis and it was kinda an emergency."

Just then the radio crackled, "George, you need any help?"

The trooper picked up the radio and said, "Everything's okay, Frank. Just a misunderstanding here. You can take off. I'll see you later." He replaced the microphone on its hook, and the trooper parked across from us on the other side of the road made a U-turn and headed south on 67.

"Officer," I continued, "I'm sorry if we did anything wrong."

"I realize he was taking a piss," he responded, "but I've got to do something."

Again he paused, and I held my breath. Cars whizzed past on their way to Indianapolis.

"Tell you what I'll do," the trooper said, turning to face me. "I'm gonna give you a ticket for letting your brother use your license."

"He has a license. He just left it at home."

"That doesn't make any difference. You're not supposed to let anyone have your license. When you come to court, have him with you, or bring his license so you can show he does have one. Maybe the judge will take that into consideration."

"Please, Officer, I'll have to miss school to go to court, and it's hard to get down here from Muncie."

He ignored me and continued, "I'm scheduling you into night court in Pendleton the middle of next month. You won't have to miss any school, and you should have thought of the inconvenience of coming down here before you gave your brother your license. Look, it's either this or I take the two drunks to jail and give your brother a ticket. Whadda you want?"

Slowly, I extended my hand for the ticket, wanting to kick myself for not listening to Miss Dora.

As I stepped out of the patrol car, a sharp Indiana wind slapped me across the face. Opening the driver's door, I told Mike to move over. He looked at me angrily. "I wanna drive, Greg. Dad said I could. . . ."

"In case you forgot, you don't have your driver's license! Move your ass over and shut up!" He slid across the front seat. After firing the ignition, I made a U-turn and headed toward Muncie. Howls of protest rose from the back.

"We're going back to Muncie," I said. "I don't want to have to baby-sit you two in Indianapolis."

Dad continued to protest. "If you don't turn around right now, I'll knock some sense into you myself. Don't forget I paid for this car. This is my car, not some snot-nosed sissy's."

"Let me know when you want to stop because I'll be glad to kick your motherfucking ass and let you stagger back to Muncie."

"You must be losin' your mind talking to me like that. Don't try to act like you're a man. You ain't worth warm piss. I remember when you were shittin' yellow and I changed your diapers. Now turn this car around."

"If you weren't so goddamned drunk," I shot back, "you'd know the state trooper is still following us. He told me to get you two back to Muncie. Do you want me to ask him if *he* can give you a ride to Indianapolis?"

As they peered out the back window at the trooper, I added, "Maybe you can tell him about the time you kissed President Kennedy, too."

Buck, now almost sober from the encounter, said, "Buster, I think Greg's right. We better head back to Muncie."

"I don't care if he is right. No son of mine's gonna call me a motherfucker and get away with it. If that boy keeps fuckin' with me, I'm gonna kill him."

Buck said softly, "You guys, just relax and take it easy."

His words did not soothe me. I wanted Dad to reach over the front seat and try to hit me. I was angry enough to stop the car and drag him back to the trooper. Dad must have sensed I was on the edge. There were no further comments from the backseat.

Three weeks passed and the date of my court appearance arrived. The previous week our car had broken down. That afternoon I stopped at the bus station to check the schedule to and from Pendleton. No buses returned to Muncie until four a.m. the next morning. I purchased three one-way tickets. Assuming the court appearance turned out satisfactorily, we would have to hitch a ride to Muncie. I pushed concern about hitchhiking to the back of my mind, knowing we could count on Dad's expertise at finding a ride.

Mike showed up late enough to make me anxious, but we quickly dressed in suits and ties and walked to Grandma's to join Dad for the trek to the station. When we entered the house, he lay on the couch in his long underwear, watching television on a set he had recently salvaged from discarded trash. I asked him why he wasn't ready.

"I don't feel well. I'm gonna stay here and rest," he said. He turned back to an afternoon game show.

"How are we going to talk to the judge without you? I need your help." Without taking his eyes off the television, he said, "Everything will be all right. Don't worry. If they send you to jail, you won't go far. The reformatory is just down the road," he added with a chuckle.

"I don't think that's funny. If it weren't for you, I wouldn't be in this predicament."

Dad shook his head. "Don't blame me for your mistakes. I wasn't stupid enough to give your brother my license, and hell, he wasn't smart enough to remember your birthday. Sometimes you two are pathetic. You can't even take care of yourselves without me around. Now you better get on downtown or you'll miss the bus, and you *will* be in trouble. There's an important program coming up. It'll have some good dialogue I can use for speeches." He turned to the television once more and took a swallow of wine.

I stood there with my fists clenched in anger, wanting to reach across the couch and punch him. Maybe that would make him act responsibly for once in his life! "That's just great," I said. "How about getting back? We don't have a ride home. The bus from Indianapolis doesn't return till morning, and I don't have money for a motel room."

Without diverting his eyes from the television, Dad said, "I've done the best job I could teaching you boys how to hustle rides. Just put your thumb out and stand in one place. Hell, you've done it before. You'll be fine. Come by tomorrow afternoon and tell me how it turns out. Don't wake me and Momma up tonight."

I stormed out of Grandma's shack with Mike in tow. We trotted down the railroad tracks to the bus station. My fury increased when I recalled how Dad had bragged to the officer that he was raising us and took full responsibility for anything we did wrong. Only the rapidly dropping temperature finally cooled me down. As we approached the new Jackson Street bus station I even chuckled at the bitter irony of it all.

The bus passed the same scenery we had seen less than a month earlier on State Road 67. Once again, the stark gray walls of the Indiana State Reformatory came into view, but this time the bus slowed, signaling the end of our journey. Air brakes hissed and the bus clattered to a stop. The driver turned his head to the back of the bus and yelled "Pendleton!"

Mike and I rushed up the aisle. Soon we found ourselves in the ominous shadow of the reformatory. The roar of the diesel engine filled the air as the bus pulled back onto the highway. A gas station attendant directed us toward the courthouse, about a mile down Anderson Avenue.

We found the small white clapboard courthouse locked and deserted. The sun had set and the air became icy. Mike and I paced back and forth in front of the building until a clerk finally arrived forty-five minutes later.

Within minutes, at least fifty people crowded into the small room. Mike and I sat in the first row, directly in front of the judge's bench. My stomach churned. What if the judge gives me a jail sentence? I wondered. What if he fines me more than I can pay? After purchasing the bus tickets, I only had twenty-four dollars. If he says twenty dollars and costs, how much are costs? Sweat dripped down my armpits. The urge to urinate overcame me, but I dared not leave my seat lest my name be called. The back of my head felt as though someone was hitting me with a flat board. When I began to experience shortness of breath, I knew I had to pull myself together. "Take three deep breaths," Dad would say to himself when he had to sober up quickly and focus his attention. I inhaled once and held it for three seconds. I exhaled. Another deep breath. This time my chest filled. The deep breaths made me realize how rapidly my heart was pounding, but I exhaled by blowing softly. I had to let go. To hell with it, I said to myself. If the fine is more than I can pay, I'll just go to jail.

Just then the rattling of chains filled the courtroom. A hush fell over the crowd. Mike and I turned to see two sheriff's deputies carrying shotguns and leading eight men in dirty prison denims, manacled and connected to each other by leg irons and waist chains. Most had several days' growth of beard and matted hair. The first two glowered at the men and women on the benches as the deputies herded them into the jury box, where they could more easily guard them. The deputies held the shotguns in the crooks of their arms and took up positions on each side. Immediately, I reconsidered my willingness to go to jail.

At seven-thirty the clerk shouted, "All rise!" Chairs scraped against the wood floor. A tall, freckle-faced man with thinning red hair swirled into the room, his black gown billowing in his wake. He took a seat at the raised podium. The first case was a shoplifter, who received a week in jail. Two drunks drew six months on the Indiana State Farm at Putnamville. A disorderly conduct charge netted the offender seven days in jail. Then there were speeding violations, each fined twenty-five dollars and court costs of ten dollars. I felt as if someone had jabbed a knife right between my navel and sternum when I realized I wouldn't have enough money.

The clerk called case after case, and men and women moved forward to stand meekly before the judge with heads bowed. I heard a familiar name, "Robert Montague." Turning toward the rear, I recognized Bob, a neighborhood friend who lived in the Projects across from Aunt Bess. He received a thirty-five-dollar fine and costs for speeding. He seemed relieved as he walked to the clerk to pay the fine. As he made his way down the aisle toward the door, I sent Mike to ask for a ride home. Mike returned victorious a few minutes later. For the first time that night I relaxed slightly, and prayed we would both be needing a ride.

Just then I saw Bob peer through the door pane. I understood. In spite of the winter weather, he preferred to wait outside rather than remain in the presence of the judge.

Finally, the room was almost empty. I was the last case. The clerk said, "Gregory H. Williams."

Walking past the wood railing, I stood in front of the judge's bench. The clerk read the charge and the judge asked me, "How do you plead?"

"Guilty, Your Honor."

"How old are you, young man?"

"Eighteen."

"Where are your parents? You know, we like to keep kids around until their parents show up."

My knees started to shake as I thought of Dad's unreliability.

The judge continued. "Sometimes kids think they can run all over Indiana and do whatever they want. Maybe I should have the deputies take you to jail until your parents get here. Do they know where you are tonight?"

I thought to myself, Actually, Your Honor, I'm quite glad my father is not here. If he were, I'm certain you would put all three of us in jail. Buster Williams is probably so drunk at this very moment he can't stand up.

Instead, I drew in a deep breath and quietly said, "We don't live with my mother, Your Honor. My dad knows where we are. He didn't come with us tonight."

I was proud of that honest statement, but the judge exploded.

"Well, why didn't he come? Does he think you're so bad that he doesn't care what the court does with you? Maybe I should put you in jail for a week to get you on the right track!"

Startled by the harshness of his language, I began to envision an endless jail term. Finally, I stammered, "Your Hon-or. He was too drunk to come tonight, sir."

Just then the state trooper who arrested me interjected. "Your Honor, the boys' father was in the car when I made the arrest. He was intoxicated. He may well be an alcoholic."

The judge asked the officer what had happened, and he recounted the story. The judge asked Mike if he had a driver's license. I'd made sure Mike had it with him before we left Miss Dora's. The judge turned to me.

"Gregory, I hope you realize what a serious offense it is to lend anyone your license. Even your brother."

"Yes sir, I do now."

"It sounds like you have enough problems without having to pay traffic fines. I'm going to take the case under advisement."

I was unable to move. I had no earthly idea what he meant. Was I on probation? What was I supposed to do?

The judge saw me hesitating.

"Go ahead, you can leave, but I want you to stay out of trouble. If I see you back here again, I promise you'll have a chance to enjoy the state's hospitality."

Finally I got the message. "Thank you very much, Your Honor."

After a quick visit to the men's room, Mike and I strode quickly from the building and raced to Bob's Ford. He immediately fired the engine and headed straight for State Road 67.

"You know, Greg," Bob said once we were on the road, "I stood outside looking at you. You sat there for an entire hour without moving once. I got nervous just watching you."

"Damn," I admitted, "I never was so scared in my entire life. When they brought in all those convicts in handcuffs and chains, I was sure I was on my way straight to the reformatory."

Just then we saw lights from the guardhouses on the prison walls. At that moment more than any other, I not only appreciated my freedom, I knew I had the power to control it. I was beginning to see that my dependence on Dad was an illusion. He often had good advice, but when it got right down to it, I couldn't count on him. His irresponsibility had given me a great gift. It made me realize that I could survive a crisis without him. I could stand up for myself. I rolled down the window to suck in the cold night air. It filled my body and I felt like a new person. Looking straight up to the stars, I felt I could conquer the world.

"Greg, I ain't no Eskimo. Gimme some slack on the window," said Bob.

We all laughed as I rolled it up.

"You don't know how much me and Mike appreciate gettin' this ride back to Muncie," I said.

"Shit, Greg, I'm glad to do it. You know, when I was looking in that window, I thought that one day you might be a judge yourself. You a damn smart boy and I never knowed anybody who ever worked harder for what they got in life. When you're a judge, congressman, or senator, don't forget old Bob.''

"Bob, I won't forget you or this night for the rest of my life.''

# Chapter 19

# Mike: Like a Moth to Flames

Later that same week, when Mike didn't return home for two days, I asked Miss Dora where he was. I discovered he had left a cryptic note on the kitchen table that he was "going to Detroit." Though Miss Dora provided love and affection, she was always a bit reluctant to be too demanding of us. I don't know if her lack of assertiveness was due to the fear of being countermanded by my father or to the fact that she simply expected us to do what we were told. Her easygoing, nondirective style worked well for me, and I developed an enormous and burdensome reputation as "Mr. Responsibility." Mike, on the other hand, was the type of kid that you had to threaten, and even then you might not be sure that he would follow orders. He seemed to have a strong inner need to be different, at least from me. Teachers, fellow students, playmates, church members, and even our large, extended Muncie family compared Mike with me, and he always suffered by comparison. Academically, Mike struggled just to stay in school, and although he showed promise of being a peer in athletics, he never had the strong will to succeed that my father had drilled into me. The more praise I received, the more I wanted. When I saw Mike try to best me at one skill or another, I worked at it until I conquered him. Basketball was

one sport in which he showed some early promise. He was one of
the stars on the Garfield Elementary basketball team that in fact won
the city championship. The better Mike became the harder I practiced. He soon gave up basketball. Although it must have all been
subconscious, I believe that he decided that the only way he could
escape from my shadow was to do something that I would either
strongly dislike or be too scared to undertake. His first choice was
boxing. Dad was an ex–Golden Gloves champion. He had received
the nickname "Buster" from his ring exploits. He tried to interest
both of us in boxing when we were around junior high school age,
and even dragged us to the Muncie Golden Gloves training site in
the old wrestling room of Central High School. I hated boxing, but
Mike seemed to have a strong interest in it. For a brief period Mike
fully committed himself to boxing, rising at six a.m. to jog with
fellows training with the Golden Gloves. The cockiness he exhibited
as he danced into the ring for his first and only fight lasted only
one round. Early in the second, after taking two hard uppercuts, he
was reeling. Panic overcame him as he began to flail at his opponent.
He was on his back and counted out well before the bell rang.

Ultimately, Mike found his niche. On the streets he could excel
and leave his naive older brother far behind. I had no desire to
"win" the dangerous games Mike began playing at age sixteen,
and I was envious of his precocious sex life only until I saw his
"women."

Mike was never a hard-core juvenile delinquent, but he sought
to emulate Dad and the role models Dad had exposed him to over
the years. He drank, gambled, had an active sex life, and mimicked
the lingo and style of the small-time hustlers, pimps, and thieves
who befriended him. Even as a youngster he seemed to have a need
to keep as much danger and excitement in his life as he could pos-
sibly generate. Although I had been thrilled to escape from the
nighttime activities at Grandma's shack, Mike was drawn there like
a moth to flames. He reveled in tagging along with Dad on his
rounds to gambling joints, bootleggers, and Muncie's whorehouses.
Mike willingly absorbed all of Dad's lessons.

Miss Dora shared my concern about Mike. Though the church
took most of her time, she had a finely tuned sixth sense about who
was doing what in the neighborhood and she kept a sharp eye on
the troublemakers. She alerted me to the fact that Mike was hanging

out with some of Muncie's worst elements. When Mike returned from Detroit he sauntered into my room wearing a new pair of sharply creased wool pants and a calf-length leather coat. Though evasive initially, he finally admitted Muncie's main distributor of marijuana gave him money for the clothes because of his help on the trip to Detroit. I listened tensely as Mike explained his assignment. On the return trip he sat in the passenger seat with the drugs in his lap. If the police attempted to pull them over, Mike was to casually lay his arm outside the window and let the drugs scatter in the wind. "You'd be throwing a lot of weed out the window," I said.

"It ain't marijuana, Greg . . . it's heroin!"

My body snapped like an electrical bolt had zinged through it. I whispered, "Mike, don't you know who used to make those heroin runs with him?"

"Who?" he asked me with his innocent eyes. In spite of his facade of worldliness, he had no inkling of the dangerous situation in which he now found himself. Miss Dora was right. Mike needed a "guardian angel." I shook my finger in his face.

"His own brother. And the only reason he has you now is that his brother was killed in a drug shoot-out six months ago!"

Mike looked shocked. At last I was beginning to get through to him, I thought. He stepped back from me. I continued. "Other drug dealers ripped him off after a dope deal and then shot him. Don't you know you're flirting with disaster?"

As Mike stood under the bare light bulb of the room I saw fear in his eyes, but he shook his head in a gesture of false bravado and tried to deflect my concern. "If somebody fucks with me, I'll set 'em on fire."

He hadn't listened to a word that I said. In my awkward and unsuccessful efforts to help Mike change course, I even threatened to fight him, but that only made him more defensive. He put up his fists. "Don't challenge me, Greg. I ain't a kid no more."

Trying to take on a parental role, I sternly forbade him to make any more trips to Detroit. If I was really emphatic he would sometimes listen to me, but it was clear that he was returning to Detroit. We argued back and forth for a while and the real reason for his strong resistance finally surfaced. It was not drugs, but a woman named Bernice.

"That's the reason I go up there, if the truth be known. Man, she's a stone fox. Last time I burned her up all night. She said, 'Mike, I'm gonna call you coffee, 'cause you grind so fine.' " He laughed.

I probed for more information about his new girlfriend when he called her a "booster." Mike reveled in the realization that he knew something that I did not. "Greg, you need to get out in the streets and live a little. You'll never learn anything spending all your time with your nose in a book. A booster is a professional shoplifter," he explained with exasperation.

Bernice had even "worked" in Muncie.

"She is the best," he continued. "She can walk in a store and clean it out. She wears booster drawers and can drop suits, sweaters, shirts, you name it, between her legs. Last week at the supermarket she even put a ham between her legs and walked out of the store."

"Damn, I sure wouldn't eat that ham. Her carrying it in her drawers. What did you do with it?"

"I gave it to Buster."

"Did he eat it?"

"Naw, he sold it to the café owner for wine money. It was on the Sunday dinner special."

As I continued to interrogate Mike, he revealed that Bernice was forty years old.

"Forty? Damn, Mike she's old enough to be our momma. What in the hell do you see in those old women? Did you tell Daddy about your *old* woman?"

"Hell, Daddy knows all about her. Last time she was in Muncie I took her by Grandma's. Dad was gonna pay me ten dollars to go to bed with her, but he only gave me five when he finished."

That absolutely floored me. Mike chuckled and told me the three of them had been in bed together when she said, "I don't know who does it better, you or your daddy. Let's go again."

It was just too unbelievable. It was hard for me to drift off to sleep that night. Mike was on the edge. I knew I had to do what I could to pull him back to safety. The next morning I lingered after breakfast to go to Central with him.

We walked north on Madison Street. In front of McDonald's I said, "Mike, you gotta stay in school. What in the hell are you gonna do if you don't have an education? Be a pimp or a gangster?"

Mike glared at me. Immediately I realized this was the wrong approach. Then he said, "Don't be bad-mouthin' pimps. I'd like to have me a stable of four or five women. Then all I'd have to do was rest and dress."

"You don't know how stupid that sounds." I heard myself saying all the wrong things, but I was impatient and exasperated.

He stuck his finger in my face. "I told you, don't be calling me stupid."

"Mike, you've got the wrong attitude. Everything that you're doing is going to lead you into trouble. The guys you run with have all spent time in prison and are on their way back. You're lucky you haven't been caught so far."

"Greg," he responded in a frustrated tone, "just goes to show you don't know what's goin' on. I am in school. I just missed last week. I even been gettin' good grades. There's just too much fightin'. Two weeks ago me and a white boy went to war on the third floor, and the teachers had to break it up. I tried to kill the mothafucker. He called me a nigger."

"How come I didn't hear about it?"

"I didn't want to tell you."

"Why not, Mike? Can't you talk to me?"

"After the fight my student teacher took me home with her and I know you wouldn't have liked that."

"Do you mean the white ex-cheerleader?"

"Yeah."

"Mike, I told you not to fuck around with her. She doesn't give a damn about you."

"Just shows you don't know shit. When we went to her house, nobody was home and I screwed her to death. She told me she wanted to run off with me."

In spite of his surface response, I could tell that my talk with him did have a temporary impact. He stopped making the dope runs to Detroit and began to attend school regularly. I was even surprised to find him doing homework one evening, apparently to impress his new girlfriend, the student teacher. Early one afternoon just after the Christmas holiday I received a telephone call from Mike's student teacher. She wanted to end their relationship. I angrily asked her why she could not tell Mike herself. "He's too immature and I don't think he'll understand. Greg, the age and race differences are just too much."

I wondered why that had only recently occurred to her. She must have read my mind. Over the phone I heard the voice of contrition. "I know I should have considered the consequences before I got involved, but I didn't, and I was wrong. I just felt you two had always received a raw deal in Muncie. I remember when my brother used to talk about how bad everyone treated you and Mike at Wilson."

Struggling to maintain my composure, I thought, That's really what I need to tell Mike. She went to bed with him because she felt sorry for him. Her honesty cooled my anger, so I listened to her apology without rebuke. With all of Mike's talk about dope, boosters, and women in Detroit, I hoped he might laugh it off. When I broke the news as gently as possible to him, his eyes began to tear. Then he pulled a mask of indifference over his face and again assumed his tough exterior. He turned away from me and headed into the street.

The following Saturday afternoon while at a movie downtown, he argued with a white boy and in the ensuing fight broke the boy's leg. Since he was still a juvenile with no serious record, the juvenile court judge placed him on unsupervised probation. He attended school for a while longer, but in the middle of winter decided to join the navy. He had to secure Dad's permission since he was underage. Certain our father would flatly reject the idea, I didn't worry about that fleeting interest. Dad always told me to go to college, and I knew he wanted Mike to at least finish high school. Yet Dad signed, and justified his action by complaining that he couldn't control Mike. Plus, Dad said, Mike would look great in a uniform.

When Mike returned from boot camp a short time later, he looked more pale and scared than ever before. I asked him how he managed a leave so quickly. With his typical braggadocio style, he boasted, "I quit."

Though only eighteen myself, I knew that the navy simply did not let enlistees who signed up for two-year terms quit whenever they fancied. It took almost a week before I discovered what really happened.

"I told them I wanted to go home, and if they didn't let me, I'd kill myself."

He handed me a paper, and I saw he had been officially discharged. His new classification was now 1-Y: "To be recalled only in time of national emergency."

Miss Dora and I wanted him to return to school, but he had other ideas. Bernice lured him back to Detroit.

Miss Dora received a letter a week later.

"Mike says he and Bernice got married," she told me. "That woman's over forty years old with two teenage kids. I just don't know what's gonna happen to that boy. He's so restless. I used to sit on the porch and watch him stroll up and down the street. He walked to the corner and stood there looking for friends to come by. Then he walked back in front of the house and stood on the corner here, like he was waitin' on something to happen. I'm afraid that marriage ain't gonna last too long."

In less than a month Mike was back in Muncie, his hand wrapped up in bandages. There had been an argument, he was cut on the hand, and he'd lost a pint and a half of blood and had twenty-seven stitches to close the wound. He proudly wore the bandages as a badge of honor, admitting his woman cut him but bragging that he knew how to handle women.

He was as aimless as ever in Muncie. Some of Miss Dora's relatives visited, and Mike decided to return to Chicago with them to look for work. I thought Chicago would offer a more safe and stable environment than what surely awaited him upon his return to Detroit, so I did not discourage the move. The family lived in a public housing project in Chicago called Cabrini Green. Little did I know that it was a notorious site of murders, robberies, and gang-related violence. Mike soon moved in with another woman living in the neighborhood, and put the relationship with Bernice behind him. We heard from him from time to time, and I always hoped for the best for my younger brother.

I have always felt a lot of guilt over the years about how Mike's life unfolded, often wondering if there was something I could have done for him that I did not. Even if I didn't fail him, what caused our lives to diverge so sharply? I believe that in his own way Dad loved both of us, but I have always wondered why he treated us so differently. Did he need for one son to fulfill his thwarted ambition, and for the other to accompany him in failure? He clearly supported my dreams, especially encouraging an education. He boasted about my accomplishments to anyone who would listen, and constantly told me I could be anything I wanted to be. For Mike it was the opposite. The consistent message he received from Dad was "You're a fuck-up just like me, and you're never going to amount to anything." Perhaps in part because Dad designated such disparate paths, the quality of my life became better and better, and the quality of Mike's continued to decline.

# Chapter 20

# Tottering Kingdoms and Crumbling Empires

By the spring semester of 1962, I needed just three classes to graduate from high school. Overcrowding at Central was still severe. The community had needed an additional high school for years, but dividing the athletic talent would have reduced the chances of winning state basketball championships. Most senior students attended classes either in mornings or afternoons. The counseling office had selected three morning classes for me, English, Civics, and P.E. For many students that might have been an ideal schedule, but I decided I wanted an afternoon math class covering trigonometry and some calculus.

It was my first visit to the closetlike counseling office tucked beneath the first-floor stairway across from the cafeteria. My only contact with Central High School guidance counselors had been during lunch hours when they stormed from the office to quiet students congregated in the hallway.

A long line snaked from the office, and it took over thirty minutes to reach the door. The room was jammed with a desk and several old-fashioned green filing cabinets. No more than four people could crowd into the room at once. When I finally reached the front of the line, a harried counselor glanced up at me from the stack of manila folders in front of her. Her sparse brown hair, knotted tightly behind her head, accented the frown lines running across her forehead.

As I requested the advanced math class, her lips pursed tightly. When she realized I wanted to spend more rather than less time in school, she gave me a quizzical look.

"Don't you know we have to accommodate over two thousand students?"

"Yes," I replied, looking directly at her. "But I still want the senior math class."

"Impossible. You can take another morning math class. See me tomorrow, when I have the class counts." She looked to the girl behind me.

"Excuse me," I said, impeding her indifferent dismissal, "I really need to change my schedule—or talk to someone who can help me."

"I'm in charge down here," she hissed. "You can't change your schedule. It is perfectly appropriate. That's final."

Frustrated by her intransigence, I glanced back to see if those behind me heard the exchange. The girl, next in line, frowned at me for taking up what she now saw as her time. Making waves was uncomfortable for me, but I was determined to make the most of my final semester. I asked, "Is there anyone else I can talk to about the change?"

Her jaws moved as she ground her teeth. "You can see the assistant principal, if you don't mind wasting your time," she replied, "but you have to bring a parent. See his secretary for an appointment."

Making the appointment was easy. The problem was getting Dad to school. That afternoon, I scoured the neighborhood for him. He wasn't at Grandma's or any of the neighborhood taverns. Finally, I reached Watson's shack in the alley off Willard Street. Katie, wearing the same old disheveled hairpiece, met me at the door. As I looked into the room filled with shouting winos, kerosene smoke, and the smell of stale beans, I was aware that little had changed in the eight years we had been in Muncie.

"Katie," I began, disregarding Dad's "Aunt Katie" order of earlier years, "is he—" Then I saw Dad on his knees at the center of the circle of gamblers, ready to roll the dice.

"Wait a minute, Billy," she said as I brushed past her and stalked toward Dad. I was no longer intimidated by Katie or the gamblers. Edging behind Dad, I saw him shake the dice and call out, "Five, Momma, five!" He rolled them across the tattered wool army blanket. He threw nine, then four, then seven. A graying but still muscular Lucius reached across to grab the money in the pot.

"Come on, Dad, I need you to go with me. We've got a serious problem."

"Let go of me, Greg," he said, wrenching away.

Again I grabbed him. "Come on, Dad, it's important. You gotta go to school with me tomorrow. I need you there, and I need you *sober.*"

"Come by Mom's in the morning."

"You'll be too drunk. Come on. You always talk about the importance of my education, but you've never been to an open house, a PTA meeting, or any parent-teacher conference."

"Greg, I said I'd go, and I meant it, dammit! I know education is your way out of Muncie." He drew his chest up like a bantam rooster. "I never want it to be said that I stood in the way of my son's academic progress!" he crowed to the rest of the men around the circle.

"Come on, I'll take you home so you can be ready in the morning."

He stood and faced me. "Look, you ain't my daddy. I'm yours. You don't tell me what to do and when to do it. I raised you. You didn't raise me."

"That ain't the way I see it," chimed in Lucius. "Greg been a daddy to both you and Mike. I seen him carry your drunken black ass home more times than I can count on my fingers and toes. That boy done raised you, whether you like it or not," he said, laughing, while the others nodded in agreement.

Dad turned and glared. "Lucius, I've got an Italian phrase for you. *Va fangu fetche mama.*"

Lucius rose from the floor. "You better not be calling me a motherfucka, Buster," he said menacingly.

I pulled Dad out of the circle and into the alley. He struggled and dragged his feet. On Second Street he leaned in the direction of Bob's Tavern, but I held fast. A day of heavy drinking had had a strong effect on him, and he was unable to resist my grip.

I was certain if I left Dad at Grandma's he would make his way back to Watson's. I tried to sneak him into Miss Dora's and put him in Mike's bed. As I guided him upstairs, he began shouting and woke Miss Dora. She ordered him to Grandma's, despite my plea that I needed to make sure he was sober in the morning.

By that time he was almost asleep on his feet, so I lifted him across my shoulder and carried him to Grandma's. Once there, I laid him on the couch, removed his tie, coat, and shoes, and threw a blanket over him. Then I walked through the tattered curtain into the back room. As I took off my clothes, I stared at the small canvas cot Grandma still kept by the toilet. So much had happened since Mike and I first shared that small space together. As I tried to sleep, I remembered the frustration, rage, and anger that had consumed me when I felt all the forces of the world massed against me and Mike as we huddled there together. Yet I had a feeling of triumph. We had survived.

The next day, we arrived at the assistant principal's office fifteen minutes early. The secretary retrieved my student file and placed it on her desk. As I glanced at the big block letters—WILLIAMS, GREGORY—I wondered what had been written about me. When the secretary left the room for a trip to the counseling office, I took my file from the desk. Dad and I read it together.

On the first page under "Color," a W for "white" had initially been entered. I remembered Dad put the W there the day we registered at Garfield Elementary School. However, parentheses were placed around the W, and a C had been written above it, obviously for "colored." Dad's statement that he was in the U.S. Army had a thick black line scratched through it; it had been replaced with "Janitor at City Hall." As I scanned the medical section, I saw for the first time that in both the fifth and seventh grades I had failed the Massachusetts Vision Test and glasses were recommended.

As I turned to the last page, I saw printed directions at the top:

This page is for the entire school life of the child. Teachers, nurses and counselors are requested to use it to record only worthwhile and significant facts in the child's file not recorded elsewhere on this card. Such observations might have to do with the solution of problems involving unusual emotional reactions, family relations, social attitudes or other conditions.

Under these words was a handwritten entry:

Father is colored—mother is white—neither of his parents lives here—He lives with Mrs. Dora Terry whom he says is no relation to him. There is a brother also—From outward appearance they both look to be white. Parents are divorced.

Though I understood the need for school officials to have information that might aid teachers, the only "counseling" I received in the Muncie school system was the warning from Mr. Bennett and Miss White not to violate the rigid rules about interracial dating. It was clear to me that the only purpose of the entry was to make sure teachers were not deceived by me or my appearance.

What troubled me most was the comment regarding my relationship with Miss Dora. There were only two ways to interpret it and both enraged me. First, there was the implication that I was lying. Clearly, the writer assumed we were related but I didn't want to acknowledge her. At no time during junior high or high school had I tried to convince anyone I was white or deny my debt to Miss Dora. Ever since the fourth grade I had shared too many experiences with her, and my black friends and relatives, to consider myself any different from them.

The second interpretation was that no sensible woman would care for two boys who weren't part of her family. This was a familiar sentiment, and I always felt it was insulting to Miss Dora. She deserved an award, not suspicion about her intelligence and integrity. No school officials had recognized the act for what it truly was— generous, kind, caring, and humanitarian. To have her goodwill questioned and belittled was more than I could bear.

Dad and I ached for a confrontation with the assistant principal about the file, yet our lives in Muncie had taught us that a confrontation over information gathered years ago would serve no purpose. We contained our anger. When escorted into his office, Dad was as dynamic and forceful as I had ever seen him. He said it was impossible to understand why I was denied the opportunity to take a special college-preparatory math class solely because of overcrowding problems at Central High School. As he sat across from the assistant principal, he recited the familiar story of how black students were discriminated against in the thirties, and that he spent his senior year building a house, which was totally unrelated to his interest in college. He leaned across the desk and said, "I'm not about to let the same thing happen to my son."

The assistant principal did not seek to defend the school's ridiculous position. He immediately signed the card.

The following morning I received a new schedule, including the senior math class. Someone added a study hall, probably to punish my challenge of authority. Study Hall Room 306 was fifteen rows across, thirty seats deep—and accommodated approximately one hundred and fifty students. I gave my class schedule to the study hall monitor, George Punzelt, my old football coach. George assigned me a vacant seat at the front of the room.

As he returned the card, he said, "Greg, you take care of the front of the room, and I'll take care of the back."

Seating was alphabetical and I took a desk behind a tall, dazzling blonde with blue-green eyes and a creamy complexion. I remembered her from Wilson Junior High School. Sara Whitney was an eighth grade cheerleader when I played on the ninth grade basketball team. Now she was a junior. She wore a stylish dress, and her perfume wafted toward me. During the Wilson years, I learned her father was a prominent farmer and horse breeder. Dad had graduated with him in 1932. Pleased with the luck to be seated behind such a beautiful girl, I gave her an emphatic hello. She responded with a friendly nod, but quickly returned to her work. Her long blond hair brushed the top of my desk. My heart raced as I sat there bowled over by her beauty. I was immediately self-conscious about my threadbare clothes. When I shifted my long legs under the short, old-fashioned desk, I brushed her with my knees. She moved forward, hunching over her desk while I savored the sensation.

After that I noticed Sara often in the hallways, and felt a pang of envy watching other boys linger around her. I became totally infatuated with her and every day took time I should have spent on my trig class thinking about how she would look, and what I could say to generate just a glimmer of interest. Though I tried mightily to draw her out I could never gain more than a quick "Hi" or "Yes" or "No" out of her. Toward the middle of the semester her standoffishness cooled my ardor, and I felt disheartened when I saw her chatting animatedly with white boys.

One day Brian Settles and I stood at the study hall door making plans to play basketball after school as Sara and her girlfriend Tricia walked past. As I slid into my seat, Tricia leaned across the aisle and asked if I knew Brian.

"He's my best friend," I responded.

"He is so cool!"

Tricia glanced around us to make sure no one was watching. Then she leaned across the aisle and said, "I'd like to meet him." Taken aback by her frankness, I promised to tell him.

The next day, I was barely in my seat before Tricia asked, "Did you tell him?"

A normal date was out of the question, so plans were made for a clandestine meeting. I served as the intermediary between Brian and Tricia, and even Sara was drawn into the excitement of watching her friend venture into forbidden territory. Finally Brian met Tricia. As she carried on excitedly about their rendezvous, Coach Punzelt strolled to the front of the room, noticed her French book, and wrote *"Ferme la bouche"* on her closed notebook. Tricia, undaunted, began to frantically jot notes. "God he's great!" "I *have* to see him again." "Greg, tell him I can get out Saturday night."

As the romance between Tricia and Brian heated up, my yearning for Sara was rekindled. I enlisted Tricia's help in my quest for Sara's attention. To my surprise, Tricia persuaded Sara to give me her phone number. For several days I called every evening and pressed for a chance to see her alone. She was noncommittal, but I continued to persist. One morning Sara agreed, but that afternoon when I phoned she had changed her mind.

She refused to explain, but I kept probing. Finally, she divulged that later that day, a white senior girl confronted her in the hallway and said she knew what was going on but wouldn't tell since she was also dating a "colored" basketball player. Sara also confided to me that her friends warned her to be careful. One of the boys who had seen us talking asked her if she had turned into a "nigger lover." Most of all, though, she was worried about her parents' reaction.

In spite of her protests, I sensed her wavering. "You don't believe in the 'Muncie Rules,' do you?"

"Of course I don't. They're not fair, but whether they're right or wrong, they still exist!"

"They'll keep on existing if we keep following 'em!" I argued. We continued to talk about ourselves for over an hour. I told her about me and my family, and our experiences in Muncie. It was the first time I had ever confided so openly in anyone. She listened so intently and seemed so sincere that I revealed more and more of myself to her. Finally, I asked one last time if she would see me. She was silent for a long moment. My palms began to sweat, but I was hopeful.

"Well"—she hesitated—"you can still call me, and we can talk in study hall."

Dejected, I said good-bye and berated myself for being so open. All my efforts had failed. I would not beg anymore.

Before I could open my books in study hall the following morning, Sara handed me a note: "When can we get together?"

Since Sara could not use the family car in the evening without a lengthy explanation, we decided to meet after school. She arrived in a Ford Edsel at the corner of Kirby and Pershing, a block from my house, around four-thirty in the afternoon. I directed her south of the city to the reservoir. We walked around the area and watched the sun set over the ten-mile-wide lake. When we returned to the car, I came up beside her, hesitated, then put my arms around her. Leaning over, I gently brushed my lips against hers. My heart beat faster and faster. Her lips parted slowly and we kissed. I felt I was in heaven.

Sara and I continued to see each other the rest of the semester. Unable to date publicly, we spent hours in her car behind an abandoned building several blocks from my house. Sara was gradually teaching me I could be trusting and open. It was a very new experience for me. I opened her eyes to a world that existed in Muncie about which she had been totally unaware. We explored each other's bodies, and shared our problems, ideas, hopes, and dreams.

Voter registration drives were in full swing in the South, and we speculated about the impact the right to vote might make there. We shared our excitement as racial barriers were challenged across the country. We read about marches, protests, and sit-ins, as well as violence directed toward the demonstrators.

Sara had not yet crossed paths with Dad, and one evening she announced her desire to meet him. The idea had absolutely no appeal to me. Dad could be so unpredictable. Sara continued to pester me until I told her the best time to catch him was when he was leaving his job at the drive-in around seven in the morning. She thought she would be able to use the family car on Saturday morning without arousing suspicion. Mike was currently on a visit to Muncie and working nights at the restaurant with Dad. The very next Saturday morning Mike woke me when he returned home at eight a.m.

"Greg, wake up! You gonna be mad as hell."

I sat up groggily in bed.

"The ole man's tryin' to take your woman. They at Grandma's."

"What?" I demanded, sensing trouble.

"Sara came by the restaurant. Dad fixed her some coffee and started telling her, 'A gorgeous, brilliant young woman like you would give me the inspiration to get my life back on track. Will you help me, Princess Charming?' You know, Dad's usual hustle—and then she drives us to Grandma's. When I hopped out and looked back over my shoulder, they were kissin' in the car."

"Don't be ridiculous! Get outta here, Mike!"

Then I began to absorb Mike's news. I knew Dad still considered himself a Don Juan, and he often bragged of his conquests. Even though he was almost fifty and staggered around town drunk, he still managed to seduce many women, some of whom were attractive.

What Mike had told me was crazy, but I continued to ponder it as I lay in bed. When I remembered that Dad's current girlfriend was twenty-five years old, I began to panic. Then I became enraged. Mike and Dad often had shared women. Dad had few scruples in matters involving wine, money, or women, but Sara was another story. I knew it was simply not possible. We trusted each other. Yet, I began to wonder if believing in her was a terrible mistake. Certain it would be useless to confront Dad, I had to talk with Sara. I fought not to lose control and telephone her immediately. I would wait for her evening call.

It was a depressing day of self-pity. The phone rang at last.

"Greg, your father is something else." She giggled.

After my long day of turmoil and suffering, her laughter irritated me. My strategy to be cool and distant dissolved, and I confronted her with an accusation of betrayal.

"Oh dear." She sighed. "Did your dad tell you that?"

I didn't answer as she continued. "I guess you want an explanation. I . . . I can't give you one. Yes, your father gave me a kiss when I dropped him off this morning. No peck on the cheek either . . . a full-fledged sexy kiss that was . . . improper. . . . I can't deny it."

I was seething inside. I felt as if Sara and Dad had both kicked me in the stomach. I let her continue.

"He's a charming man. Both he and Mike filled my head with so much flattery it wasn't until later I realized I'd been steamrollered by praise. They've got some incredible lines, those two! Is your dad always that way, Greg? He wasn't falling-down drunk, but he was pretty tanked up. I was certainly not drinking, but felt . . . intoxicated. It's like I dreamed the encounter."

Finally, I relaxed slightly and listened to her babble on, trying to make sense of what had happened. I couldn't understand it either. Dad was just . . . Dad. I might have learned more than my father did when he was in treatment for alcoholism. At times like these I recalled the Serenity Prayer I'd seen on the wall at Nash Rehabilitation Center: "God grant me the courage to accept the things I cannot change." I knew by now I could not change my father, and he constantly challenged me to forgive him. The alternative would be to be consumed by anger and resentment.

Graduation was June 6. I saved money from my part-time jobs for a new, black, double-breasted wool suit to wear to the ceremony. I asked Miss Dora to come with me.

"I'd like to go, Greg, but my feet hurt too much for the long walk downtown. But I'm proud of you, just like you was my own boy."

Though she wanted the best for me, she would almost never venture outside the refuge of the church and into any place where she had to associate with white people.

I gave Miss Dora a hug and a kiss, and she handed me a card with three dollars in it. I wanted to express my sentiments, but I still couldn't articulate my profound feelings of love and gratitude to her. I prayed she knew how much she meant to me.

Brian, Carl, and I walked to the Muncie Fieldhouse together. Brian offered us some Ancient Age whiskey from a bottle he carried, but we were feeling too good without it. The graduating seniors formed two lines in the hallway inside the fieldhouse. Boys in purple caps and gowns were on one side, and girls all in white were on the other. The girls talked excitedly with each other. I took my place in line, and was silent as I listened to the din of voices from inside the basketball arena. As we moved down the hall for the last time as Muncie Central students, I stared at the walls covered with pictures of the Bearcat State Basketball Championship teams of 1928,

1931, 1951, and 1952. My picture would never hang on the field-house wall, but I knew I had accomplished a great deal during my years in Muncie. Just being able to walk into that auditorium to receive my diploma was to overcome tremendous odds. All 660 of us stood together and were pronounced graduated "en masse."

As we floated from the basketball arena to the strains of "Pomp and Circumstance," I was pleasantly surprised to find my mother's youngest sister waiting for me in the hallway. She had been away from Muncie for a number of years while her husband was in the military. My tears flowed freely as I realized she cared enough about me to search the paper for the time and date of the graduation, and then find me in the huge crowd. She was the only member of my mother's family to acknowledge my graduation. She handed me a card with a gift, and then disappeared into the sea of parents and well-wishers.

Dad had been gone for almost a week. Grandma heard he was in Anderson. There was no doubt that he knew the date and time of my graduation. He had spoken of little else for the past month. I wondered if he was in jail. Surely, he wouldn't let me down, not tonight. I searched the crowd. At last, I spied his homburg tilted at a rakish angle, headed toward me. Almost sober, he was beaming.

"I'm proud of you, son. I walked the entire fifteen miles from Anderson, just to be here. This is just the first step, but it was the hardest. Making it this far means you can achieve all your dreams. Next is college, then law school. I can't help you much anymore. It's up to you now. Just remember, the best is yet to be."

Dad handed me a box and was about to leave when Brian and Carl arrived. He paused long enough to give all three of us his blessing.

"Gentlemen, as you go upon the highways and byways of life, may your journey be filled with high hopes, good companions, and the best of everything. You have muddied the waters of the stream called Muncie and emerged victorious. You, who Muncie would try to conquer, have turned into conquerors yourself. In this mad, mad, sad, sad world of tottering kingdoms and crumbling empires, I know that the days of discrimination and prejudice are numbered when we can send forward from Muncie three young men like you with big shoulders, defying attack and contradiction, ready to take any blows that might be rained down upon you. I salute you, and bid you adieu."

With that, Dad twirled his hat through his fingers like a baton and then weaved through the crowd.

I opened the box. Inside was a tan pocket secretary with embossed gold letters: GREG H. WILLIAMS, ESQUIRE.

Both Carl and Brian admired it. Then Brian asked if I was ready for the black students' graduation party.

"You guys go ahead. I've got some things to do first."

Sara picked me up near my house, and we celebrated alone.

# Chapter 21

# Your Truly Mother

Though college had been my dream for years, I was so naive about the admission process that my entire senior year passed without my filing a single application. I believed college would somehow just happen. It wasn't until the euphoria of high school graduation faded that I realized I must turn my full attention to getting into college. Although I was in the top ten percent of my high school class, I had received virtually no guidance about college. As always, the major obstacle was money. Tuition at Ball State was only one hundred dollars a quarter, but I realized that the only way I could afford college would be to find a full-time job and delay my educational plans for at least a year.

One afternoon while downtown seeking work, I spoke briefly with the father of a football teammate. He was a realtor at that time, but he had previously been a very successful high school coach. We talked about football, and he was surprised to learn that I had received no help from my coaches in obtaining an athletic scholarship. He still maintained contacts in the coaching ranks, and expressed a willingness to make some calls on my behalf.

When I checked with him two days later, he told me he had spoken with a Ball State football coach. The coach was unable to promise a scholarship, but encouraged me to try out for the team in the fall, and in the meantime was willing to recommend me for one of the few summer jobs filled by athletes at the university. Immediately, I accepted the offer. That same day I walked to Ball State and filed my application for admission.

The job paid $1.50 an hour for a forty-hour workweek. That was the most money I had ever earned. The summer work crew was comprised of basketball and football players. Two Iranian soccer players later joined the group. Only two of the other athletes were black.

When I arrived at the stadium the first day of work, my co-workers were sprawled on bags of powder concrete mix in a large storage room. One fellow was collecting change for a trip to buy doughnuts and milk. It was clear not much work was expected. Only when our foreman arrived was there movement off the bags. He assigned us tasks of painting, cleaning, and mowing grass. We worked for about forty-five minutes, then the doughnuts arrived.

In the afternoon we did a bit more work, but as the sun bore down on the football field we again returned to the storage shed and played cards while we alternated watching for the foreman. Even though I was thankful to have a job, I did not challenge the established routine.

Our relationships began to unravel from the hours of dawdling in the storage room and making fun of each other. Most of the fellows were pampered high school athletes, not accustomed to being the butt of jokes. One of the black athletes chided an awkward six-foot, eight-inch farm boy from southern Indiana about his affection for country music. The farm boy muttered a racist insult, and then claimed he had been misunderstood. Only the four-thirty whistle for quitting time prevented that exchange from escalating into a physical altercation.

One afternoon after work, I walked with the two black athletes to the student union. As we crossed University Avenue, we saw one of our Iranian co-workers driving toward town. He approached the intersection and pulled into the far right lane to make a turn. His right blinker flashed off and on. As we neared the intersection, the stoplight changed twice yet he did not move. He was still sitting there impatiently when we reached his car. Leaning in his passenger-side window, I informed him that he was in the parking lane. He looked at me blankly, then frowned as he realized his mistake. We stood on the sidewalk doubled over with laughter.

"What you niggers laugh at?" he exploded. "Fuck you!"

We were stunned into silence. Though our co-worker was very friendly with the awkward farm kid, we had assumed that his brown skin made him more tolerant than other members of the crew. Before we could respond, he sped into the traffic lane, barely missing a collision with another car.

In July the athletic director surprised us with an unannounced visit. He threatened to fire all of us if he caught us loafing again. From that point on I worked hard and some of the other guys joined me. The camaraderie of the group still continued to disintegrate. The job ended in early August, and though I needed the money, I wasn't sorry.

I knew the chances of obtaining a football scholarship were slight, but once practice began it was clear there were no scholarships to distribute. I decided to seek a basketball scholarship instead. Ball State had only one gym, and practice times were limited. Freshmen, being at the bottom of the priority list, were given a seven a.m. practice time. For me that meant a predawn bus ride across town. I loved basketball, and though I often found myself guarding players five and six inches taller, I managed to dominate them. Praise from my teammates boosted my confidence, but after the final team selections the coach also indicated I would not receive a scholarship. I quit the basketball team and turned to my studies, hoping my summer savings would last through the winter.

In spite of nagging financial problems, my first-quarter classes opened up a whole new world. In my World Civilization class, Dr. Ferrill's incisive analyses of world events, sprinkled with a combination of historical anecdotes, were absolutely fascinating. He constantly urged us to digest and assimilate knowledge, and to develop a broad worldview. He reinforced the advice Dad had given over the years. I learned more about the privileges and responsibilities of a college education in that course than in any other during my entire college career.

Dr. Bennett's psychology course revealed the inner workings of the mind, and was the perfect complement to Dr. Ferrill's course. Under Dr. Bennett's direction I began to research issues such as prejudice, aggression and intolerance, and even interracial marriage. My high scores on the Ball State entrance exams exempted me from the basic English class, and I enrolled in an upper-level literature course. Few topics were off-limits during discussions—sex, race, politics. I began to feel truly at ease. That first quarter was a whirlwind of growing, maturing, studying, learning, writing, and thinking. When the grades arrived in early December, I tore open the envelope and discovered I had an A– average.

Sara arranged to graduate from high school a semester early, and began college at Ball State in January of 1963 while still living at home. Although we attempted to conceal our relationship, she faced growing suspicion from her parents and friends. Her parents received anonymous phone calls in the middle of the night reporting that their daughter was dating a "nigger." One late-night caller told them my name. Sara's mother and father woke her, demanding to see my photo in her school yearbook. She showed it to them, and they were baffled. They demanded explanations, but she continued to be evasive.

Sara's former friends ostracized her. Sometimes she confided their taunts and insults to me in tears. I knew only too well how painful it was, but I was powerless to protect her. Her home life grew worse. She longed to escape her parents' control. She began working as much as possible with the hope of transferring to a college far away from Muncie.

In the end, however, it was her parents who left Muncie. Her father accepted a job at a horse farm in Ocala, Florida. Sara moved in with her grandmother, and continued to attend Ball State. Her grandmother was a staunch conservative and an alcoholic, but Sara immersed herself in her classes, her job, and a new group of more liberal-minded friends at the university. She spent most of her time with a small group of civil rights activists on campus who shocked Muncie with demonstrations and protest marches. Their first victory was to win official desegregation of off-campus housing. Up to that time, black students either lived in the college dormitories or in one of Muncie's two black neighborhoods, far from the campus. Blatant segregation prevented them from living in the often cheaper and more convenient rooming houses near the university. Sara's group, the Muncie Interrelations Council, maintained a vigil outside the off-campus housing office until the embarrassed administration finally declared that homeowners and landlords who discriminated on the basis of race would not be authorized to rent to any Ball State student.

The campus atmosphere seemed isolated from the community. In fact, for a time we almost forgot we were in Muncie. We were tired of secrecy, and began to attend lectures and campus events together. It was a happy, freeing time for me. Emboldened, I visited Sara at her grandmother's, and was a hit with the elderly woman.

One Saturday I accompanied Sara to a cousin's wedding. As I circulated through the crowd of strangers I saw the Muncie realtor who had helped me secure the summer job at Ball State. My friendly hello was met by a cold response. The next day he took it upon himself to apprise Sara's grandmother of my racial heritage. While Sara was studying at the Ball State library, her grandmother, in a drunken rage, threw all of Sara's possessions into the driveway. When Sara arrived home that night, her grandmother would not allow her to enter the house. While Sara loaded her things into her car, her grandmother stood on the porch shouting, "You deceived me. I never want to see you again. You have disgraced the family."

Sara's parents flew immediately to Muncie. I wanted to talk with them and let them get to know me. They refused. Everyone in her family began to pressure Sara to end our relationship. When she resisted, her parents threatened to withdraw all financial support.

Sara moved into a rooming house near campus and took a second part-time job. She became moody and depressed, constantly changing her mind about a relationship that was causing her so much pain. Desperate to keep us together, I did whatever she wanted. Yet the more malleable I became, the more we seemed to drift apart. Soon confusion and tension dominated our time together. By March of 1963 our relationship ended, just as my summer savings ran out.

Though devastated by the loss of Sara, my immediate concern was staying in school. One of the summer supervisors of the Ball State stadium crew had told me to come and see him when I was "hungry." By January, I was on his doorstep. The best he could offer was a position as a part-time janitor from four to seven in the evening in the Practical Arts Building, for seventy-five cents an hour. It was a long drop from the summer athlete's pay of $1.50 an hour, but I had no choice. I took it, but $11.25 a week was not enough for food and clothing. I needed an additional job. I found a second one as a kitchen worker at Ball Memorial Hospital, washing dishes, mopping floors, and unloading delivery trucks Saturdays and Sundays from eleven a.m. until seven p.m., also for seventy-five cents an hour. That thirty-hour work week allowed me to finish my first year of college. Although tuition costs were low, I knew $23.00 a week would not support me through my sophomore year. I didn't know where to turn for help.

One afternoon I was stopped on the street by Minnie Jolly, a black political activist, and a friend of my father. She asked about school, and I told her I was running out of money. She suggested I talk to Dr. Ferrill. Minnie knew Dr. Ferrill from their long association in the local Democratic party. She told me that he had been pleased that I earned one of the few A's in his class. I visited Dr. Ferrill at his office in the Arts and Sciences Building.

He leaned forward in his chair and removed the pipe from his mouth. "I might be able to help," he said. "Since the governor is a Democrat, we now control the state road crews. I'll call Democratic Party Headquarters in Indianapolis and see if I can get you on for the summer. Of course, you realize you would have to travel all over the state and the accommodations are Spartan."

I shifted to the edge of my seat and said, "That doesn't bother me in the least. I just need a job so I can stay in school."

He leaned back again, and took another draw on his pipe. "Don't worry, Greg. I think we can work out something. You know, I'm glad you came in to see me. I've been wanting to talk to you."

Alarm bells went off in my head. I hoped this was not going to be another version of Miss White's monologue. Surely not, I said to myself as I looked around his office, cluttered with books about life and history far from the constrictions and pettiness of Muncie. This man had done nothing but help me expand my own limited horizons. I was anxious to hear what he had to say.

"Greg, what are your career plans after you finish your B.A.?"

I exhaled with relief, and told him I wanted to be a lawyer.

"Well, I'm sure you will be successful, but I would like to encourage you to think about academic life. You're putting together a fine record, and we need people with a rich background like yours in the university community. Don't dismiss teaching out of hand." I pondered Dr. Ferrill's words: "with a rich background like yours." No one had ever characterized my background so positively before, and it filled me with happiness and gratitude. I was overwhelmed that he considered me good enough to one day be a professor.

"Thank you very much, Dr. Ferrill. I really like history, but my long-term interest is politics, and I feel a law degree would be more helpful."

"I understand, Greg. That was the same choice my brother made. Still, give university life some thought." He paused, then added, "You know, with your grades, you might be eligible for an academic scholarship. Why don't you drop by the financial aid office and fill out an application?"

I thanked him for the suggestion, and arranged to check back with him about the road crew in a week.

I sat on the steps outside the Administration Building reading the financial aid forms. They included questions about parents' income and assets, my income and assets, and my checking and banking accounts. I was overcome by self-pity when I realized I would have to put zeros in all the boxes. Convinced no one would believe my financial situation was so desperate, I dropped the application in the trash can at the corner of the building.

While Dr. Ferrill was looking into the summer job possibility, Dad learned that the new Republican sheriff was looking for deputies. The only black on the Sheriff's Department planned to join the Muncie Police Department, so there was some pressure on the sheriff to hire a black replacement. Dad arranged for me to meet an important black Republican who was willing to contact the sheriff on my behalf. Dad also prevailed upon Allen Weir, a lawyer active in local Republican politics, to inform the sheriff of my interest in the job. Both men spoke highly of me to the sheriff, but he made it clear in his conversations with my patrons that no one would dictate his decision. Yet he was willing to meet with me, and within a few days I sat in his office.

The sheriff was a twenty-year veteran of the FBI, and his deadpan expression made it difficult to gain any sense of how the interview was progressing. He said he was pleased with my grades and knew of my athletic achievements on the Bearcat basketball and football teams. My own interest soared when I learned the job paid $300 a month. I knew I could stretch that salary to finish my undergraduate degree.

A week passed without word from the sheriff, but I learned that he contacted several black Republicans to find out more about me. While all of them recommended me highly, his inquiries did produce some negative reaction. A local black minister, also a Republican, began to circulate the news that he opposed my appointment. He accused the sheriff of planning to pay off the black community by hiring me, while preserving the outward appearance of a "lily-white" department. Although I knew the minister only slightly, his daughter had been a classmate of mine at Central High School. She was a pleasant, quiet girl, and I had a good relationship with her. When I learned of her father's opposition, I felt betrayed.

Dad told me not to worry. "Greg, you've got a lot to learn about politics. The Reverend is a 'Johnny-come-lately.' Nobody's gonna pay any attention to that old man."

The controversy forced me to move beyond my own feelings and consider more carefully the minister's view. There *was* a need for a visible black presence on the department. It *was* important for Muncie and Delaware County to see black people in positions of authority. I considered withdrawing my name from consideration.

That week, one of Aunt Bess's grandsons, my cousin Jewitt Hayes, arrived in Muncie for a brief visit. Jewitt worked as a parole officer in Pittsburgh. Whenever he visited Muncie he spent time with me. I saw him as he was leaving Aunt Bess's, and he asked me to ride with him to Whitely to play basketball. As we crossed town, I shared my dilemma with him.

"That old preacher don't know a damn thing about who you are and what you can do. You want to get through school, boy. That's what you have to do. If you get the job, just do the best you can. Let the politicians worry about who's black and who isn't. Nobody in Muncie ever gave you any breaks just because you looked white. You've had to take just as much crap as anybody I know, black or white. You deserve that job just as much as anyone. If you're in a position to arrest some brothers, you are gonna be fair—not like some of the hillbillies they got on the department. You always gonna have people crackin' about you bein' black or sayin' you ain't black enough. Damn, cousin, you paid your dues!"

An anxious week passed as I waited for the sheriff to make a decision. The pressure against hiring me mounted, but the sheriff had a stubborn streak. He summoned me to the jail for a second meeting. His face disclosed absolutely nothing about his inner feelings. He leaned back in the wooden chair and his head touched the bars on the window.

"Greg, do you fully understand the responsibility of the job? You'd be in charge of the jail, and we have some real bad actors in here. Do you think you can handle these fellows?"

"Yes sir," I said, leaning forward to impress him with my sincerity and interest. "In fact, I know a lot of them. We grew up in the same neighborhood."

"I know you did, and that raises another point. If you have to arrest some of your friends, could you do it?"

I hadn't really thought about that, but quickly decided if I was going to do the job, I wasn't going to do it halfway. "Yes sir. If I find them violating the law, I would have no problem arresting them."

"Let me be blunt, Greg. I have known your father for many years. When I was in the FBI and he worked at City Hall, I saw him often. I know he's an alcoholic. Now, I don't believe in holding the sins of the father against the son, but I simply can't have Buster hanging around the jail drunk, disrupting our work. Is that a problem I would have to worry about?"

"Sheriff, my dad will never come into this jail as long as I work here. We've talked about the job, and he knows it's the only chance I have to finish my education. I've already told him that if he did come here, I would arrest him."

For the first time the sheriff's poker face betrayed him, as I detected a glimmer of surprise.

"I believe you would. One more thing, Greg. Are you sure you'll be able to continue school and hold down a full-time job? You're going to have a forty-hours-plus workweek in addition to your fifteen hours of college classes. During the summer we do twelve-hour shifts so everyone can take vacation. Can you do it?"

"Sir, I know it's going to be hard, but I don't have any alternative. I need this job. I have good grades, and I know I can make it through school. I'll do my best, and I will never do anything to embarrass you."

"I believe you, and I want to hire you. The only thing that troubles me is your age. You're only nineteen years old. You'll be one of the youngest deputy sheriffs in the state of Indiana. This job is a lot of responsibility."

He paused. I drew in a deep breath and said, "Sheriff, I've had a lot of responsibility for a long time."

His stony face revealed only the slightest hint of satisfaction. Then he said, "What the hell. I want you to start on the first of July."

My first assignment was as turnkey at the jail. I answered telephone calls, dispatched cars to fights and accidents, and dealt with the hundreds of other problems into which the police are called. I also completed the paperwork and the booking procedure for all prisoners and even transported some to Indiana's state correctional institutions. Though my shift ended at eleven p.m., it was often past one in the morning before I arrived home.

Occasionally, I saw old friends in my new job. The first group of convicted burglars I took in shackles and chains to the Indiana State Prison in Michigan City included the father of one of my close friends from the Madison Street YMCA playground. A week later I placed handcuffs on my old nemesis Reggie from my first playground fight. I felt great sadness when he was taken to the Indiana State Reformatory at Pendleton.

Once my future plans appeared financially possible, I found myself drawn into a wider world. In August 1963, Martin Luther King, Jr., prepared to lead a "March on Washington" to force President Kennedy and Congress to address problems of segregation and discrimination in the United States. News of the march was on the minds of almost every black person in Muncie. Was this the beginning of a new era? Was life going to change for black Americans? Would change come to Muncie? As I sat watching the television at the jail and saw the throngs of people at the Lincoln Memorial, I yearned to be part of that moment in history. Over the black-and-white screen, I heard the inspirational words of Dr. King and vowed to dedicate my life to making the world a better place than I had found in Muncie. How could I fulfill that commitment?

As I sat at my desk berating myself for not taking time off to "March on Washington" and exhibit the courage of my conviction, the entrance bell rang. Two white police officers held an obviously intoxicated black man between them on the steps. One officer was a small nondescript balding man. The other was almost six feet tall, and powerfully built, with muscles bulging in his short-sleeved shirt. He had a burr haircut and wore metal-rimmed glasses. I was struck by the fact that he wore thin black leather gloves. Since he wasn't a motorcycle cop, the gloves seemed incongruous. He had the prisoner's arm intertwined with his beyond the ninety-degree angle. He was administering the painful "come-along" hold. The prisoner, even though drunk, virtually stood on his toes as the larger officer strained to bend the prisoner's wrist even farther. The prisoner moaned with pain. I noticed bruises around his face and forehead. One eye was swollen shut. There was blood on his shirt, but none of the facial abrasions were bleeding.

I asked what had happened.

"He fell trying to get in the car," responded the beefy officer, smirking as he moved behind the prisoner. He grabbed him by the neck and pushed him roughly through the door. The man stumbled, and I reached for his arm to keep him from falling. The officer shoved him to the hallway booking area. I handed them a form, then returned to the office to answer a radio call. All of a sudden I heard, "Asshole, speak up!"

*Bap! Bap!*

I raced into the hallway just as the leather-gloved officer drew back his fist. He stopped and glared at me.

"What do you want?"

I said nothing, but watched him intently.

"Why don't you go on back to the desk while I finish with our prisoner?" he said threateningly.

"I'll just wait here."

"Suit yourself. I may have to convince our boy here to answer a few questions, then I'll turn him over to you."

Firmly I said, "The sheriff told me that once they walk in the front door they belong to the county, so I guess he's already in my custody."

"Yeah, but it's my arrest, and I gotta talk to him."

"Go ahead and talk to him. I'll wait."

"Here, you take him then," he said, thrusting the already completed form in my face.

"What about patting him down, fellows?" I said, looking at the officers. "I thought you guys were supposed to do that."

"You said he belonged to you, smart-ass. Take care of it yourself. Don't get your hands wet, though. He just pissed his pants. I don't want to soil my gloves with scum like him."

As they walked outside, I overheard one say, "You'd think he was a nigger himself, the way he sprang out of the office to protect that coon."

After placing the prisoner in the cell, I called the sheriff at home. He asked me if I saw the officers hit the man. I had not. He asked me how certain I was the bruises on his face came from the encounter in the jail. I was uncertain. He asked what I wanted to do. I wanted to see the officers punished for their acts, but knew I couldn't prove what they had done. We were at a stalemate. We talked about the political implications of the sheriff's department accusing local police officers of misconduct. "But," he added, "I'm not going to have any prisoners mistreated in my jail. What do you want to do?" he asked.

"I guess we can't do anything but forget it. I don't have enough proof."

The sheriff tried to console me by reminding me that I would soon be on regular patrol myself. "You'll be calling the shots and making arrests, Greg. I know you're going to continue to do a good job for me."

When classes began that fall at Ball State I was relieved to have the money to be able to continue. However, my routine was exhausting. Classes began at eight a.m. and ended at two in the afternoon. Promptly at three every afternoon I reported in uniform to the jail and was on duty at least until eleven p.m. More often than not it was past midnight when I left to go home to study for my classes. One evening while sitting at the radio desk just before the shift change, I leafed through the *Muncie Press* and noticed the announcement of the death of my mother's oldest sister in the obituary column. Two nights later, while on duty at the jail, I received a phone call from Walter, one of my mother's brothers.

In a deep voice he said, "Greg, your mother is in town and wants to see you and Mike."

My heart skipped a beat and I sucked in my breath.

"She's afraid to ask you herself. Afraid you boys might turn her down."

I realized I was gripping the phone so tightly my hand ached.

He continued. "She's gonna be here for a couple of days. Would you like to talk to her?"

I had waited ten long, lonely years for this call. In those first few years in Muncie not a day passed that I didn't fall asleep hoping she would call or write. Yet we heard nothing, day after day, month after month, year after year. The pain of rejection, of begging my cousins for small bits of information about her, of having my hopes dashed time after time, had nearly cauterized me. Now, when she seemed gone forever and when we accepted we would never see her again, she came back.

He paused, waiting for an answer. I had decided, but I couldn't speak for Mike.

"Greg, you there?" he asked.

"Yeah," I responded. "I'll talk to Mike after I get off work. I'll call you," I said coldly, and hung up the phone without waiting for a response.

Mike was now back in Muncie. He had left Chicago for good in midsummer, and was back to his rootless, restless, and aimless routine in Muncie. As soon as my shift ended, I searched for him at his favorite hangouts. There was a loud and rowdy crowd near the playground, but Mike was nowhere in sight. After turning down an offer to join buddies for a beer, I drove past Joe's Barbecue and the pool hall. Just as I was ready to give up my search, I found Mike at Tish's Chicken Shack.

Mike and I sat on the curb outside Tish's. The memory of Mike and me sitting on the cold sidewalk on the corner of Kirby and Monroe ten years earlier skipped through my mind. Until that Easter Sunday weekend, we had expected to see Mom, but Dad's bitter words dashed our hopes. That night we were mere boys of nine and ten. Our lives were in the hands of an alcoholic father. Our mother had fled. Now we were adults. It was a heady feeling finally to have some power over the woman who had wounded me so deeply. I vowed to punish her for all those years, for all those times I ached for her presence.

"Greg, you're right." Mike nodded in agreement. "She let us down, but she's still our momma. I believe she loved us. She just didn't come and see us."

"She came to Muncie almost every summer," I said. "Yet not once did she drive across town and see us. I haven't seen her for ten years and as far as I'm concerned it can be ten more."

"What about Sissy and the baby? Don't you want to hear about them and find out how they're doing? I bet they wanted to see us as much as we wanted to see them."

"Yeah," I admitted grudgingly. "I'd like to see them, or at least hear about them."

We talked for a while longer, then I called my uncle to tell him —we were on our way.

As we entered the old neighborhood, I recognized some of the plain frame houses from years past when we first visited Muncie as small children. They had seemed so grand and large, sitting on high sloping hills. Those carefree days had ended so abruptly. I couldn't remember the last time I had been in this part of town. The houses looked much smaller now. We walked up the steep concrete steps. I rapped loudly on the door, my "deputy sheriff" scowl ready for my cousins who had ignored me all those years in school.

A short pale woman opened the inner door and moved cautiously to the screen. Peering through the wire mesh, I strained to recognize her. She didn't look like my uncle's wife. Then it hit me. I was looking at my mother. If we had passed on the street, I would not have known her. My last memories were of a tall, beautiful woman with long auburn hair. Now I towered over a small woman whose eyes moved with uncertainty. As she stepped onto the porch, I searched in vain for something familiar—the curl of her lip, the color of her hair, even the smell of her soap. Yet nothing was familiar. She was my mother, but she was a stranger.

As she embraced me, my anger melted and joy swept over me. My reservoir of grief broke, and tears streamed down my face. I was so happy to see her, to touch her, to be close to her. After ten years of struggling to control my emotions they now overwhelmed me. I squeezed her tightly, thankful that Mike had convinced me to see her.

She turned to Mike. Tears streamed down his face. He trembled and shook as they embraced. His tough exterior, hardened over the years, dissolved with her touch. At that moment he regressed to the sensitive nine-year-old who had needed so much protection. Sobbing uncontrollably, he haltingly asked, "Momma . . . why . . . didn't we hear anything from you all those years? Why . . . didn't you at least write to us?"

"Mike," she said, pulling away from him and looking directly into his face, "I did write, and try to contact you." She paused and said, "I sent letters and money for Mom to give to you boys. She must not have done it. . . ."

I turned up the collar on my deputy sheriff's jacket. The feelings of love and warmth began to vanish into the night as I struggled to comprehend her words. Although I knew what a heartless woman my Grandmother Cook could be, I couldn't bring myself to believe my mother's excuse. How could she expect us to believe her when we had heard nothing? Rivers of tears streaked Mike's cheek and his body shook in spasms. "Mom," he asked, "why . . . why didn't you come to see us?"

"I did, boys. I came to see you a lot."

"When did you come to see us?" I said accusingly. "Did you try to see us, and Dad didn't tell us?"

"Well, you boys didn't see me, but I saw you. Every time I came to Muncie, I had them take me over to Kirby Avenue, and we sat across the street from Dora Terry's house and watched you boys leave for school. I remember one June morning just like it was yesterday. Billy, you looked so neat and clean dressed up in a suit. You must have had some program at the school. When you two walked out the gate, it was all I could do to keep from jumping out of the car and running across the street to hug you."

That must have been the day of my elementary school graduation, I thought. The day I *didn't* receive the award for best student. My shoulders slumped as I realized I had been rejected by my school and my mother on the same day.

"Why didn't you get out of the car? You were less than thirty feet away from us!"

"Billy, I thought Tony might be around, and I didn't want to create a big fuss. He might have beaten me again. You know he used to beat me all the time."

"But you had your brothers with you."

"Yeah, but we were in the colored area, and Tony might have had some friends around."

"Nobody would have bothered you," I protested bitterly. "Miss

Dora wouldn't have minded you knocking on the door. Even Grandma came by the house once."

"I know, but we just didn't feel safe. Son, I hope you're never in a situation when your children are close enough for you to touch, but you can't say one word to them. It was terrible for me."

As she drew back toward the door I realized we were making her very uncomfortable. Slowly, I regained my defenses. I realized my own mother was like so many others. I couldn't tell her what I really felt. It was time to change the subject. I asked her about Tony Junior and Sissy.

She fished through her purse and drew out pictures of Tony Junior, Sissy, and her new baby. We stared at the small snapshots under the reflected glow of the street corner light, but it was hard to see more than broad features. Her husband, Bob, was white. Sissy, who was just learning to write her name when the family broke up, had only two years left in high school. Tony Junior, the toddler, was now a ninth grader.

Mom continued.

"Boys, I've talked to Bob. He has agreed to adopt you just like he did the other two kids."

I reeled back on the porch. She can't be serious, I thought. First she abandoned us, then she did not even acknowledge the existence of the woman who had saved our lives. Thankful that the darkness concealed my anger, I stood silently as she continued.

"You know, when I divorced Tony I got custody of all the children, including you two. You're under my control. Now Bob's willing to give you his name."

The more she talked, the less sense she made. My mother acted as if she had been gone for a month, and was returning to make a very ordinary request.

Speechless, I scrutinized her face. I looked at Mike. Surely he didn't believe her line of crap. I thought Mike knew all about being hustled, but he smiled wistfully as Mom painted an enchanting picture of him joining the family in Virginia, finishing high school, and finding a job. The frigid night wind rattled the leafless trees in the background. I wondered if our mother had heard about Mike's marriages to two black women in their forties, his numerous stepchildren, and his life in one of Chicago's roughest drug-infested ghettos.

The warmth of the first embrace had evaporated. I shuffled my feet to ward off the chill. I didn't want the meeting to end, but our reunion had taken an absurd twist. I wanted to scream, "This is all ten years too late! Where were you when we really needed you?" We stood less than a foot apart, desperately trying to reach out to each other, yet we were unable to connect. We lived in different worlds. The distance between us was far more than miles and years. I didn't want to start over. I wanted an apology for the years of neglect. I wanted her to say, just once, "I'm sorry I wasn't there for you boys, and I prayed every night someone was holding you and protecting you the way I wanted to." I wanted her to say she thanked God for giving us Miss Dora. But my mother was only concerned with her own distorted reality.

"Yeah, we got a little piece of land on a mountainside," she continued. "One day we're gonna build a summerhouse. . . ."

I tried to break into her monologue. "Mom, it wasn't easy for us—"

She cut me off with a sharp gesture. "I know that," she said. "I know all about it."

"You wouldn't believe how religious Sissy has become," she continued. "And Anthony, I think he might even be a priest."

"Mom, there's a lot of prejudice in Muncie," I said, trying once more.

"I know that, honey. I grew up here, don't forget. . . . Like I said, Bob is willing to adopt you boys and take you away from all this."

The conditions for becoming part of her life became very clear to me. We could reenter her world if we rejected the one in which we had lived for the past ten years. She knew little about our life in Muncie, nor did she want to know. Gaining acceptance to her world required that we deny our black heritage and pretend that the people and circumstances of our life in Muncie did not exist. We were to forget we were "colored" boys. She expected us to move back into her life without a past, without roots, without feelings for the people who had sheltered and cared for us when our need was greatest. I knew that was something we could never do.

We stood on the porch for almost two hours while she made detailed plans for Mike to move to Virginia, live with them, and finish high school. My summer vacation could be spent with them, and we would become one big happy family. She must have thought I was crying with happiness, yet they were tears of lost hope. I had wanted to hear those exact words for so long. Now when they finally came, they were too late. After a final hug, Mike and I walked down the steps. He talked excitedly of going to Virginia, but I felt farther away from my mother than I had at any time in my life.

I stayed in the deputy sheriff job for three years, working and attending classes full-time. Whenever the load seemed impossible to bear, I recalled those first few months in Muncie. I reminded myself that if I could make it through those days, all other obstacles could be overcome. After graduation I moved to Washington, D.C., to pursue my dream of becoming a lawyer. I worked full-time as a high school history teacher, and pursued a master's, a law degree, and then a doctorate. It was a brutal schedule, and from time to time the future looked bleak. One November when I was particularly discouraged and about to give up, I received a note from Miss Dora, and knew I had to persevere.

*Wedny Oct 31, 1967*

*My dear son greg only a few line to let you know that i gat your seet and loveli letter. same time go well and doing pretty good. hope your are well and duen finne. Mike was here last week and stay 2 night. he look well and was glad to seen him. greg I thank about you every day and night and get lonesom and want to see you and wish you was still in Muncie. But I know you are try to go to school and try to wark and be a lawyer and I hope I will live to see you make it. I wish I had maney to help you some But I dont have it Im just a poor old lady. Buster is duin pretty good now he's been sober two months. now he look so much better go nice and clean. he com by evury morning to see how Im feal. well it get cold her now and that near wenter now you write when you can Because I all way want to hear from you*

*love all way, your truly mother*
*Dora Smith*

Sara and I found each other again and were married in 1969. Miss Dora and Dad witnessed the civil rights revolution on television, but their lives remained unchanged by it. I am grateful they were able to know our two oldest children, Natalia Dora and Zachary.

Miss Dora passed away in 1975. In 1991 Sara returned from a summer of volunteer work in El Progresso, Honduras, and said she'd met seven-year-old twin boys who needed a home. Carlos and Anthony have brought great joy to us. Their presence makes me realize all over again what a miracle it was for Miss Dora, at age fifty-two, with such limited resources, to take on the job of raising Mike and me. Not a day goes by that I don't think about her, and thank God for putting us under her protection and care.

After I left Muncie, I spent years trying to convince Dad to quit drinking. He dismissed me with the proclamation, "Don't worry about me, Greg, I'm gonna live to a hundred or die trying." He did quit shortly before Miss Dora's death. Still, the years of hard drinking claimed the ever-youthful Buster Williams at the age of sixty-one. He achieved one of his precious goals—to die sober. At Gill Funeral Home, just two blocks from the house of my youth, I greeted over two hundred people who paid him their final respects—judges, lawyers, the mayor-elect, former mayors, city councilmen, police officers, city workers, pimps, prostitutes, winos, and just friends. The next day there was a column in the *Muncie Star*:

# A NOTE ON BUSTER

... A man of charming personality liked by everyone, that was James Anthony (Buster) Williams who died unexpectedly Nov. 21 at age 61. Intelligent ... and up on modern events, Buster had friends in every walk of life and liked to do small, unsolicited kindnesses to please them. ...

Buster and his friendly greeting or wave of the hand will be remembered and missed.

My black grandmother and my white grandmother both died in the 1970s. They lived within two miles of each other, but they never met. In 1974 my brother Mike was blinded in a shooting in an Indianapolis bar. He lives in Indiana. A support group, Adult Children of Alcoholics, helped him rebuild his life. Sister Adele of the Benet Learning Center of Fort Wayne, Indiana, worked long hours with Mike to help him finish high school and begin college classes. My half brother, Jimmy, died of cancer in 1992.

Brian, still my closest friend, is an airline pilot living in the Southeast. Another good friend became an automobile factory executive. A third had a career as a professional basketball player, two others are college administrators and teachers. Yet for every one who made it, there were too many who were unable to break the mold Muncie cast for them. It pains me to remember those promising young lives lost to drugs, alcohol, barroom brawls, and prison.

I often think about life in Muncie and even sometimes in the middle of the night, halfway between sleep and consciousness, I go to the place where that bewildered boy of long ago still dwells in me, and my eyes fill with tears. We share the disbelief that all the things that happened to him in those early years of his life could have occurred. We cry together, and I tell him that he is now in a safe place and that a wiser and stronger friend is here to protect him. But the wounds are deep, the scars on his soul ache, and he is able to draw little solace from my presence. He wishes me well, but in his little manly way asks why it had to happen to him. Was there some deeper reason for the turn of events of his life, or was he just the victim of circumstance?

I do believe that there was some reason I was called upon to live the life that I was given. Maybe to share it with others in the hope that no child will have to experience what I did. In spite of all the pain and grief of my early years, I am grateful to have been able to view the world from a place few men or women have stood. I realize now that I am bound to live out my life in the middle of our society and hope that I can be a bridge between races, shouldering the heavy burden that almost destroyed my youth.

I was fortunate to be able to achieve my goal of becoming a lawyer, and later my dream of being a law professor. I have held positions that even in my wildest fantasies during the nights at 601½ Railroad Street I could not envision for myself. Yet when I stand in front of students, my mind often wanders back to the pain and rejection of the Muncie years. Almost as if it were yesterday, I vividly recall watching Dad being beaten by the police, and the day we were chased from the "white" waiting room in Louisville. I never felt more impotent and powerless to control my life than I did in those days. When I think of those times, I remember what Dad used to say:

"Son, one day this will all pale into insignificance."

He was wrong. Muncie has never paled into insignificance. It has lived inside me forever.

The typeface used in this book is a version of Palatino, originally designed in 1950 by Hermann Zapf (b. 1918), one of the most prolific contemporary type designers, who has also created Melior and Optima. Palatino was first used to set the introduction of a book of Zapf's hand lettering, in an edition of eighty copies on Japan paper handbound by his wife, Gudrun von Hesse—also a type designer of note; the book sold out quickly and Zapf's name was made. (Remarkably, the lettering had actually been done when the self-taught calligrapher was only twenty-one.) Intended mainly for "display" (title pages, headings), Palatino owes its appearance both to calligraphy and the requirements of the cheap German paper at the time—perhaps why it is also one of the best-looking fonts on low-end computer printers. It was soon used to set text, however, causing Zapf to redraw its more elaborate letters.